ANGERS, FANTASIES AND GHOSTLY FEARS

Angers, Fantasies and Ghostly Fears

NINETEENTH-CENTURY WOMEN FROM WALES AND ENGLISH-LANGUAGE POETRY

Catherine Brennan

UNIVERSITY OF WALES PRESS
CARDIFF
2003

British Library Cataloguing-in-Publication Data.
A catalogue record for this book is available from the British Library.

ISBN 0–7083–1764–2 paperback

Published with the financial support of the Arts Council of Wales

Typeset at University of Wales Press
Printed in Great Britain by Dinefwr Press, Llandybïe

For Alexandra and Michael, and for my Welsh family,
with love and thanks

Contents

Acknowledgements

This work has materialized with the help of many people. I want particularly to thank the following: Alex and Mike, whose trust and faith have inspired me, and my family in Wales whose love and fierce pride have always been there.

I am indebted to Jane Aaron – her guidance and generosity of spirit have made the book possible – and to my friends and colleagues in England and Wales, whose support, moral, intellectual, emotional and practical, has been so important – especially Dianne Gash, Diane Warren, Jeff Messem, Veronica Spencer, Sue Harper, Verena Wright, Katie Gramich, Allan D'All, Lorraine Newhouse and Stella Pratt. Duncan Campbell and Ceinwen Jones of University of Wales Press have been supportive and endlessly patient editors; I thank them for their contributions to this book. I am also grateful to the young people of First Base, who have taught me so much about strength and courage in adversity, and about the real meaning of politics.

Introduction

In October 1997 Gillian Clarke, the contemporary English-language Welsh poet, responded to the narrow 'Yes' result of the previous month's Welsh Assembly referendum with a reflection on the future of Welsh literature in British literary studies. She rallied Welsh writers with the assertion:

> The evidence that the nation has always existed lies in our literature . . . One of the most exciting challenges in the recent past has come from the brilliant young playwright Ed Thomas. His clear meaning is, if we want to be a nation we, the artists, must build it in the imaginations of the people. Let's to it.[1]

Clarke dared Welsh artists to channel post-devolution energy into expressions of new understandings of Welshness arising out of Wales's newly won status. She acknowledged the advances made in recent decades in terms of institutional perceptions of Welsh literature, noting that

> the Welsh Arts Council and the Welsh Academy worked for a generation to persuade teachers and examination boards to value the work of Welsh writers. The excuse for its neglect was 'It's not good enough', or 'It's too local'. Now this work is valued at all levels and appears on examination boards throughout Britain.[2]

The challenge to the cultural hegemony of 'English' canonical authority which is implied in Clarke's comments here must inevitably be accelerated, I would argue, by the effects of devolution in Wales.

Contemporary post-colonial criticism has, of course, been long concerned with the reassessment of so-called 'English' literature. In their 1989 work, *The Empire Writes Back: Theory and Practice in Post-colonial Literatures*, Bill Ashcroft, Gareth Griffiths and Helen Tiffin, for example, argue that post-colonial literatures written in English have historically been relegated to 'marginal and subordinate' positions in relation to 'English' literature.[3] Post-colonial critical theory provides a stimulating and potentially fruitful perspective for analysis of the position of Welsh literature written in English. Implicit in the assertion made by Ashcroft, Griffiths and Tiffin, however, is the assumption that all 'post-colonial literatures' emerge from a non-European base. In the large body of post-colonial theory produced over recent decades little or no attention has been paid to writing by Welsh artists. It seems to me that, given this critical vacuum in post-colonial theory, a reconsideration of English-language texts by Welsh writers may prove timely. In analysing work produced by Welsh writers in the past, it may be possible to access the repository of national identity which Gillian Clarke argues is constituted in Welsh literature; at the same time, new dimensions may be added to understandings of post-coloniality which will supplement current theoretical perspectives.

Many post-colonial critics have identified the nineteenth century as a crucial period in the formation of Anglocentric cultural dominance in literature. In focusing on English-language poetry written by Welsh women throughout the nineteenth century, this study aims to generate insights which may complexify theoretical and historical accounts of gender, class and national identity in the period.

Sandra Gilbert and Susan Gubar have taken Virginia Woolf's idea of the ill-fated career of 'Judith Shakespeare' as a starting-point for their work *Shakespeare's Sisters: Feminist Essays on Women Poets*; they cite Woolf's recognition of the particular difficulties encountered by the woman poet in coming to terms with 'all those obstacles that discourage women from attempting the pen'.[4] Imagining Shakespeare's frustrated poet sister, Woolf asked 'who shall measure the heat and violence of the poet's heart when caught and mangled in a woman's body? – she killed herself one winter night and lies buried at some crossroads where the omnibuses now stop outside the Elephant and Castle.'[5] As Gilbert and Gubar observe, whilst a significant body of feminist criticism which has emerged since the mid-1970s is concerned with the links between sexual and creative identity in prose fiction by women, there has been a relative paucity of critical material which explores 'the problems as well as the triumphs of women poets'.[6] To some extent this neglect has been

addressed in recent years by the work of feminist critics such as Angela
Leighton, Margaret Reynolds and Margaret Homans, whose scholarship
provides a useful map of the hitherto barely charted territory of
nineteenth-century women's poetry. Nevertheless, as Gilbert and Gubar
point out, the relationship between gender and creativity as enacted by
the woman poet is a 'profoundly controversial subject',[7] which has by no
means been exhausted by existing studies. The nineteenth century, as
Angela Leighton has noted, is a period during which the woman poet as
'a self-professed, rather than just self-supporting, writer, appears almost for
the first time in history'.[8]

The act of poetic self-profession which Leighton notes entails, for the
nineteenth-century woman writer, complex intersections of gender,
genre and tradition. It is in considering another of Virginia Woolf's
famous adages – 'As a woman I have no country'[9] – that questions arise
about ways in which the issue of national identity may also play its part in
the construction of a writer's subjectivity and, for the woman poet, affect
her sense of herself as a woman, a poet and a member of a particular class
and religious grouping.

However, Woolf insists on the irrelevance of nationhood for women.
In feminist terms the strategic potential of Woolf's argument in relation to
'liberty, justice and peace' is attractive.[10] Woolf's dialectic is extremely
persuasive in terms of women's subject position as members of what she
calls the 'Outsiders' Society'; it is particularly compelling when read in the
light of post-Freudian and post-structuralist theoretical perspectives on
psychology and language.[11] Woolf is compelled, however, to qualify her
declamatory stance somewhat in order to account for the 'irrational'
identification experienced by some women with the culture or landscape
of their homeland: 'And if, when reason has had its say, still some
obstinate emotion remains . . . this drop of pure, if irrational, emotion she
will make serve her to give to England first what she desires of peace and
freedom for the whole world.'[12]

I am interested in investigating poetry produced by women whose
experience of this 'irrational' connection implies an intensified
marginality, rather than the act of affinity with the mainstream which
Woolf's argument suggests. I intend to examine the work of nineteenth-
century Welsh women poets who were marginalized doubly, by their
gender and by their nationality, from the dominant discourse of
imperialist British patriarchy. I am concerned with the connections
between national identity and the female subject, particularly when the
subject in question identifies with a white minority culture but also aspires
to acceptance within the literary hegemony of the ascendant power.

In part, the project entails an exploratory foray into the still largely concealed territory of nineteenth-century Welsh women's poetry. Numerous feminist critics have argued convincingly in recent decades for the value of 'unearthing . . . lost works by women writers and the documentation of their lives and careers'.[13] Elaine Showalter, notably, has discussed the importance of establishing a 'female tradition' of nineteenth-century women's writing which connects the 'holes and hiatuses' between the landmarks represented by the happy few well-known nineteenth-century literary women. I would argue that an exploration of work produced by Welsh women in the period may provide supplementary material with which to bridge the lacunae and interstices of the primarily Anglocentric tradition of nineteenth-century women's poetry in English.

This book represents an early mapping of the terrain. The writers discussed have been selected, in part, on the basis of their chronological positioning across the century. I am interested in the web of historically specific influences which operate in the production of these texts. In concentrating on a period of such intense and rapid technological, political, demographic and topographic change, it seems useful to examine the output of writers who worked at various specific points throughout the century. The writers have also been chosen because their experiences exemplify a spectrum of diverse species of Welshness. Much theoretical work has been done on the elusiveness of national identity. Eric Hobsbawn, for example, in his book *Nations and Nationalism Since 1780*, refers to the fact that,

> in spite of the claims of those who belong to [a nation] that it is in some ways primary and fundamental for the social existence, or even the individual identification of its members, no satisfactory criterion can be discovered for deciding which of the many human collectivities should be labeled in this way.[14]

Given these problems of definition, it may be productive to explore the work of writers who are representative of the heterogeneity of experience which Hobsbawm indicates.

To these ends, then, I focus on the writing of seven poets whose lives and work span the nineteenth century, beginning with Jane Cave (*c*.1754–1813), moving through Ann Julia Hatton (1764–1839), Felicia Hemans (1793–1835), Maria James (1795–1868), Sarah Williams (1838–68) Emily Pfeiffer (1827–90), and concluding with Anna Walter Thomas (1839–1920). All of these women have in common, I would argue, a deeply felt connection with Wales. Jane Cave, Maria James and Emily Pfeiffer were born in Wales; Ann Julia Hatton, Felicia Hemans and Anna Walter Thomas were born in England but moved to Wales and lived there for most of their lives; Hemans and Thomas demonstrated their enthusiasm for their new home by learning Welsh. Although Sarah Williams was born and lived in London, she was Welsh at least on her father's side, visited Wales regularly, and seems to have retained profound emotional links with the country. All of these writers draw, in their poetry, on their experiences of Wales and Welsh identity.

It is notable that in each case the writer's attachment to Wales is mitigated by a corresponding and, arguably, equally meaningful association with England or, in the case of James, America. Research in the area of English-language poetry by Welsh women in the period yields no significant material by writers who were born and bred in Wales and who remained there throughout their lives and writing careers. The issue of language is clearly a significant contributory factor in this phenomenon. In 1850 two out of three people in Wales spoke Welsh, and most of them were monoglot. In his book, *A History of Wales*, John Davies comments on the 'vitality of Welsh language activity in the period 1850–80 . . . Welsh was the only language of the mass of people'.[15] In focusing on English-language poetry, then, this study concerns itself with what was in effect a minority language in Wales at the time, and one whose poets not surprisingly emerge out of material (geographic) relationships with English-speaking culture. In his book *Mid-Victorian Wales: The Observers and the Observed*, Ieuan Gwynedd Jones undertakes a detailed analysis of language and social change in the period, noting that Welsh-language culture in the Victorian era was based upon 'a working-class consciousness'.[16] Jones examines a range of prizewinning eisteddfod essays and observes that 'always the argument recurs that the Welsh language, because of its age-old, organic connection with liberty, is the working man's best defence against oppression'.[17] Conversely, as Jones argues, 'the virtually unanimous opinion of the Welsh elite – the educational, religious, commercial and political leaders of Victorian Wales – [was] that the disappearance of the [Welsh] language was inevitable and a good thing'.[18]

It is clear, then, that use of the English language in the period, particularly in the area of literary endeavour, is closely connected to issues of class. The writing careers of the seven poets selected for this study corroborate the sociolinguistic hierarchy identified by Jones. With one exception, the poets emerged out of the middle ranks of British society, which were burgeoning at the beginning of the nineteenth century and increasing in economic and cultural dominance as the epoch progressed. Although Ann Julia Hatton was a member of a distinguished acting family, and therefore difficult to locate precisely in terms of social status, only Maria James can be categorized as a specifically working-class poet. Cave, Hatton, Hemans, Williams, Pfeiffer and Thomas wrote in English as a matter of course since, even in the case of those who were born in Wales, English was the mother tongue of their class grouping; James, originally a monoglot Welsh-speaker, was compelled by economic adversity to emigrate to the United States, where English was the only viable language for literary expression.

Thus, in embarking upon this exploration, I acknowledge its limitations in terms of scope. I would suggest, however, that parameters demarcated by the intersections of gender, class, language and national identity constitute at the same time a framework through which to generate new readings of the poems. It is my intention to deal with the seven women poets in individual chapters and in chronological order. Before embarking on this exploration, however, it is necessary to present, firstly, an account of the methodology I intend to follow, and, secondly, a historical overview of the class, gender and national contexts of their work, and of the way in which those contexts changed during the century.

* * *

Methodologically my approach draws extensively on theoretical notions of culture and society developed through the large and often disparate body of so-called Marxist feminist critical thought. In very broad terms, Marxist approaches to literary criticism advocate readings of literary form and style which yield insights into the writer's relationship with the society in which she lives. Frederic Jameson, for example, has asserted that: 'A Marxist criticism would reconstruct the inner form of a literary work, as both disguise and revelation of the concrete . . . the surface of the work is a kind of mystification of the concrete.'[19] Mary Poovey has applied the same argument to the issue of women's writing:

> the very act of a woman writing during a period in which self-assertion was considered 'unladylike' exposes the contradictions inherent in propriety: just as the inhibitions visible in her writing constitute a record of her historical oppression, so the work proclaims her momentary, probably unconscious, defiance.[20]

Poovey argues that the often uneven surface of nineteenth-century women's writing may be read as a manifestation of the inner tensions involved in writing at a time when self-assertion of any kind was considered to be at odds with feminine norms.

In her essay 'Pandora's Box: Subjectivity, Class and Sexuality in Socialist Feminist Criticism', Cora Kaplan discusses a number of conceptual difficulties inherent in the relationship between Marxist and feminist approaches to text. Kaplan notes the way in which within the discourse of Marxist feminist criticism 'psychoanalytic perspectives have yet to be integrated with social economic and political analysis'.[21] By comparing two roughly contemporary Marxist feminist analyses of Charlotte Bronte's *Villette*, Kaplan problematizes any theoretical methodology which fails to 'come to grips with the relationship between female subjectivity and class identity'.[22] Kaplan maintains:

> The ways in which class is lived by men and women, like the ways in which sexual difference is lived, are only partly open to voluntary self-conscious political negotiation. The unconscious processes that construct subjective identity are also the structures through which class is lived and understood, through which political subjection and rebellion are organized . . . literary texts give these simultaneous inscriptions narrative form, pointing towards and opening up the fragmentary nature of social and psychic identity, drawing out the ways in which social meaning is psychically represented.[23]

I propose to adopt the mode of reading which Kaplan advocates, incorporating psychological as well as social understandings of text and context. My analyses of the poems will therefore draw on a range of post-Freudian theoretical perspectives on language and identity. I would argue, however, that such an interpretative approach must equally incorporate some consideration of the national identity of the writing subject, particularly when considering texts which emerge out of the nineteenth century, the apogee of British imperialism. I would further suggest that the application of this method to work by Welsh women of the period may generate insights into the operations of gendered subjectivity which will supplement current feminist understandings of literature and history. Gayatri Chakravorty Spivak begins her essay 'Three Women's Texts and a Critique of Imperialism' with the assertion: 'It should not be possible to read nineteenth-century British literature without remembering that imperialism, understood as England's social mission, was a crucial part of the cultural representation of England to the English.'[24] Spivak's thesis

involves a stimulating analysis of Mary Shelley's *Frankenstein*, Charlotte
Brontë's *Jane Eyre* and Jean Rhys's *Wide Sargasso Sea*; her readings expose
the literary mechanics through which is achieved the othering of
colonized cultures, and the ways in which this process contributes to the
self-identification of the colonizers as 'English'. I propose an exploration
of literature produced in the period by women writers for whom the
process of self-identification to which Spivak refers may be problematized
not only by their gender, an issue which Spivak explores in depth, but
also by the more intensely marginal formation of subject positions
engendered by their various associations with Wales.[25]

In order to develop the theoretical apparatus through which readings
may be made in terms of the poets' experience of Welshness, it is
necessary first to ground discussion in consideration of the concept of
national identity. The irrational essence of nationhood and national
identity is a theme explored by numerous analysts who do not concern
themselves with Virginia Woolf's feminist agenda. Benedict Anderson, for
example, has discussed national identity in terms of what he calls
'imagined communities';[26] similarly, Eric Hobsbawm makes plain his
conviction that 'nationalism requires too much belief in what is patently
not so'.[27] Hobsbawm makes a meticulous and cogent case for the mythic
construction and function of national identities, particularly throughout
the nineteenth-century 'Age of Revolution', noting that the concept of
nation 'belongs exclusively to a particular, and historically recent
period'.[28] Having detailed a range of sources for the emergence and wide-
spread popularity of the 'concept of nation' in the period, Hobsbawm
goes on to demonstrate the inadequacy of available criteria by which to
define it. He examines the importance of language, ethnicity, religion and
political history, systematically assessing and rejecting each as a viable
indicator of national identity. Thus, whilst rejecting the notion that
national identity has any basis in 'the real experience of most human
beings',[29] he acknowledges the rapid development of its popular appeal
throughout the nineteenth century, and the concomitant political force
which it came to represent. Hobsbawm sees national identities, then, as
'dual phenomena, constructed essentially from above, but which cannot
be understood unless also analysed from below, that is in terms of the
assumptions, hopes, needs, longings and interests of ordinary people'.[30]
I am persuaded by the scholarship of Anderson, Hobsbawm and others
of the imagined status of national identity; however, the centrality
of invention in the construction of nation, I would argue, in no way
diminishes the emotional force experienced by those who, for whatever
reason, identify with it. Gwyn A. Williams, in charting the history of

Welsh nationhood, has acknowledged the supple fictionality of national identity: 'The Welsh as a people have lived by making and remaking themselves in generation after generation . . . Wales is an artefact which the Welsh produce . . . The Welsh or their effective movers and shapers have repeatedly employed history to make a usable past.'[31] Williams thus historicizes national identity without disregarding its significance to the people who consider themselves to be Welsh. In the course of this book I intend to proceed from this premise in pursuit of an understanding of the 'assumptions, hopes, needs, longings and interests' of seven nineteenth-century women poets, all of whom sustained links with Wales which were sufficiently significant to structure thematically a range of works in their respective oeuvres.

★ ★ ★

I began by discussing the potential to this study of the large corpus of so-called post-colonial theory. I have already referred to the work of Gayatri Chakravorty Spivak, who is one contributor to this body of thought. In the introduction to *The Post-colonial Studies Reader*, Bill Ashcroft, Gareth Griffiths and Helen Tiffin outline the project of post-colonial literary criticism: 'Post-colonial theory involves discussion about experience of various kinds including migration . . . suppression, resistance, representation, difference . . . gender, place, and responses to the influential master discourses of imperial Europe.'[32] Clearly, discussion of this kind is potentially useful to the analysis of texts by Welsh women poets, whose subject position in terms of gender, genre, geography and political power may be fragmented and marginalized in relation to dominant cultural canons. Difficulties arise, however, when attempting to apply the term 'post-colonial' to the Welsh context. Conceptual resistance to the notion of nineteenth-century Wales as a colony of England emerges from legitimate concerns over terminology. Wales was certainly conquered and colonized during the Middle Ages. John Davies refers to the defeat of Llywelyn ap Gruffudd in 1282 as marking the year when 'the whole of Wales was thrown to the ground'.[33] Gwyn A. Williams relates in graphic terms the well-rehearsed mechanisms of colonial domination which were brought to bear in subjugating the Welsh people to the rule of the English conquerors.[34]

Despite the brutal form of the early conquest, however, from a legislative point of view the Welsh have enjoyed parity with the English since the Acts of Union were passed in 1536 and 1543. As John Davies notes, 'thereafter in the eyes of the law everyone living in Wales was English'.[35]

This equivocal privilege was achieved, of course, at the cost of Welsh as the language of public life. Nevertheless, it can be argued that what has happened to Wales since 1536 has been a gradual, though hopefully now curtailed, process of provincialization rather than of colonization, as it is customarily defined. Wales the nation thus became a province of London, rather than a colony of England. I would suggest, however, that, in relating post-colonial criticism to Welsh texts, this is a problem of nomenclature and not of insurmountable theoretical substance.

Ashcroft et al. establish a fairly inclusive definition of the terminology: 'We use the term "post-colonial" . . . to cover all the culture affected by the imperial process from the moment of colonization to the present day. This is because there is a continuity of preoccupations throughout the historical process initiated by European imperial aggression.'[36] I propose in the course of this study to adopt the terms of reference set out by Ashcroft et al. Given these definitions, the problematic nature of the Welsh context in terms of the colonization process is resolved as a matter of chronological proximity. Indeed, I would suggest that an examination of texts which emerge out of a sense of marginality through provincialization may succeed in rendering more complex the discourse of post-colonial theory, which so far has taken little account of the literatures of Wales, or, for that matter, of Ireland or Scotland.

* * *

My specific purpose here is to examine the work of these writers in terms of its dramatization of their links with Wales. In view of the extent of critical neglect involved, it seems important, however, also to establish a sense of the poems in relation to the more general issues of class and gender, the ways in which the two intersect, and the ways in which the Welsh question may inform these themes. In the course of researching the material in terms of the juxtapositions of class, gender and Welsh identity, the issue of religion has been a recurring theme. Without exception the poets engage with the concept of Christian spirituality, and this is often a theme which informs their depiction of Wales and Welsh identity. In cases where religion figures in the verse as an aspect of the individual poet's Welshness, I intend to analyse their constructions of spirituality in relation to the historical development of Christian dogma and practice in England and Wales during the nineteenth century.

I would argue that the poems yield, as a result of the methodological approach detailed above, a range of readings in relation to each of the three areas of investigation, where the work of each poet generates analyses informed by specific conditions of literary and political history. In order to illustrate this discursive premise in this introductory chapter, I will make preliminary reference to various examples of the poets' work in considering each thematic strand.

Of the seven writers considered here, only Felicia Hemans received significant critical attention in the last century.[37] A few poems by Jane Cave and Emily Pfeiffer have been included in recent anthologies; there is also a limited bibliography of articles of a largely 'local flavour' on Cave, Pfeiffer and Hatton, but broadly speaking the poetry of Sarah Williams, Maria James and Anna Walter Thomas has remained unpublished and unregarded for roughly a hundred years.[38]

The area of class is an interesting point at which to begin this preliminary survey. As previously noted, the overwhelming majority of the poets examined here may be categorized broadly as belonging to the middle class and it is this perspective, therefore, which they bring to their writing. Within this apparently narrow scope, however, there is a spectrum of difference between them in terms of their treatment of class issues in the poems, and this offers potential for useful historical perspectives on this turbulent period.

The first of the poets discussed, and chronologically the earliest, is Jane Cave, whose writing career began in the 1770s. It is not possible to refer confidently to the existence of a discrete British middle class in this period. Indeed, it was only during the last decades of the eighteenth century that the middle class, as distinct from the power base of landed wealth in British society, began to form out of the converging interests of a range of heterogeneous 'middling groups'. This formation was not fully consolidated in terms of political power until the Reform Act of 1932.[39] Jane Cave belonged to the diverse and shifting middle strata of late eighteenth-century British society. A reading of Cave's work in terms of ideas about class evidences, I would argue, the ambiguous and transitional status of this social grouping at the time. Through close analysis of Cave's use of formal patterning, thematic content and linguistic device, a picture emerges of a class subjectivity fraught with artistic, economic and political tensions. The patrons on whom Cave relied for financial support include a number of aristocratic and gentry figures; her stylistic preference is for neoclassical forms, already outmoded by her time of writing, and closely linked to eighteenth-century aristocratic culture. Yet at the same time the content of certain of her poems points explicitly to an acute dissatisfaction with aristocratic values, and an urge to identify with an alternative meritocracy seen as morally superior. Cave's work may thus be read as an index of the equivocal self-assertion involved in the formation of the nascent middle class in late eighteenth-century Britain. Visible in Cave's poetry, I suggest, are traces of a process of identification of difference in moral terms, combined with resentful consciousness of political and to some extent economic disenfranchisement.

The work of Sarah Williams, or 'Sadie', as she called herself, by contrast suggests a poet who is more secure in her class identity. Her writing career took place during the 1860s, at the height of Victorian bourgeois domination. By 1859 the industrial and commercial classes which, by reason of their wealth and control of economic life, came to dominate English society and culture after the middle decades of the century, had stamped upon English development an impress peculiarly their own.[40]

There is no hint in verse by Williams of the struggle for class independence or the imperative for self-assertion noted in earlier poetic offerings such as those by Jane Cave. By the 1860s the cultural ascendancy of the middle class in Britain was an incontrovertible and all-pervasive reality. The aristocracy and gentry barely feature in Williams's poems, and there is certainly no sense in which the upper classes can be seen to jeopardize the poet's middle-class assurance. Tellingly, what does impinge on the poet's consciousness of class identity is the lurking presence of the urban poor, which she tends to figure as an endearing yet potentially powerful entity. In his analysis, *Mid-Victorian Britain*, Geoffrey Best describes the general mood of social accord prevalent during the middle decades of the nineteenth century and refers to an overwhelming sense of mid-Victorian calm.[41]

Depictions by Williams of the city working class in her poetry offer interesting insights into bourgeois experience during this period of apparently supreme self-confidence and stability. I would argue that analysis of the poems allows a complex and nuanced view of 'mid-Victorian calm' which may be read as giving expression to Victorian bourgeois anxieties about inequality and deprivation which were unvoiced in explicit cultural representations of the period.

In the case of Maria James, critical reading of the poems permits access to the creative process of a nineteenth-century working-class poet. Chronologically James falls between Cave and Williams; her only volume of verse appeared in 1839. James and her family left Wales in the early years of the nineteenth century. These were years in which the Enclosure Acts (1793–1818) transformed forever the topographic, economic and demographic landscape of rural north Wales. As a result of the combined economic pressures of war with France, rapid industrialization in south Wales and – perhaps most significantly – a final drive towards absolute control by the landowning rich, massive areas of Welsh farmland were enclosed. For many of the poor of north Wales's farming communities, who were already suffering terrible hardship during the famine years of 1795–7 and 1799–1801, enclosure was the final impetus for flight into the 'New World' across the Atlantic.[42] The family of Maria James appears to have been part of the human tide whose fate Gwyn A. Williams describes: 'In the northern Llŷn peninsula farmers and fishermen in revolt against enclosures decimated the population of their community in an independent movement into upstate New York . . . while behind them thousands trapped in poverty clamoured to get away.'[43] Gwyn A. Williams refers to these as the years of 'the rage to go to America', when the United States appeared to beckon the Welsh poor with the promise of boundless opportunity.[44] Once in the States, James found employment as a domestic servant with an American family. Her particular position as economic refugee and domestic servant, dependent upon her employers for shelter and income, provides an interesting and unusual perspective on the reality of the 'American dream' for one Welsh emigrant. Representations of class identity in James's verse are richly suggestive of the frustrations of life as an immigrant worker in the land of opportunity. Readings expose tensions between her economically driven need to conform to the behaviour expected of a loyal servant in a foreign land and her disenchanted sense of herself as a poet. Some useful scholarship has taken place in recent years which focuses on poetry written by working-class women during the nineteenth century;[45] what poems by Maria James offer is a rare opportunity to investigate work by a poet whose material survival has been achieved with the promise of freedom and prosperity, yet at the cost of belief in such possibilities.

★ ★ ★

Clearly, then, the chronological structure of this book facilitates analysis of a number of perspectives on class identity throughout the nineteenth century. The work of each of the poets examined yields insights into aspects of the experience of class at a particular moment in the period. Of course, since these are women writers, it is important to consider whether and in what ways readings of class position evinced through the verse may be mitigated by the poets' experiences of gender identity. Leonore Davidoff and Catherine Hall make the point that 'gender and class always operate together, that consciousness of class always takes a gendered form'.[46] Proceeding from this assumption, readings of work by the poets discussed here may be even more complex. What, for example, does Jane

Cave's approach to the evolving position of her own 'middling' class group tell us about the importance of gender difference in the formation of middle-class ideology and conduct at the turn of the eighteenth and nineteenth centuries? To what extent does Sarah Williams's identification in her poems with the consummate self-confidence of her class contribute to an understanding of the function of gender in consolidating and propagating bourgeois ideology at its cultural, political and economic apogee? And, further, what tensions are discernible in the texture of the verse between the constructions of femininity entailed in establishing and maintaining those respective systems and the lived experience of the nineteenth-century woman poet? In the case of Maria James, the converse form of analysis may also be useful; it is interesting to consider, for example, the ways in which gender informs the particular class perspective of an emigrant worker as dramatized through her verse. Her position as housemaid and still-poor emigrant may be said to reconfigure our assessment of familiar tropes in nineteenth-century women's verse, such as domesticity, freedom and confinement.

Indeed, the work of all seven poets offers ample material for a general investigation of the issue of gender in relation to nineteenth-century women's poetry. The nineteenth century, of course, saw the rise to prominence of the so-called 'woman question'. The cult of domesticity, which to a large extent defined dominant bourgeois value systems at the height of the Victorian era, relied upon particular understandings of the 'proper' place of women in society.

Connections between individual women's experiences, the 'woman question' and women's writing are complex, inconsistent and often contradictory. Clearly, these links need to be carefully historicized in relation to each individual poet. However, a brief look at the course of the struggle for women's political rights through the period indicates the intensity of the tension inherent between the prescribed propriety and the movement towards women's equal treatment under the law. In the early days of the century, middle-ranking women's involvement in political and philanthropic activities, such as campaigns for prison reform, the eradication of alcoholism and prostitution and, perhaps most significantly, the abolition of slavery, precipitated vociferous public debate about their appropriate 'mission' in life. By the 1830s serious arguments for women's rights were being voiced in various periodicals and meeting halls around Britain.[47] In 1832 MPs refused to consider the enfranchisement of women, and in fact, with the Reform Act of that year, the exclusion of women from political representation became enshrined in legislation for the first time, through the use of the words 'male person'.[48]

When, in 1867, John Stuart Mill's amendment to the Second Reform Act proposing limited female enfranchisement was defeated, the campaign for women's suffrage began in earnest. Despite almost two decades of intense democratic lobbying, the Third Reform Act in 1884 enfranchised virtually all men whilst women remained completely powerless at parliamentary level. It was at this point that militant suffragism, later brought to prominence by famous advocates such as Emmeline Pankhurst, began to develop among campaigners demoralized by what they saw as the failure of democracy. Throughout the century developments in women's history, such as those described above, served to deepen the complex and already widespread social anxieties over the 'woman question'. It is potentially useful, then, to consider the work of the poets selected here in the light of chronological developments across the century, and in terms of their – often deeply encoded – responses to issues of gender.

The range of perspectives includes, for example, that of Ann Julia Hatton, a character already possessed of a chequered history and a dubious moral reputation before she ever took up the pen name 'Ann of Swansea'. Hatton's volume of verse, *Poetic Trifles*, on which I base my discussion, was published in 1811; she wrote, therefore, at a time when women's lives were increasingly becoming controlled through a plethora of institutional mechanisms. The division of gender roles into so-called separate spheres, with the private domestic space firmly defined as women's domain, was, as Davidoff and Hall describe in meticulous detail, a vital element in the rise and dominion of the bourgeoisie.[49] Feminist critics have shown how establishing women's status as private domestic creatures entailed the systematic regulation of the female body through a network of discourses including law, medicine, religion and the family.[50] A key strategy in the operation of these discourses was the double standard in sexual morality. Hatton's poetry seems to me to be extremely interesting in this regard. As a member of a family of actors Hatton's class status was ambiguous, but in terms of education and income she was certainly more closely aligned with the 'middling groups' than with the lower classes. Hatton was also seen to be a morally transgressive woman, and endured public censure and significant material sanctions as a result of her disreputable conduct. Her perspective, then, was that of one who was subject to the inequities of the double standard, and yet also aspirant, to some extent, to the social class whose interests were supported by its abuses. Perhaps unsurprisingly, Hatton's poems are often preoccupied with explorations of erotic love; an examination of the literary strategies employed in these excursions offers an opportunity to investigate the poet's responses to the moral and social code which both defined and constrained her as a woman and a writer.

One poet who has been credited with single-handedly 'making the shift [among nineteenth-century women poets] . . . to a Victorian ethic of home' is Felicia Hemans.[51] Although Hemans died in 1835, two years before Queen Victoria acceded to the throne, she is considered by many critics to be a primary archetype and instrument of Victorian domestic sensibility in literary culture.[52] Her prolific popular output of poetic works, many of which still endure as standard anthology pieces, has enshrined Hermans as a cause célèbre among nineteenth-century women poets. An entire industry of literary criticism has grown around her work in recent years, much of it evincing readings from a feminist critical perspective, and in this way she is unique among the largely unknown poets to whom I refer here. Notwithstanding the already large corpus of available material, Hemans is an important figure in terms of the gender history of the period, and a consideration of her work in relation to this area is potentially valuable to the study. In my assessment of Hemans's work I make a brief survey of selected interpretations in the current range, and consider them in the light of my own analyses of her poems.

An interesting contrast to Hatton's marginal and somewhat reviled position and Hemans's defining conservative respectability is Anna Walter Thomas, something of a 'bluestocking' figure who was writing at the end of the century, and who occupied very different social circumstances from those of either Hatton or Hemans. Thomas, alone among the poets discussed here, was by birth a member of the upper echelons of nineteenth-century British society. Born into a gentry family of some intellectual distinction, Thomas and a number of her sisters married Oxbridge scholars and were able, through their husbands' connections and access, as well as their own impressive gifts, to pursue academic eminence of sorts for themselves. Unlike the other poets selected, Thomas did not publish volumes of verse. The two available poems are both prizewinning National Eisteddfod entries submitted in 1883 and 1892 respectively. Thomas was thus writing from an unusually privileged social position, at a point in the century when debate over the 'woman question' was reaching a political and cultural peak. Thomas's engagement with gender issues in the poems may allow access to an understanding of the ways in which a woman of her many advantages, and during a period of such intense gender-political controversy, was able to process the juxtaposition of her propitious social status with the impediment of her gender identity.

I have spent some time discussing the scope of the study in terms of gender and class issues, but I turn now to the real core of the project, which is the consideration of the seven poets in terms of their links with Wales. Regardless of the specificity of their individual circumstances, all of these women identify to some extent with Wales whilst, nevertheless, writing in English for an English literary market. I am concerned in this book to examine the ways in which the poets negotiate the inherent tensions of this position, and, further, to consider what the insights gained from such an investigation may add to an understanding of the relationships between gender and national identity in the context of Welsh–English relations in the period. In order to ground discussion, it is necessary to reflect on the historical background to the literary works.

The history of Wales in the early nineteenth century may be characterized as a narrative of incorporation. Linda Colley, in her book *Britons: Forging the Nation 1707–1837*, makes the point that at the turn of the eighteenth and nineteenth centuries a process of consolidation was under way between the politically dominant English centre and its Celtic peripheries. Colley locates the incorporative drive in the English need for additional renewable resources, human as well as financial, in the face of war with France and the increasing demands of empire building and maintenance:

> The growing need to raise taxes and cannonfodder from the island as a whole (and from that other island across the Irish Sea) forced those elite Englishmen who initially monopolized civilian power in London to accept a quota of Scots, Anglo-Irish and Welshmen into their ranks. Moreover, the elastic empire that resulted from Wars with France increasingly depended on Britons who were not English for government, exploration and exploitation.[53]

The 'Welshmen' to whom Colley here refers are, of course, the landed masters of Wales, who were entitled to enlist the majority of the country's inhabitants to the functions of tax and cannon fodder. As Jane Aaron has argued, however, 'Colley presents this process as essentially one of gain for all concerned . . . one may still query to what extent any of [the] "substantial profits" filtered back to the people of Scotland, Ireland and Wales.'[54] Aaron makes an interesting case for the 'wooing' of Wales in literature published by English presses in the early part of the century. She cites a number of fictional works of the period which depict Wales as charming and picaresque with much to offer the new British order, and examines the novels of several Welsh women writers, including Ann Julia Hatton, in an effort to determine their responses to the incorporative process. The poetry of women writing in this period, such as Jane Cave and Ann Julia Hatton, may offer equally fruitful sites for investigation. Their different perspectives in terms of social hierarchies of respectability has the potential, I would argue, to produce useful readings of the ways in which identification with Wales may mitigate an understanding of the Anglicizing process for those who were not of the elite group of immediate beneficiaries.

By the middle of the nineteenth century the landowning elite of Wales had been successfully incorporated into the English/British mainstream, to the apparent satisfaction of all the leading parties, and any wooing of Wales by England had summarily ceased to be necessary or desirable. The Anglicization of the people of Wales in the middle to late part of the century involved less a process of seduction than one of exploitation and abasement. The rapid industrialization of Wales in the mid-nineteenth century, with its social deprivations and demographic upheavals, has been well documented.[55] Representations of Wales and the Welsh which emerged at this point from English authors, both literary and sociological, depicted a rough and inhospitable country inhabited by a people whose ignorance and lawlessness were matched only by their spiritual destitution and moral dereliction, particularly that of its women.[56] I will return to this point in my discussion of religious issues in the Welsh context, but it is clear that poetry by Welsh women, some of whom lived and worked in England and all of whom aspired to success in the English literary canon of the period, constitutes a potentially rewarding territory for explorations in the histories of Wales, England and women's writing. The poetry of Felicia Hemans is intriguing, for example; whilst considering herself to be a 'naturalized Welsh woman', and writing at length on Welsh topics, Hemans nevertheless penned a number of English literature's most memorable panegyrics to British imperialism. Amid the wealth of critical material available on Hemans, little attention has been paid to her Welsh connections. It seems to me that analysis of her Welsh poems is long overdue in a literary critical evaluation of the period. Less famous work, however, by writers such as Sarah Williams or Emily Jane Pfeiffer, may also prove useful. Both poets deploy Welsh settings in their verse, and explore Welshness as a significant theme. I am equally concerned to discover the ways in which these lesser-known women attempt to reconcile their claims to Welsh identity with the demands of 'British' codes of respectability and patriotism at the height of British imperial dominance.

In the course of researching the poetry, it has become clear that an element which is often important in the poets' various senses of themselves as Welsh women is that of religion. This is perhaps not surprising when considering work which was produced in a century during which religious identity was a vital criterion in determining legal, political and social status. Calvinistic Methodism, the Nonconformist denomination which thrived in nineteenth-century Wales, initially remained a tendency within the established Church decades after the Baptists and Independents had broken away; Calvinistic Methodism was not established as a denomination in its own right until 1811. It developed as a distinctive and separate movement from either English-based Wesleyan Methodism or other Nonconformist sects throughout the nineteenth century. The Toleration Act of 1689 had allowed freedom of worship to Protestant dissenters, though Roman Catholics remained beyond the pale. By the beginning of the nineteenth century significant concessions had been made to dissenters, resulting in forty-five of their number having become sitting Members of Parliament by 1807, although they were still excluded from ministerial or administrative office, from commissions in the armed forces and from the universities. In 1828 the Test and Corporation Acts, which had disbarred Nonconformists from holding government office, were repealed; and the following year the Catholic Emancipation Act was passed, allowing Catholics, too, equal consideration under the law, though suspicion of their loyalty endured. By the mid-nineteenth century the religious momentum had radically shifted to the extent that, as David Thomson asserts,

> the most generally accepted and practised form of Christianity was that which may be broadly called evangelicism . . . It was the period when the so-called 'nonconformist conscience' permeated English life and manners – even amongst conformists . . . In 1846 the Evangelicals formed the 'Evangelical Alliance' which united all English Protestants, Anglicans, and Nonconformists alike, in a common resistance to Roman Catholicism and all its influences.[57]

At the same time the rise of the Oxford or Tractarian movement in England at the mid-point in the century, with its suspiciously Catholic sensibility and emphasis on ritual, caused what Thomson describes as 'liturgical warfare within the Church',[58] resulting in a renewed public concern with ecclesiastical and religious matters.

Clearly, then, religious faith and observance was a central element in the way nineteenth-century Britons viewed themselves. In the case of Welsh identity, religious allegiance became a still more intensely crucial determining factor. Ieuan Gwynedd Jones notes the sustained growth of membership of religious organizations in Wales during the middle decades of the nineteenth century, making the point that 'this religious

expansion was largely confined to the Nonconformist denominations'.[59]
Jones goes on to detail the profound and widespread influence of these on
the general consciousness of Welsh people.

> Religion in these communities was not a divisive force . . . it was a
> unifying one . . . They proclaimed not divisiveness but a fundamental
> harmony based on the essential of belief. To claim that this quality of
> believing was universal . . . would be foolish . . . But it was this substantial
> minority of the population which established the moral universe within
> which the vast bulk of the population lived.[60]

The domination of Nonconformity over Welsh communal consciousness
persisted throughout the nineteenth century. What engendered the
explicit linking, during the middle of the nineteenth century, of Welsh
national identity with Nonconformist religious practice was the attitude
and conduct towards Wales of the English establishment itself. Early in
the nineteenth century it was already obvious that the Church of England
had lost its foothold in Wales; as Williams remarks: 'in the first years of
the new century growth [in Nonconformist membership] became
torrential'.[61] The Church, however, was apparently unconcerned to
address the situation; according to Ieuan Gwynedd Jones the reasons for
this *laissez faire* attitude were rooted in political expediency:

> None of the £1 million voted by Parliament in 1818 for building new
> churches, and only a minuscule part of the additional grant of £500,000 in
> 1824, came to Wales . . . [This] was the result of political calculation, namely,
> that the threat to public order originated mainly, or was invariably to be
> found, in very large towns and cities of which there were none in Wales.[62]

Rapid and intense industrialization during the 1830s changed this view
entirely, and after the Merthyr and Newport risings, of 1831 and 1839
respectively, Wales began to be viewed with increasing anxiety from the
English centre. Wales, and particularly the hotbed of potential insurrec-
tion in the industrial south, became subject to careful surveillance. As
Jones observes, 'what was found sharpened the apprehension of the
establishment of what was held to be a necessary congruence between
right beliefs and proper conduct'.[63]

I have already discussed the tendencies of the literary establishment
in its depictions of Wales and the Welsh at the time. But it was at this
point also that both Church and State intervened by initiating copious
numbers of enquiries designed to investigate all aspects of the conduct of

communities emerging from outside the moral influence of the established Church. The most significant of these studies produced the notorious 1847 'Blue Books', the *Reports of the Commissioners of Inquiry into the State of Education in Wales*. Jones argues that the purpose of the report was 'to demonstrate a need and to justify the adoption of forms of educational provision designed to return a people to their old allegiances'.[64] Regardless of the level of conscious calculation involved in devising the aims of the project, there is clear evidence that its results were used to attempt to 'shame' the Welsh into moral, political and religious conformity. The report comprised the published findings of a government enquiry, ostensibly into the state of education in Wales. As Gwyn A. Williams and John Davies both allow, it was accurate enough in its description of the woefully inadequate educational provision in Wales at the time. What it also did, however, was to discuss the sexual morality of the Welsh, with Welsh women coming in for particular criticism; it concluded that a combination of Nonconformist religious practice and adherence to the Welsh language had produced a nation 'uniquely lax in their sexual habits'.[65] Gwyn A. Williams describes in characteristically vivid terms one, presumably unanticipated, result of the report's publication: 'The Saxon Night of the Long Knives was recalled as the Report was stigmatized as *brad*, the Treason of the Blue Books. A form of Welsh nationalism, peculiarly Dissenter and Welsh-speaking, was stung into life.'[66] It is difficult to overestimate the impact of the 1847 report upon Welsh cultural life in the second half of the nineteenth century. Responses to the report were varied and complex, but few areas of Welsh culture remained unengaged with the national identity crisis experienced in its aftermath. One side effect was that Nonconformism, the Welsh language and Welsh women's supposed sexual immorality became inextricably linked in the outside world's perception of Wales and the Welsh; and these factors were no less crucial to the way the Welsh saw and presented themselves.

Inevitably, then, the act of writing as woman and a poet during this period, already encumbered by constraints imposed by Victorian patriarchal codes of femininity, was further problematized for the Welsh woman poet. If Welshness was synonymous in British culture with a linguistic and religious infrastructure which spawned an uncivilized population mothered by unchaste women, the poets' engagement with issues of Welsh identity may well provide new perspectives on the vexed relationship between women and Victorian patriarchy.

Ieuan Gwynedd Jones makes the point that, in addition to these intersections among religion, gender and Welsh identity, the 1847 report also highlighted implications in terms of class consciousness: '[The report] more completely than almost any other source . . . shows the extent to which different social classes adhered to different forms of religion, but also the extent to which, even before 1847, there had developed a perception that the clergy were the servants of one class against another.'[67]

It seems to me that what the work of these seven Welsh women poets offers is the chance to explore, not only their individual contributions to an understanding of class, gender, religion and Welshness in the nineteenth century, but also, and perhaps more importantly, the ways in which a marginalized sense of national identity may inflect the representation of experience in all of these areas. In examining the poetry of Jane Cave, Ann Julia Hatton, Maria James, Felicia Hemans, Sarah Williams, Emily Pfeiffer and Anna Walter Thomas, it is possible to interrogate Virginia Woolf's claims for the tragedy of 'Judith Shakespeare' and the problems of women and national identity; for these writers, in their lives and their poetic practices, enact the tensions envisaged by Woolf. But as Welsh women theirs is a drama which is stretched across a network of forces more fraught than Woolf could imagine, and more interesting because of that.

1

Surface and inner tension in the poetry of Jane Cave

This chapter is concerned with the literary output of Jane Cave, later Winscom, a now little-known writer who enjoyed a considerable degree of success as a poet at the turn of the eighteenth and nineteenth centuries. In particular, the chapter engages with the way in which the poems may be read as problematizing Cave's sense of her Welsh roots. I am concerned with interrogating the hitherto unproblematic homogenization of Cave's work into the English literary mainstream. I intend to question whether many of the poems in Cave's oeuvre may be seen as demonstrating a tension between the poet's aspirations to the canon of English poetry and her identity as an expatriate Welsh woman.

Jane Cave was born and brought up in south Wales, the daughter of an Englishman who worked as an exciseman in Talgarth, Breconshire, for many of his daughter's formative years. Whilst stationed with the Excise in Talgarth, John Cave came into contact with Howel Harris and his religious community at Trefecca, and was converted to fervent Calvinistic Methodism. Jane Cave herself left Wales as a young adult; she was married to another exciseman by the name of Winscom in 1785 and she bore him two sons. She is known to have lived in Bristol and Winchester before returning to the land of her birth where she died in Newport, Monmouthshire, in 1813.

Cave's volume of verse, *Poems on Various Subjects, Entertaining, Elegiac and Religious*, went into four editions between 1783 and 1794; by the time of the fourth edition it boasted a list of some two thousand eminent subscribers. It is to be hoped that Jane Cave enjoyed her popularity while it lasted, for her work remained unpublished between 1794 and 1989.

In his essay on 'Poets of Breconshire', Roland Mathias speculated on the source of Cave's initial popularity, discounting in no uncertain terms the possibility of anything more impressive than 'a technical competence, a sententious approach to religion and a flair for using the personal as a starting point for occasional poems'.[1] She has been getting some better press more recently, however, and, interestingly, English critics have been demonstrating greater appreciation of her work than Mathias's sweepingly negative view. A brief selection of Cave's poetry appears in the 1989 *Oxford Anthology of Eighteenth-century Women Poets*, edited by Roger Lonsdale, and the volume is promoted as consisting of 'a hundred witty women glistening and pulsing with spirits before us'.[2] Cave, however, seems to have been inclined to share Roland Mathias's low opinion of her work. Her prefatory note 'To the Subscribers' seems typical of the self-abnegatory tone of much eighteenth-century women's writing which Alice Browne has referred to as 'pathetic expression of bravado which show how little some women thought of their own work':[3]

> Ye gen'rous patrons of a female's muse,
> 'Ere you my works with studious eye peruse,
> My pen would first in humble strains impart
> The genuine dictates of a grateful heart;
> Thanks to my friends – and should my labours please,
> Crown'd are my wishes, and my heart's at ease,
> My time improv'd, my musing hours well spent,
> If these conspire to give my friends content:
> But Seward, Steele or More, hope to see,
> With gentle candour read, 'The Author's Plea'.[4]

The emphasis is on humility and gratitude to the purchasers of her poetry. She also claims to suffer from an inferiority complex with regard to the work of some of her celebrated contemporaries, namely Anna Seward, Anne Steele and Hannah More. However, the deferential modesty of this introduction belies the confidence and even temerity of many of the verses which succeed it in the volume. Stylistically Cave's work is conservative for the period, a feature which, as Lonsdale's volume demonstrates, it shares with that of many of her female contemporaries. Elaine Showalter has discussed women writers' historical appropriation of so-called 'masculine genres' in terms of their lack of self-confidence.[5] A reading of Cave's poems, however, presents a supplementary possibility – which is that her use of the retrospective style is part of a strategy of self-conscious masking, and, perhaps, an unconscious process of containment of the potentially subversive ideas which it frames. I have already discussed my intention to adopt a broadly Marxist approach to the poems.

What I propose is that this interpretative approach may legitimately be applied to Cave's work, and may generate readings which illuminate its conditions of production not only in terms of the artist's experience of gender and class but also with regard to her relation to Wales. My intention is ultimately to explore the ways in which this proposition may affect an interpretation of Cave as a Welsh-born writer. Before embarking on that exploration, however, I want to examine the way in which her poetry may be read in these terms with reference to the familiar issues of gender and class which have precipitated the interest of Lonsdale and others in her work.

★ ★ ★

Firstly, then, I turn to the question of sexual politics. 'The Author's Plea', referred to in the 'Note to the Subscribers' is the first piece in *Poems on Various Subjects*, and appears in all editions. It opens in her customary apologetic tone as it describes 'perhaps a thousand faults and more', which a critical perusal of the book is likely to reveal.[6] However, the poet's defence of her shortcomings is constructed in a lively comparison between the freedom of her youth and the constraints of responsible adulthood which, in its understanding of economic factors, prefigures Virgina Woolf's seminal plea for a 'room of one's own' a century and a half later:

> So when the muses come on anxious wing,
> I bid them fly where peaceful leisure rests,
> 'Tis vain in me to entertain such guests . . .
> Now duty's call I never must refuse,
> I rise, and with a sigh myself excuse . . . [7]

The late eighteenth-century 'feminist' agenda has been seen as divided into three areas of concern, namely: inequalities in women's education, in women's legal and economic position, and in the prevalent double standard of sexual morality.[8] So how does Jane Cave fit into this paradigm? Access to education is certainly one of her concerns. In 'The Author's Plea', for instance, she acknowledges that it is only 'Fortune' which is responsible for the extent of the development of each individual's intellectual and creative potential:

> By books and study fructify the mind,
> And lead the genius where it was inclin'd;

> The inauspicious dame deny'd that I
> Should thus, where nature's self inclin'd apply . . . [9]

The poet sees herself as caught in a trap where nature has equipped her to do what fortune will not allow. The implication is that womanhood does not preclude rational and creative intellect, and that it is therefore social convention, rather than divine decree, which is the agent of the poet's ill-fortune.

The issue of women's legal and economic status is addressed most directly in Cave's work in her humorous poem 'An Elegy on a Maiden Name'. Her tilt at the proprietary patriarchal convention takes the form of a witty and good-natured farewell to the single life:

> Adieu dear name which birth and nature gave,
> Lo! At the altar I've interr'd a Cave;
> For there it fell, expir'd and found a grave. [10]

The approach is one of mock-melodrama, the tone exuberant and optimistic. However, the imagery of death and burial, aside from the irresistible conceit borne of the name itself, connotes an instinct on the part of the poet that she is relinquishing not merely her name but her 'nature'. The obvious contradiction that the maiden name itself is a patrilineal inheritance is explained by the poet describing her attachment to it in terms of a precious legacy from her mother:

> But ah! The loss of Cave I must deplore,
> For that dead name the tend'rest mother bore. [11]

The poet's perception of the bond with her maiden name and 'nature' may thus be read as a more visceral and essentially female connection than the legal force of patriarchal convention to which she now succumbs. She is compelled by circumstance to make the commitment, however, and in doing so can only hope for the best:

> May I find in you
> A friend and husband – faithful, wise and true. [12]

According to the evidence provided in two of Cave's later poems dedicated to her unborn child, this was a vain hope – by then the tone has shifted to one of bitterness and disappointment; she advises her child, if a daughter, ominously of the dangers inherent in choosing a husband:

> Their tempers and defects they hide,
> Till they obtain the wish'd-for bride,
> And then they cast the veil aside.[13]

The same two poems, 'To My Unborn Child if a Son' and 'To My Unborn Child if a Daughter', are useful indices of the poet's perception of her society's sexual double standard. And it is here that her most strident and unambiguously 'feminist' attitudes are revealed. Cave first addresses her unborn child as a son. This poem concentrates on urging his caution in choosing a wife, but, once certain of his choice, to treat her with the utmost consideration:

> And if you find the maid is she,
> Who may through life your helpmate be,
> Then court her heart, with honour court,
> Nor dare to make a nymph your sport.[14]

Tellingly, the mother's greatest concern for her unborn son is that he should not abuse the woman who gives up her liberty for his sake. The earlier cheerful surrender of her own freedom seems paramount in her mind when considering his future. She abhors the possibility that he might

> With ardour seek – her love to obtain –
> Then to desert and give her pain,
> Involve in grief who had been free,
> Content and happy but for thee.[15]

The twin poem, 'To My Unborn Child if a Daughter', is also a sour statement on the nature of the poet's own marital experience. It is a scathing indictment of the moral failings of mankind, and, by implication, of the unequal code which permits, and even endorses, men's morally reprehensible behaviour towards their wives:

> For such the deep deceits of men,
> And such their power o'er female hearts,
> We cannot penetrate their arts . . .
> Thus after each precaution taken,
> Too oft' we find ourselves mistaken.[16]

The emotional and spiritual value of female relationships is a recurrent theme in Cave's poetry; the titles listed in the table of contents to all editions of her volume provides ample evidence of this preoccupation. Of the 1794 version of the list, which numbers some sixty pieces, twenty-three announce the author's concern with women-centred associations; it includes, for example, such offerings as 'On the Marriage of a Lady, to Whom the Author was Bridemaid', 'On the Death of Mrs Mayberry of Brecon', 'On the Death of an Only Child Written at the Mother's Request', 'On the Death of Mrs Blake, who died in child-bed (of her sixth child)', and 'To a Lady who Lent the Author (tho' quite a Stranger) Two Valuable Volumes and Co.'.

The strength of Cave's imagined bond with her daughter is clear from the example of the poem cited above. She also refers to the benign and powerful influence of her own mother who died at the age of forty-four in poems such as 'Elegy on a Maiden Name' and 'On the Death of the Author's Mother'. And in an elegiac poem dedicated to 'Mrs Powell of Bristol', Cave mourns the loss of another important and formative friendship:

> Thou wert my friend from early youth,
> E'er either took the name of wife;
> No fickle friend, but such in truth,
> Whose friendship ended but with life.[17]

The relationship is depicted as fundamental, powerful, and prior in terms of emotional seniority, as well as chronology, when compared to the more cosmetic attachment of marriage. Cave's connections with women are often central to her poetry. Much of her oeuvre is preoccupied with concerns which continue to be crucial to women's experience: childbirth, child care, infant mortality and women's health issues. The relationships with her mother, her imagined daughter and her female friends are empowering in practical and poetic terms. Adrienne Rich coined the term 'lesbian continuum' to describe 'a range through each woman's life . . . of woman-identified experience of positive and nurturing female associations . . . to embrace many forms of primary intensity between and among women.'[18] To a great extent, Cave's poetry is evidence of her sensitivity to the value of such a continuum, two hundred years before her currently distinguished 'sister' gave it a name. I would argue, then, that Cave's poetic engagement with the 'woman question' of her time offers a lively, often bold contribution to a feminist history of the period.

In view of the confident nature of her ideas, Cave's consistent stylistic conservatism is intriguing. She favours the rhyming couplet and iambic metre preferred by the male aficionados of an earlier era in that century who claimed to revere the artistic and political values of classical antiquity. In attempting to account for this strategy I have referred to the poet's unconscious urges; in order to engage more systematically with this concept, it is necessary to refer to the basic tenets of the theories of psychoanalysis. Sigmund Freud's assertion that literary production, for example, may be interpreted as symbolic of the relationship between the artist's conscious and unconscious thought-processes is relevant to an exploration of Cave's use of stylistic convention.[19] Received wisdom has traditionally divided human behaviour according to gendered categories – where the faculties of rationality and logic, and the capacity for considered positive action, are regarded as essentially male attributes, whilst emotional, visceral and variegated responses are more closely associated with the female nature. Such classification has never been more entrenched, nor has more value been attributed to the supposedly male factors than in the early eighteenth-century period which Cave's formal patterning imitates. Freud's work only reasserts ancient gender divisions, and much post-Freudian feminist scholarship has been concerned with interrogating these stereotypes. Hélène Cixous, for example, has stressed the subversive essence of female creativity in opposition to the 'logocentrism' of male-engendered western rationality.[20] For Cave, however, the act of imposing patriarchal structure on radical concepts may in itself represent a subliminal urge – namely to contain and control the ideas which have the potential to threaten not just the political status quo, but the emotional and material well-being of the poet herself. In this reading the poet's deployment of the framework of logocentric discourse, rather than being a symptom of timid conformity, becomes an instrument of her own creative strength. The poet's determination to achieve self-expression is inhibited by the patriarchal bias of her society, but she is not silenced – nor does she forgo the opportunity for material gain in its pursuit. Her conscious and unconscious mental processes combine to spawn sometimes ungraceful but nevertheless compelling testimony to the ideological and aesthetic forces which shape her as a women and an artist.

Cave's attitudes towards issues of class divisions are perhaps even more remarkable for an eighteenth-century woman poet than is her instinct for gender-political debate. Categorizing Jane Cave as a member of a particular class group is in itself a precarious undertaking. In attempting to assess her position, patrimonial rank is the most effective gauge available; the social and economic status of her father and husband must therefore serve as the primary benchmarks of Cave's class position. In his 1980 work *Something to Declare*, Graham Smith, archivist and librarian to HM

Customs and Excise, describes the entry requirements of the eighteenth-century exciseman, such as Mr Cave or Mr Winscom:

> The more complicated work of the Excise [compared with Customs], with the diversity of manufacturing processes to be controlled, demanded a higher standard of education from its entrants . . . Applicants were required to understand 'the first four rules of arithmetick (sic) and write with a fair hand'. Their application had to be supported by a person of substance, and they had to obtain training in the art of gauging.[21]

Smith also remarks that

> There was no shortage of recruits . . . despite the hazardous nature of the work and the general unpopularity of their calling, life was not too unattractive. Compared with similar posts, revenue officers were relatively well paid. With the possible exception of officers of the armed forces, it would be difficult to find a trade or profession with salary or prospects comparable with the Excise.[22]

Jane Cave, as the daughter of one such officer, was clearly educated to a standard where she was capable of earning her living, perhaps as an upper-rank domestic servant, a lady's maid or a housekeeper, and certainly, for a time, as a writer. In their influential study *Family Fortunes: Men and Women of the English Middle Class 1780–1850*, Leonore Davidoff and Catherine Hall attempt to demarcate eighteenth-century class boundaries; they see the middle class as distinct from the aristocracy primarily through the middle-class 'imperative . . . to actively seek . . . an income rather than expect to live from rents and the emoluments of office while spending their time in honour-enhancing activities such as politics, hunting or social appearances'.[23] Davidoff and Hall also offer an interesting definition of what they term 'the middle-class provincial intellectuals' who are distinguishable as such 'by virtue of their literacy and capacity to articulate . . . publishing pamphlets, manuals, tracts, sermons, poetry, writing in local newspapers and church magazines [and] in locally published books produced by subscription'.[24] Despite their scrupulous efforts towards a definition, Davidoff and Hall never achieve complete clarity, interchanging throughout their account one approximate term with another: 'middling class', 'middle ranks', 'middle strata' and 'middle groups' all seem to be synonyms for one another in their text. However, for the purposes of this book, and with the scholarship of Davidoff and Hall in mind, Jane Cave may be identified as belonging to the burgeoning provincial lower-middle rank of eighteenth-century Britain. She may certainly be viewed as part of the section of society which is easily differentiated from the aristocratic and landed echelons, many members of which are numbered among her list of subscribers.

In the tone and content of much of Cave's verse she aligns herself firmly with the more humble and wage-earning ranks. A particularly striking example of Cave's class consciousness can be found in her 'Poem Occasioned by a Lady's Doubting whether the Author Composed an Elegy to which her Name is Affix'd'. The context so clearly described in the title is presumably autobiographical; the tone is one of stinging rebuke, the poet referring to the elegy in question as 'what she [the Lady] did on Sunday see'. [25] There is a breathless immediacy about the lightly punctuated opening four lines which reinforces the impression that the incident involving the sceptical aristocrat has taken place very recently, and the sting is still keenly felt:

> If Lady B. will condescend
> To read these lines which I have penned,
> Perhaps it may her doubts confute,
> And she'll no more my word dispute . . .[26]

The tone of angry retort is sustained as she continues:

> You'd hate a base perfidious youth,
> Such my disgust to all untruth.
> A gen'rous mind is never prone
> To claim a merit not her own:
> I would disdain t'affix my name
> To that which is another's claim.

The poet is defending herself here at the level of personal integrity. Her implicit claim to possess a 'gen'rous mind' in line eight cleverly exploits the iambic metre in order to cast aspersions upon the Lady's own magnanimity of spirit: in reading the line, the stress must fall on the first syllable of 'gen'rous', which immediately suggests the semantic possibility of an alternative to generosity; the addressee could hardly fail to perceive the implied snub. From line thirteen onwards, however, the tone modulates into rational argument as the poet turns to consolidate the indignant defence of her literary honour on the grounds of a vindication of the moral and intellectual capacities of the lower classes, and makes a thinly veiled diatribe against what she sees as the unmerited and slothful vanities of the aristrocracy.

The poet's contempt for the Lady's skill as a critic is clear at once. The negative 'condescend' in line one connotes unjustified self-importance on the part of the titled subject. The poetic convention of omitting the full names of living characters is deployed to the utmost advantage of the poet's purpose here. The subject is anonymous, save for the epithet of her social station – and linked with the verb 'condescend', which implies inflated self-opinion, her title itself becomes a stinging rebuke. Lady B. is subjected to a lecture which further asserts in declamatory fashion that desirable attributes such as intelligence and moral virtue are not confined to, nor even inclined to reside with, the upper classes:

> Of beauteous form Heaven made me not,
> (Nor has soft affluence been my lot,)
> But fix'd me in a humbler station,
> Than those at court in highest fashion.
> But there are beauties of the mind,
> Which are not to the great confin'd,
> Wisdom does not erect her seat
> Always in palaces of state;
> This blessing Heav'n dispenses round;
> She's sometimes in a cottage found;
> And tho' she is a guest majestic,
> May deign to dwell in a domestic.

The poet's tone is heavy with irony as she goes on to demonstrate her unwillingness to make idle boasts about her ability, whilst asserting the skill which the Lady has disputed:

> Yet of this great celestial guest,
> I dare not boast my self possess't,
> But this would represent to you,
> As wisdom does, the muses do,
> No def'rence show to wealth or ease,
> But pay their visits as they please.
> Sometimes they deign to call on me,
> And tune my mind to poetry;
> But ah! they're fled, I'll drop my pen,
> Nor raise it till they call again.[27]

Cave's flair for satire is evident here, and the poem is sharp and funny, even two centuries after the event. What I find interesting, however, is the light this piece sheds on the attitude of a British lower-rank woman to the unjust nature of the social system which defines her status and that of the vast majority of her peers. Linda Colley, in her work, *Britons: Forging the Nation, 1707–1837*, has discussed the feat of self-conscious reinvention accomplished by the ruling order in the aftermath of the American War of Independence: 'Many of them now took care to appear scrupulously religious and morally impeccable . . . [they displayed] relentless hard work, complete professionalism, an uncompromising private virtue and an ostentatious patriotism.'[28] And in her chapter on 'Woman Power' Colley describes the increasing emphasis on separate spheres for male and female activity throughout the period during which Cave was writing: 'The confines of the home were the boundaries of [the eighteenth-century woman's] kingdom . . . Her contribution to the nation was essentially private and always indirect.'[29] I would argue that the evidence of Cave's 'Poem Occasioned by a Lady's Doubting . . .' points to at least one female Briton who was not entirely convinced by the remodelled moral ascendancy of the British upper classes, and who was, furthermore, unprepared to acquiesce in the apolitical role ascribed in that society to someone of her social rank and gender. The rhyming couplet – a form promoted early in the century primarily by supporters of the class which the poem berates – is an interesting vehicle for these outspoken sentiments. The poet's attitudes are masked by her apparent homage to the neoclassical canon. I would argue that this conservatism can be read as symbolic of the poet's resistance – it may be unconscious resistance – to her own status as a dangerous outsider to the cultural system to which her work aspires, but to which it also offers a challenge.

★ ★ ★

I have dwelt at length, then, on establishing Jane Cave's credentials as a contributor to Roger Lonsdale's aforementioned collection in terms of class and sexual politics. Another implicit tenet of that anthology, however, is that the work in question is universally 'English'.[30] Of the six Cave poems included by Lonsdale, none are chosen from the half dozen in her volume *Poems on Various Subjects, Entertaining, Elegiac and Religious* which relate to Wales. In Lonsdale's wielding of the anthologic form, the national identity of a poet such as Jane Cave and, indeed, the premise of a national tradition from which she might have emerged, is rendered invisible by the assimilation of her work into the mainstream of English literary culture. What interests me more, however, than the attitude of the English literary establishment is that Cave herself seems to have been inclined to efface traces of her own Welshness from her work during the course of her writing career. In the first, 1783, edition of *Poems on Various Subjects* Cave incorporates several pieces which are explicitly Welsh in theme, but these have disappeared by the time of publication of the fourth and final edition in 1794.

In her book, *Britons*, Linda Colley has described the process by which Britain was forged as a nation during the eighteenth century; she stresses the centrality of Protestantism as a powerful unifying factor in establishing a British consciousness, defined against the dangerous 'other' of France and Catholicism. Colley, however, also recognizes that the union was superimposed 'on much older alignments and loyalties'.[31] An examination of any history of Wales in the period will demonstrate the extent of cultural divergence from the mainstream Anglo-British experience, particularly in the sphere of religious practice, and particularly in the geographic region of south Wales where Cave grew up.[32] Methodism, of course, was a radical movement within the Anglican Church, and its influence in the period was by no means confined to Wales. However, Welsh Calvinistic Methodism, as founded by Howel Harris, to whom Cave dedicates an elegy, was a variation unique to Wales at the time and was very different, in its emphasis on emotional release, from the more restrained English Wesleyan Methodism. In attempting to establish the extent of Jane Cave's identification of Methodist practice with her Welsh childhood, the experience of her English father is very relevant. John Cave was a native of Gillingham in Dorset. After his conversion to Methodism, and when his tenure as an excise officer in Talgarth had expired, he decided to return to Gillingham in order, as Roland Mathias puts it, 'to infuse life and enthusiasm into churchmanship'.[33] However, John Cave found himself rejected by the local clergy and congregation alike, and returned to Wales, setting up in business as a glover in Brecon. In 1781 John Cave published an 'Epistle to the inhabitants of Gillingham, Dorset wherein is a looking glass for the faithful',[34] in which he chides his former neighbours for their treatment of him and his religious message. It is not clear whether Jane Cave accompanied her father on his 'mission' to England; she may have done, as her marriage did not take place until 1783. In any case the frustrations of John Cave (with whom Jane retained close emotional ties throughout his life) would inevitably have had a strong influence on his daughter. In a poem dedicated to her father on the occasion of his eighty-first birthday Cave describes the impact of his passionate religious practice:

My mind retains from infant years
How oft he kneel'd dissolved in tears,
And wrestling on his suit preferr'd,
Till God was present there.[35]

I would contend, then, that it is feasible to read Jane Cave's view of Methodist fervency as closely associated with her Welsh background.

In his essay 'The New Enthusiasts', Geraint Jenkins gives an account of the influence of the renowned Methodist evangelists – notably Howel Harris – as crucial to the cultural 'remaking' of Wales in the eighteenth century: 'One of the most powerful influences in the remaking of Wales in the eighteenth century was enthusiasm. Those who counted themselves enthusiasts were characterized by the consciousness of a New Birth, infectious zeal, warm personal piety and pulpit eloquence.'[36] Although legal toleration of Nonconformist Protestantism had been institutionalized in Britain since 1689, the religious practice Jenkins depicts is radically different from the official Anglican doctrine of the British state. His essay gives ample textual evidence of the disdainful attitude of many English observers. One commentator remarked in 1752 of a Breconshire gathering, for example, that 'The Manner of the Itinerant's holding-forth is generally very boisterous and shocking, and adapted, to the best of their skill, to alarm the Imagination, and to raise a Ferment in the Passions, often attended with screaming and trembling of the Body'.[37] Jenkins describes the religious background in which Cave grew up; the attitude of contemporary English commentators on Welsh religious practices illustrates the 'othering' of such experience, carried out by agents of the dominant culture in which Cave later came to live and to which she attempted to belong.

Colley's stated aim is to fill the 'human vacuum' of textbook history by uncovering the 'identity, actions and ideas of those men and women who were prepared to support the existing order'.[38] The work of a Welsh writer of the period, such as Cave, whose biography suggests that the 'Britonizing' process to which Colley refers was a reality of lived experience, yields a corpus of human impressions with which to fill the 'vacuum'. The very existence in Colley's book of a separate section on 'Woman Power' testifies to the marginality of available evidence of women's experiences – the mainstream of documentation is male-centred history. Rediscovered creative writing by Welsh women of the period is, I would suggest, doubly valuable to a comprehensive view of evolving eighteenth-century Britain. In this chapter one of my aims is to challenge the assumption that the work of a poet from a Welsh background, such as

Jane Cave, can be homogenized seamlessly into the dominant canon of English literature. I will analyse closely some of Cave's early poems in order to investigate her apparent ambivalence towards her Welsh origins and to ascertain whether it is also signalled in the textual fabric of her writing.

In the introduction to their 1989 work, *The Empire Writes Back: Theory and Practice in Post-colonial Literatures*, Ashcroft, Griffiths and Tiffin assert that in the construction of the British Empire literature was crucial to the process of colonization; any deviance from the 'privileging norm' of English literature was sensed as a threat to the claims of the imperial centre. More than this, however, the ultimate incorporation of marginal literary forms was also partly due to collusion on the part of the colonized.[39]

In the light of this contention, then, it is not surprising to observe that the formal properties of Cave's poem 'Thoughts which Occurred to the Author at Llanwrtid [sic] in Breconshire, in walking home from Dol-y-Coed House to the Well', one of the few explicitly Welsh pieces to appear in all editions, owes much to the influence of the large body of English work written much earlier in the same century. In common with most of her work, the piece consists of iambic rhyming couplets – a form which, in the heyday of the eighteenth-century neoclassical period, was deployed in order to reflect the advocacy of order, reason and control in cultural and political life, and to celebrate the practice of the same qualities in poetic craft. It is potentially useful, therefore, to attempt to establish the extent, if any, of Jane Cave's ambivalence towards the forces of rationality so entrenched in the by then outdated literary culture which she persisted in imitating, which were so antithetical to the cultural aesthetic of her native historical community.[40]

Cave begins her piece by extolling the virtues of tranquil rationality in rural outdoor surroundings:

> Sweet, silent, solitary place,
> Where I majestic footsteps trace,
> Where Reason may ascend her throne.
> And meditation reign alone . . .[41]

These are, so far, fairly representative sentiments for early eighteenth-century neoclassical descriptive verse. The speaker's initial salute to the scenery as a stimulant to her faculties of reason is at odds with a post-Romantic reader's impressions of the transcendental sublimity of Welsh topography. In *The Prelude*, for example, William Wordsworth's imagination is lifted to its greatest heights by contemplation of the Snowdon range.[42] There is evidence, however, that earlier in the popular imagination of the English reading public, and certainly by the time Cave wrote this piece, Wales was already viewed as a wild and romantic location – more likely to engender passionate awe than the rational thought which Cave's speaker claims.[43] But as Cave's poem continues it is possible to detect a shift in the early idyllic tenor which is at variance with the cerebral excursion of the opening lines; this fluctuation, it seems to me, can be directly linked to the poet's handling of the theme of religion. Cave's Welsh retreat is linked in a fundamental way to the speaker's sense of Christian divinity. The textual evidence of 'Thoughts which Occurred to the Author . . .' suggests that, as an expatriate Welsh woman poet, the issue of religion is crucial to her sense of selfhood in all components of her identity. In her use of the neoclassical descriptive verse form, the sense of Cave's Welshness is communicated through her close weaving of landscape and religion, the physical with the metaphysical. The land itself is depicted as existing in a close relationship with the divine; it is in her characterization of this bond that Cave betrays the divided sense of self which I have asserted. In the speaker's opening remarks on the psychological effects of the Welsh surroundings – 'Where Reason may ascend her throne/ And meditation reign alone'[44] – the reader is thus immediately alerted to a sense of the imposition of alien values on to the native landscape. Indeed, the early descriptions of the Breconshire environment with its 'sweet songsters', 'fragrant fields' and 'green pasture' might, for example, have been written seventy years earlier: its terminology and mood are similar to these of many Augustan depictions of rural idylls, for example, Alexander Pope's 1713 poem, 'Windsor Forest'.[45]

The impression of strained control persists in the poem for twelve lines. Welsh scenery is subordinated to the neoclassical English poetic paradigm; passionate Welsh Methodist fervour is suppressed in favour of the genteel Anglican tone. But, at line twelve, the scene of 'ordered variety' suddenly becomes literally overshadowed by the powerful and hitherto repressed presence of the Welsh mountains. The reader becomes aware that the speaker is surrounded 'Before, behind, on either side'[46] by these imposing giants. The picture of civilized nature which has been described is in fact dominated by the encompassing circle of 'stupendous' hills.[47] The feature of mountainous Welsh topography is a significant one to the speaker; the unruliness of the landscape compared with the earlier Anglicized derivative marks the beginning of the speaker's unrestrained religious rapture, as if the altitude brings her closer to God:

Four ponderous hills stupendous rise,
As if to teach my heart and eyes
To send their wishes to the skies:
Thither my thoughts and eyes ascend,
Where wonders still more wond'rous blend . . .
The radiant region of the day,
With matchless majesty display,
More of the great unfathom'd all
Than doth the whole terrestrial ball.
My eyes recoil, the rays so bright,
Tho' short the gaze, dissolve my sight:
If such thy power, great work divine,
How mighty His who bade thee shine![48]

The hills are described as 'ponderous'; this is an interesting image which implies both impressive physical presence and deep contemplation. The hills thus become a symbol of the duality of the speaker's torn consciousness, embodying the effects of passionate awe and rational meditation. The hills are further personified in the simile 'As if to teach my heart and eyes / To send their wishes to the skies'; the land of the speaker's birth is metaphorized as a council of tribal elders from whom her sense of God and self has been learned.

As it continues, the poem exhibits further signs of literary ambivalence. Whilst the language becomes increasingly extravagant, the formal arrangement continues to adhere to the iambic couplet metre, and, despite the euphoria of the tone, an attempt is made to maintain the structure of rational contemplative progression. The speaker's meditation on the theme of God in nature moves through a number of discursive phases in the course of the poem. In recognition of neoclassical fashion, Cave's subject attempts to advance from descriptions of the scene of her meditation, through the nature of her topic and her reactions to it, to a form of poetic culmination. However, in Cave's case, the shifts are in mood rather than in rationale. Her speaker's train of thought is rooted in her emotional responses to the land in which she senses the presence of God, rather than in her faculties of reason.

In contrast to 'Thoughts which Occurred to the Author . . .' which survives in all versions of the volume, Cave deletes her elegy 'On the Death of the Reverend Mr Howel Harris' from later editions. In terms of the theory of poetic repression of political and cultural marginality which I have been attempting to advance here, this is an interesting omission for the poem is perhaps the most overtly Welsh in theme of Cave's oeuvre.

The elegy is an exuberant tribute to the man whose evangelical fire effected the conversion of her English father to Calvinistic Methodism. By the 1794 edition of *Poems on Various Subjects* the elegy had disappeared, along with a similar tribute to the 'Reverend Mr Watkins of Llanursk' (*sic*).

In another of the poems which appears in all editions, 'On Hearing the Reverend Mr R - - - - - - D. Read the Morning Service, and Preach in Saint Thomas' Church, WINCHESTER', Cave explores her dissatisfaction with the Anglican faith in which she worshipped during her years of exile in England. The poem is an important document in divining the dialectic which shapes her inner life, torn between the two very different cultures that define her as a person and a poet. As so often in her work, the piece begins with a respectful nod towards neoclassical values of rational contemplation and acknowledges the possibility of achieving grace through quiet meditation:

> When plac'd within the consecrated aisle,
> In pensive solitude I sat a while;
> At length with all the grace that Heav'n inspires,
> All that solemnity the church requires,
> Began the sacred order of the day . . . [49]

But, as soon as the clergyman opens his mouth, dissatisfactions arise. The chief complaint inspired by the performance of the unfortunate Reverend R - - - - - - D., and, by implication, that of the Anglican practice in general, is that his delivery of the Christian message lacks passion – 'As tho' no truth, or soul, or God were there'. The imagery used to describe the service is musical, but the tone is ironic: 'With such a cadence he dismiss'd each clause / As should enforce GOD'S eternal laws'.[50] Reverend R - - - - - - D.'s 'cadence' is an uninspiring intonation. The enervated musical experience is compared unfavourably even with the spurious excitement of a stage entertainment:

> While lesser truths delivered on the stage
> Or even fictions with the mind engage;
> Because the player labours through his part,
> To claim attention and affect the heart.[51]

The poem, which opens in terms of respect for the virtues of reason and order, and attempts to adhere to the stylistic form which celebrates the same features, shifts to become a plea for the eduction of that fire and zeal in religious practice so often observed at the time in the Methodist services Cave would have experienced in her youth. An attempt is made to present the poet's demands for change in the form of a reasoned case, but the core of the poet's argument is her conviction that religion should consist not merely of love, but also of passionate celebration, which can be inspired only by charismatic presentation, a feature she evidently sees as lacking in the Anglican approach. That this piece is retained in all editions of the volume may owe something to the fact that it is not immediately identifiable as the Calvinistic Methodist polemic which it is; but its survival is surely significant also of the strength and depth of Cave's feelings on the issue.

The radical post-colonial theorist Frantz Fanon writes of the relationship of the colonized subject to the culture of the colonizing power:

> Every colonized people – in other words, every people in whose soul an inferiority complex has been created by the death and burial of its local cultural originality – finds itself face to face with the language of the civilizing nation; that is, with the culture of the mother country . . . To speak a language is to take on a world, a culture.[52]

Jane Cave's poetry on Welsh topics seems to me to demonstrate one woman's experience of such a confrontation. It is tempting to speculate that, as the daughter and later wife of two English tax collectors, Cave's personal status as a Welsh woman may have been more intensely fractured than most. Her position as a dependant of two agents of the colonial machine may well have exacerbated in her the sense of alienation which Fanon recognizes. But these tensions are obscured in the present-day revival of interest in her work. The denial of Cave's ethnological background in the sweep of the anthologizer's editorial pencil signals the ignorant, and perhaps defensive, colonial drive towards cultural absorption as described by post-colonial theorists such as Ashcroft et al. The evidence of Cave's own similar process of progressive ethnic abnegation signals the impulse of the colonized subject to achieve that absorption for herself. The textual witness of Cave's poems on Welsh themes is testimony to the troubled efforts of a woman writer, doubly marginalized by her gender and her nationality from the dominant discourse of British patriarchy, to come to terms with what Fanon has termed 'the language of the civilizing nation'.[53]

★ ★ ★

In summation, I offer my readings of the work of Jane Cave as evidence of her value to the feminist programme of 'reanimating' neglected women writers. Much of Cave's poetry provides insight into the position of the late eighteenth-century lower-rank woman and her perceptions of the male-dominated and class-divided world in which she was compelled to exist; it affords analysis of the experience of the woman writer in the face of a male-centred literary canon. I have also suggested that it may yield a supplementary theory to the common explanation of the woman writer's imitation of venerable 'male' genres and styles. Mimeticism such as Cave's may be a reflection not only of a lack of confidence on the part of the woman poet, but also sometimes of an unconscious urge to contain the potentially subversive audacity of her ideas.

I have attempted to extend this notion of stylistic retrospection as repressive device to an examination of Cave's position as twice-marginalized Welsh woman subject. I would posit that analysis of her poems which relate to Wales allows the feasibility of such an interpretation. Cave's persistent deployment of the iambic couplet, beloved of practitioners of the earlier, neoclassical period, is doubly relevant to an exploration of her status as a Welsh woman poet. The sensibility of the earlier period was concerned with the preservation of a distinctly English literary and political establishment. The classical versification of many of her poems commands an apparatus with which to attempt to quell the fires of indignant marginality, but it is ultimately inadequate to disguise the controversial nature of the poems' value systems or the intensity of the emotion which they engender in their creator.

2

Ann Julia Hatton and ambivalent exile

> My First's a bird that did appear
> When Kings and nobles lov'd good cheer
> Should ornament their table;
> And oft it hath in Poet's brain,
> Inspir'd a melancholy strain,
> And eke a pleasing fable.
> My Second has alas! been seen
> To raise a barrier between
> A fair one and her lover;
> My Whole's a town, its name to hit
> Requires but very little wit
> In a moment you'll discover.[1]

So quips Ann Julia Hatton, the self-styled 'Ann of Swansea', on the subject of her adopted Welsh home. The riddle makes effervescent use of the epigrammatic form, but its imagery is ambiguous and strangely gloomy. The sea is depicted as unequivocally negative, the sorrowful exclamation 'alas' prefixing an image of separation and pain. In this chapter I will explore Hatton's poetry in terms of what may be a more uneasy relationship with Wales than her adopted pen-name suggests.

There could scarcely be a more extreme contrast than that between the pious and supremely respectable Jane Cave and her younger near-contemporary, the outrageous Ann Julia Hatton. Hatton gained notoriety during the first three decades of the nineteenth century for the scandals of her personal life and, in addition, some recognition and commercial success for her writing which she published under the pseudonym 'Ann of Swansea'.

The adoption of the pen-name suggests that Hatton, although not Welsh by blood or birth, felt some identification with Wales. My purpose here is to explore the poetry of this largely forgotten author in terms of its stylistic and thematic properties, and in relation to the usual categories of class and gender, but with a particular focus on the light it may shed on the nature and extent of Hatton's sense of her own Welshness which, as I have already suggested, may entail problematic issues of identity. I begin with brief biographical details by way of a general introduction, and in order to account for Hatton's Welsh connections. Ann Julia Hatton was born in Worcester in 1764, a younger daughter of the Kemble family, the re-nowned theatrical dynasty. The Kembles claimed for themselves a link with the ancient and aristocratic Catholics after whom the village of Kemble in Wiltshire is named, and who later migrated to Herefordshire. This connection is obscure and unsubstantiated, but it is certain that Hatton's father, Roger Kemble, was born in Hereford in 1721.[2] Hatton's eldest sister was the celebrated tragic actress Sarah Siddons (who incidentally was herself born at a Brecon inn); another sister, Elizabeth Whitlock, achieved similar fame during her own lifetime for her work on the American stage. Ann Hatton is known to have spent some of her childhood in south Wales, whilst her parents worked in itinerant theatre companies there. At nineteen she married an actor named Curtis, who had unfortunately neglected to mention the existence of a prior and still lawful wife. Upon the revelation of his bigamy, the unscrupulous Curtis abandoned Hatton in a state of extreme poverty, to alleviate which she was compelled into desperate measures. In a 1971 essay 'Ann of Swansea', Ivor Bromham describes her involvement around this time with a notorious medical charlatan calling himself 'Doctor' Graham. Bromham recounts how she is believed to have delivered lectures at Graham's 'Temple of Health' in London 'on the most unbecoming and bawdy subjects'.[3] At this period, Hatton is also known to have used her position as 'Mrs Siddons' sister' to solicit public charity. Around 1783, she attempted suicide in Westminster Abbey; her family, who presumably had hitherto been silenced by their disgust at her bigamous marriage and subsequent activities, now intervened and settled a generous annuity on her, on the condition that she resided no less than a hundred and fifty miles from London. Biographies of Sarah Siddons take a uniformly dim view of Hatton's conduct: in his book, *Sarah Siddons: Portrait of an Actress*, Roger Manvell refers to Hatton as a 'troublesome sister', and as the Kemble family's 'greatest failure [who] ended a debased sort of exhibitionist';[4] Yvonne Ffrench describes her as the 'mysterious sister, Ann . . . a large and squinting woman . . . with the soul of an adventuress and a talent for associating herself with notorious persons and inconvenient activities';[5] Kathleen Mackenzie is even more graphically detailed in her condemnatory description:

> Anne Kemble [was] the only member of the family who had not done well. Anne was a terrible trouble to them all because she drank heavily and was always making scenes, she loved notoriety . . . it was very distressing and embarrassing for all the Kembles.[6]

Hatton was clearly a tiresome relative for the illustrious Kembles and it must have been some relief to them when, in 1792, Hatton married the widower William Hatton and settled into relatively decent obscurity. The Hattons left together for America, returning seven years later to settle in the Swansea area. William Hatton died in 1806, and it is at about this time that Hatton adopted the pen-name 'Ann of Swansea'. In 1783, at about the period of her desertion by Curtis, she had published a short volume of verse entitled *Poems on Miscellaneous Subjects by Ann Curtis, Sister of Mrs Siddons*. The book was issued by subscription and boasted among its subscribers several members of the British aristocracy. Between 1811 and 1831 she published a second volume of poems, *Poetic Trifles* (1811), and numerous novels, the first in 1813 entitled *Cambrian Pictures, or Every One Has Errors*, all published under the pseudonym 'Ann of Swansea'.

I am indebted to Bromham for his biographical scholarship on Hatton. In addition, Moira Dearnley's recent research has, excitingly, uncovered a number of previously unpublished poems and provided useful insights into Hatton's life in Swansea.[7] Some interesting critical work has also been done recently on the novels of 'Ann of Swansea', particularly on *Cambrian Pictures*.[8] However, very little attempt has been made hitherto to explore the poems in depth. It is on the neglected *Poetic Trifles*, and on some of the unpublished manuscript poems, therefore, that I focus my analysis in this chapter.

Before turning to the poems themselves, it is necessary first to ground discussion in a consideration of the literary context from which Hatton's poems emerge. Hatton's oeuvre, perhaps most particularly her novels, but also to some extent her poetry, are profoundly influenced by the late eighteenth-century cult of sensibility. Janet Todd's book *Sensibility: An Introduction* details the development from the middle of the eighteenth century of the literary movement which dominated all genres from the 1740s to the 1770s, and whose residual influence may be detected in Gothic and later Romantic works. Todd shows how sentimentalism, the key component in the literature of sensibility, manifested itself across all literary forms and 'involved the arousal of pathos through conventional situations, stock familial characters and rhetorical devices. Such literature buttonholes the reader and demands an emotional, even physical response.'[9] In a detailed and systematic study, Todd discusses the issues of religion, class, gender and location, among others, in relation to sentimental literature. She notes, for example, the importance in the genre of sensibility of Method-ism, with its focus on the 'loving kindness of Jesus',[10] and its emphasis on enthusiastic emotional response. She also details the way in which, against a social background of increasing 'middle and trading class' eminence, combined with a slowly developing working class, sentimental literature tended to depict a world peopled by dynamic yet pious merchants, exquisitely feeling aristocrats and their devotedly loyal servants. Todd also examines how the social position of women in the period, defined and confined by the complementary and repressive ideologies of separate spheres and the sexual double standard, contributed to the appearance of a 'new sentimental and susceptible woman' in literature written by both sexes. Women's chastity, for centuries demanded as a criterion for Christian living, became a political and economic imperative in the eighteenth century. Women's moral influence was felt to be of paramount importance in society; in literature of the period the figure of the virtuous woman became society's moral signifier, her body a site of patriarchal propriety but also the repository of a range of anxieties about her potential for disorder. If the sentimental woman was pure and morally influential, she was also, as Todd notes, 'peculiarly susceptible to influence'.[11] Thus, in sentimental literature, women are depicted as emotional creatures given to fits of weeping, fainting and blushing; as Todd notes, however, such susceptibility always entails the potential for or the threat of 'erratic and deranged' behaviour. She suggests that in sentimental literature an idealized woman emerges, sensitive yet pious and passive – glorying in her essentially powerless moral influence. This position, of course, presented some significant contradictions for women as producers of sentimental literature, and many women writers 'reliably learned to depict themselves as helpless ladies, moral monitors and chaste entertainers'.[12]

The poetry of Ann Julia Hatton is extremely interesting in relation to these conventions. It is additionally compelling when considering another key element of sentimental literature, that of place. The early nineteenth century saw the decline of the literary dominance of London, and a corresponding upsurge of interest in, as Janet Todd puts it, 'distant picturesque parts, Wales or Northumbria for example'.[13] Todd details the ways in which rustic provincial locations were idealized in sentimental literature of the period, often by writers with no first-hand connection with or experience of these areas. Todd acknowledges that 'some authors combined their actual location with the literary image of rural retreat';[14] her discussion of place in writing of the period focuses, however, on its use as a purely literary device. In this chapter I will explore the possibility that in the poetry of Ann Julia Hatton location is a more significant and telling resource than the cosmetic deployment Todd suggests. It seems to me that the work of a woman writer who is connected to Wales by blood, birth or circumstantial accident offers interesting possibilities for a consideration of the ways in which she conforms to or deviates from the widespread paradigm.

★ ★ ★

Hatton's upbringing, like Jane Cave's, included a significant degree of indoctrination in the Methodist faith. It could be assumed, therefore, that this early influence predisposed her to her subsequent identification with that culture which so ardently embraced Methodism during this epoch, the Welsh culture, and that her religious sense was thus a significant marker of her Welsh identity, as was the case with Cave. But, from the evidence of her literary endeavours at least, it is difficult to formulate this type of argument in relation to Hatton.

A great many of the poems in *Poetic Trifles* concentrate on romantic and erotic love. Religion is not a subject to which Hatton gives significant explicit attention. Unlike Jane Cave's, Hatton's sense of her own spirituality is not clearly defined. Her religious upbringing, in line with prevailing conventions concerning mixed marriages, meant that the sons of the family were brought up in their father's Catholic faith whilst the girls were raised in line with their mother's Methodism. Accordingly, the Kemble sons were baptized Catholic, and at least two of Hatton's brothers were sent to prominent Catholic boys' schools, including the Benedictine Douai School near Reading. The girls' spiritual education, however, was undertaken by their staunchly Methodist mother. In her speculative and hugely deferential biography of Sarah Siddons, Kathleen Mackenzie lingers over anecdotes which demonstrate the young Sarah Kemble's religious devotion. There is little evidence that Sarah Kemble's young sister Ann derived the same gift of faith from her mother's nurturing offices. *Poetic Trifles* is virtually devoid of all but a passing reference to God. Although the unpublished manuscript poems written in Hatton's old age are marginally more promising in this regard, it is difficult to discern in Hatton's poetry any real sense of spiritual or religious devotion. Unlike that of Jane Cave, Hatton's Methodist background provides neither spiritual sustenance nor poetic resource. It certainly seems to have no connection with her sense of herself as a Welsh woman poet by adoption.

★ ★ ★

I turn now to the issue of class. Hatton's own class position is ambiguous. Notwithstanding the Kembles' precarious pretensions to aristocratic breeding, the acting profession in which they excelled was entering a transitional phase in terms of its social status during the mid- to late eighteenth-century period. Through the first decades of the century acting had been considered an 'insecure and socially disreputable life'. As Roger Manvell observes: 'the status of the players was always in doubt . . . The sterner religious elements in the community were staunchly against letting them gain any sort of foothold, bringing sin and damnation in their wake.'[15] Hatton's father, Roger Kemble, had joined forces in 1752 with his father-in-law, John Ward, who, along with a small number of actor-managers, was attempting to develop in the profession a degree of respectability and social status. By the 1760s, when itinerant theatre companies were still generally thought to be the lowest and most 'utterly degraded' branch of the acting business, the Kemble ensemble was regarded as a fairly reputable group. Roger Kemble seems, at any rate, to have made a reasonable living out of his endeavours, and appears also to have educated his children as well as the family's nomadic lifestyle would allow. Although the Kemble daughters received some formal schooling when the company's schedule permitted, it was their mother, Mrs Sally Kemble, who primarily delivered her daughters' education. After her colourful early experiences in acting and public life, Hatton is known to have attempted a career in teaching,[16] and clearly achieved some success as a writer. Hatton apparently aspired to membership of society's middle strata and, in terms of educational and financial resources, was more clearly aligned with this than with any other class grouping. But as a member of an acting family, and as a scandalous woman in her own right, her position can also be regarded as insecure and peripheral, not only in relation to the middle ranks, but also to society as a whole.

The poems themselves, whilst rarely engaging explicitly with issues of social hierarchy, seem nevertheless to reflect the contradictory and precarious nature of Hatton's class identity. Like Jane Cave, Hatton relied on the patronage of a number of aristocratic subscribers. As in Cave's case, however, there is evidence to suggest that Hatton's apparent obsequiousness to her benefactors may have masked less yielding attitudes to class privilege. Janet Todd, in her discussion of class in terms of the cult of sensibility, identifies contradictory impulses operating in the poetry and prose of the period. On the one hand sensibility was often depicted as residing exclusively in the 'higher and more genteel orders',[17] whilst in other texts 'a meritocracy of feeling' was insisted upon, where all ranks were seen as equally capable of reacting sentimentally. In Hatton's poem dedicated 'To Mary' an interesting slant is applied to this dichotomy. Over nine stanzas, 'To Mary' constructs an argument for the corrupt and corrupting influence of the upper classes. Whilst the poor female addressee is certainly depicted as passive and mild, she is nevertheless shown to have the capacity for strong sentimental feeling; that capacity is,

however, negatively encoded in this poem, and seen as developing out of
the pollutant effects of contact with the privileged elite:

> Ah, simple maid, that gentle breast,
> The pillow now of peace and rest,
> May heave with woe, may swell with care,
> May prove the pangs of fell despair;
> Then let no vagrant wishes find
> An entrance to thy spotless mind,
>   My sweet, my artless Mary.
>
> For should'st thou quit the mountain's side
> Where tranquil now thy moments glide,
> And mingle with the rich and vain,
> Who scorn the daughters of the plain,
> Thy unsophisticated heart
> May change its present ease for smart,
>   My sweet, my artless Mary.[18]

Hatton depicts not a meritocracy of feeling here so much as a moral
hierarchy of emotion, in which the poverty and obscurity of Mary's social
position corresponds with her gentility of heart and, perhaps more
significantly, with her moral and spiritual purity.

In Hatton's poem the idea is implied that sensibility is the preserve of
the 'genteel and upper classes', but this is juxtaposed against an inversion
of the dominant ethic, where the humble 'maid', Mary, is seen to be in
danger of becoming infected by proximity to aristocratic sensibility.
Sensibility, far from acting as a source of moral authority, is liable to spoil
Mary's present 'spotless mind'. The semantic conjunction of wealth and
vanity in line ten, connotes a link between class privilege and moral
turpitude. Paradoxically, however, the poet locates the threat of moral
violation not in Mary's assimilation into the world of the 'rich and vain',
but in the likelihood of her rejection by them. It is the contempt of the
privileged classes for the 'daughters of the plain' which jeopardizes their
moral well-being in Hatton's scheme. By stanza three it becomes clear
that it is the aspiration towards upward social mobility in a rigid system
which imperils the poor girl's soul:

> Then let not pride's fallacious ray
> Seduce thee from the humble way;
> Ambition dazzles to destroy . . .[19]

The somewhat tortured ethical logic of the piece presents a jaundiced view of class structures. It is tempting to speculate that Hatton's own experience of rejection and thwarted ambition affected the formulation of social morality expressed here. In any case, however, Hatton's manipulation of the conventions of sentimental literature in the poem have a potentially equalizing effect in terms of class; this is not because she insists upon the 'meritocracy of feeling' which Todd discusses, but rather because she impugns the moral fibre of the species of sensibility residing in 'genteel and upper classes'.

In her long poem, 'Hoel's Harp', Hatton once again examines the relationship between society's privileged elite and their subordinates. The poem is set in medieval Wales and narrates the tale of the blind harpist, Hoel, once celebrated in 'many a noble hall', now forced to beg a living from the charity of local villagers. In wrenchingly sentimental style, the piece describes the wretched injustice of Hoel's plight:

> This harp in many a noble hall,
> Has spread delight and mirth around;
> And many a castle's moated wall,
> Thus echoed its melodious sound:
> And oft the Chieftain's greedy ear
> Has drunk its martial–sounding lays:
> And many a highborn maiden's tear,
> Bestow'd on me delicious praise:
> But age has damp'd my bosom's fire,
> Genius and strength at once expire;
> My hand now feebly sweeps the string
> From which no streams of rapture spring.
> Yet still to memory 'twill impart,
> When midst its chord my fingers move,
> Events recorded on my heart . . . [20]

Janet Todd remarks on the prevalence, in sentimental literature, of fantasies of service as 'familial and feudal'.[21] As already outlined, Todd accounts for this phenomenon as a form of compensation for the employing classes' fear of burgeoning servant-class solidarity. In Hatton's poem the depiction of feudal power relations can scarcely be characterized as ideal or familial. In 'Hoel's Harp' the feudal system is depicted as socially irresponsible and exploitative of its lower orders. The poet thus identifies the weakened figure of the blind harpist as one of the inevitable casualties of an unequal and uncaring social model; it is only the random kindnesses of the poor which sustains him. If, as Todd argues, much sentimental literature was concerned to depict idealized master-servant relations, Hatton is clearly working against the popular tide. In 'Hoel's Harp' and in 'To Mary', the poet's interest is in the plight of the socially disenfranchised, and, I would argue, in excoriating the systems which limit them. Hatton relies upon the thematic and tonal resources of sentimental literature, but in doing so her approaches to issues of class indicate a resistance to the political status quo.

★ ★ ★

Hatton's concern with marginality and oppression, visible in her treatment of class in the poems, is more explicit in her approaches to issues of gender. In the short 'Epigram', which appears in *Poetic Trifles*, Hatton plays with the notion of gendered difference, adopting a male persona:

> Jane vows, I said, that she had angel features,
> I swear 'tis monstrously provoking.
> That women are such weak and silly creatures;
> They take for earnest what is only joking;
> And worse, she says that sighing at her feet
> I vow'd that she alone possess't my heart;
> Now, if I did, allow me to repeat,
> My speech was, like her beauty *formed by art*.[22]

Hatton mocks the fabled capriciousness of male devotion; she also satirizes the speaker's and, by implication, all men's misapprehension of the way women perceive the world. But the tone is gently teasing, the reader cannot help but be amused by the speaker's bewildered protestations, particularly, perhaps, when armed with the knowledge of its female authorship. The rather more caustic closing line, however, whilst lampooning the speaker's frustrated spite, can also be seen to evince humour from women's supposed tendency to artificiality. This piece, published in 1811, when the poet was a woman in her forties, suggests her mirth at the gendered machinations of romantic love. A later poem, 'The Mirror', written in Hatton's last years and unpublished in her lifetime, reveals a far less cheerful attitude towards the same subject. The poem is worth reproducing in its entirety:

As yet no wrinkles in thy face appear;
Thy bosom has no stain of yellow hue;
And still meandering as a streamlet clear,
Thy veins disclose a bright and healthy blue.
As yet there's lustre sparkling in thine eye,
Thy dewy lips a crimson tint disclose;
And still unfaded on thy cheek doth lie
The glowing colour of the summer rose.
'Tis thus my mirror most deceitful says
That time to me, but little harm hath done;
Vain as I am, and fond perhaps of praise,
This flattery my belief has never won:–
Credulity alas! is woman's bane –
By adulation thousands are betray'd –
Deceitful mirror! O, pronounce again,
Unsay the falsehoods, thou hast lately said!
Tell me, that vainly blooms the polish'd mind
When youth's gay rosy hours away have flown.
Tell me, that man can seldom – *never* find,
Beauty, or charm, in *intellect alone*.[23]

Here, in a genuinely poignant exploration, the poet acknowledges the vanity, artifice and self-delusion which the speaker, as an old woman, employs for her emotional survival. In a world, which places value on women's superficial conformity to particular aesthetic standards, youth, beauty and their absence become serious issues. Whereas in the 'Epigram' women's artifice in beauty is seen as legitimate cosmetic resourcefulness, in 'The Mirror' it is figured as tragic self-deception. In the 'Epigram' women's credulity is depicted as humorous gullibility to men's romantic ruses, in 'The Mirror' it has become the pitiful last resort of lonely old age. In the final two lines of 'The Mirror' it becomes clear that the source of the speaker's agony is the miserable converse reality of the same gendered difference which she so light-heartedly celebrates in the 'Epigram'. In the 'Epigram' the depiction of difference remains implicitly essentialist: the male speaker declares 'women are such weak and silly creatures'; in 'The Mirror' Hatton locates women's foolishness and vulnerability in the attitudes of men and, by implication, in the system which promotes and supports their prejudice.

I have already discussed Janet Todd's view that the growing importance of the sexual double standard in late eighteenth-century culture instilled in women writers of sentimental literature the need to depict themselves as passive, virtuous and harmless entertainers. Hatton is an intriguing figure in this respect. The spicy reputation born of her early adventures no doubt enhanced the commercial success of Hatton's books; in Ivor Bromham's account of her life, his attempt to lionize her as a local south Wales heroine involves the assertion that 'Ann's poems seem to reveal that [the] unbecoming actions [of her youth] occasioned her deep regret and sorrow in later years'.[24] A glance at some of the poems in *Poetic Trifles* reveals, however, that, though it is possible that Hatton regretted causing pain to her family, she remained undaunted about expressing the rather 'unbecoming' themes of which Bromham somewhat prudishly complains. In one poem dedicated to an anonymous lover, for example, Hatton describes the temptation of sexual passion in graphically physical terms:

> I confess, dear seducer, afraid of the bliss,
> I scarce dare allow to thy pleadings a kiss;
> For so warm are thy pressures, so sweet is thy breath,
> I fear 'twill to reason and virtue be death.[25]

The tone is mischievous, and the sensuality so vivid that despite the protestations of self-discipline and denial the thrust of the piece is manifestly lustful. In later stanzas the speaker accounts for her reticence in terms which clearly acknowledge the centrality of the prevalent double standard in sexual morality in controlling women's carnal instincts:

> And would'st thou for one little moment of joy,
> The peace of my bosom for ever destroy?
> Oh! would'st thou condemn me,
> Existing through years
> To sully each day with my blushes and tears . . .
>
> No, no, let us banish such sensual desire,
> Dismissing weak love for a loftier fire;
> Turn from me thy eyes, for too much they implore,
> I'll still be thy friend – but *I will be no more*.[26]

The poet asserts women's capacity for sexual desire, but in her self-denial the speaker recognizes that it is she, and not her male suitor, who would suffer the condemnation of society for an act in which they both share. The blushes and tears of passionate longing, the speaker protests, could too easily become transmuted for woman into those of shame and destitution. Here Hatton once again vitiates conventional uses of sentimental resources. In Hatton's scheme, women's susceptibility to influence and propensity to bodily displays of emotion may be read as symptoms of their subjection to confining patriarchal ideologies of gender difference. In an addendum placed after this piece the poet underscores her endorsement of its expostulations:

> *This poem is a translation from the French. The prudish may think it too glowing a confession – I consider it charming!

In a dexterous manoeuvre the poet manages simultaneously to affirm and disown the poem. The exclamatory punctuation suggests her self-conscious delight in confounding her critics.

Hatton's penchant for writing and continuing to publish this kind of risqué verse may be interpreted as a literary manifestation of the socially subversive impulse which powered her youthful adventures. I would argue that these poems may be read in general terms as the spirited response of a woman writer who was punished for her early unruliness against the sexual double standard, and who was compelled to exist in a geographically and politically marginalized sphere in a manner which compounds the material and psychological sidelining of all women, and particularly rebellious women, during this historical period. In her poem 'A Man Without Deceit' it is possible to discern Hatton's playfulness with the conventions of eighteenth-century 'masculine' genres. The un-ascribed epigraph which immediately follows the poem's title reads 'Shew me a thing on earth so rare / I'll own all miracles are true'. The poet's intention to satirize masculine value systems is obvious as she abruptly dispels the reader's expectations of eulogy in favour of a humorous, if rather scathing, dismissal of male integrity. The piece is composed of scrupulously regular octosyllabic rhyming couplets; in its rhetorical and exclamatory tone it draws on the 'high' style of many early eighteenth-century poetic epistles:

> Could I but hope at last to meet
> The man who never us'd deceit;
> Whose lip no falsehood ever stain'd
> Whose tongue no bosom ever pain'd;
> And from whose clear and steady eye
> No wily glances learn to fly:
> Oh! I would journey where the sun
> His shining course hath never run . . .
> Could I at last but hope to find
> A man with pure and honest mind.[27]

Imitation of the masculine genre is self-conscious and cynical. Techniques previously used to extol the inalienable strengths and virtues of a male economy are deployed here to the opposite effect. Hyperbole and exaggeration dominate the poet's claim that she is prepared to go through any trial in order to find an honest man; she makes clear in her overstatement the ludicrously slender chance of succeeding in such a quest. Hatton's manipulations of the ancient narrative conventions of trial and quest in this poem are overtly disruptive of their traditionally male associations. The poet imagines herself as a hero, undertaking a series of exotically sited trials in the course of a quest, in this case to discover that mythical creature – the honest man. With tongue explicitly in cheek, she mocks the impulse to conquer which figures in accounts of male achievement throughout history. In lines seven to fourteen the poet takes a satiric swipe at the age-old mythology which defines violent domination as heroic, and which sanctions, even canonizes, the colonial drive. Were she but to discover an honest man at the end of her journey she would willingly travel to new worlds

> . . . where the sun
> His shining course hath never run;
> With untir'd step would gladly haste
> O'er burning moor and sandy waste:
> I'd brave the tiger's secret hold,
> I'd face the serpent's scaly fold . . .[28]

She is decrying, by implication, not only the integrity of men, but also the intrusive hostility of male urges, and the art forms which enshrine them – including, of course, the venerable male art form she is utilizing herself.

It seems to me that Hatton's approaches to questions of gender in her poetry evidence a self-consciously subversive impulse. In many cases the poetry dramatizes Hatton's marginal position in terms of dominant gendered morality. I want to turn now to an exploration of the ways in which Hatton's subject position as self-elected Welsh woman poet may inform the verse.

★ ★ ★

Much recent post-colonial feminist work has concentrated on parallels between the 'othered' position of the colonized subject and that of women in many societies. In her essay 'The Only Free People in the

Empire: Gender Difference in Colonial Discourse' Bridget Orr considers the 'identification and desire for the other' which is visible in the travel writings of Lady Mary Wortley Montagu.[29] She notices certain moments in her texts which suggest the breakdown of the incorporative drive in 'a moment of admiration and wonder'.[30] Orr's paper makes some very useful connections between post-colonial and feminist discourses; but she is specifically concerned with the relation of a woman who is 'internal other' (Wortley Montagu) to the 'external other' of a colonized people (in this case, the Turks whom Montagu encountered during her husband's ambassadorship in Turkey, 1716–18). What Hatton's poetry offers is the opportunity to examine the work of a woman whose connection with the 'external other' is imposed and indefinite; whose experience of living in a colonized country appears to have produced a degree of dialogism between self and other in which identification with the colonized exceeds that of the enthusiastic traveller. In terms of the issue of Hatton's position as an exiled poet in a colonized country, many of her poems on Welsh themes offer interesting insights.

Hatton's debt to the cult of sensibility is visible in a number of her later poems, particularly those on Welsh themes. Much of Hatton's poetry demonstrates a preoccupation with wild nature, with folk culture and with the power of the imagination. The aforementioned 'Hoel's Harp', for example, evokes the bardic culture of a medieval Wales. Under the influence of late eighteenth-century work by the editors of medieval British texts, and the imitators of such material such as Chatterton and MacPherson,[31] the non-classical past had developed into a popular site for poetic excursions by practitioners of the genre of sensibility; Coleridge's 'Christabel', written between 1797 and 1800, and Scott's 'The Lay of the Last Minstrel', published in 1805, are notable examples of the trend towards utilizing medievalism as a poetic resource. Hatton is clearly influenced by the fashion; her poem narrates the story of an old, blind harpist who though weak and close to death carries with him a wealth of communal memory; the old man is depicted as a source of both folk culture and tribal history. Gwyn A. Williams has described such performers in medieval Welsh culture as the 'remembrancers of a dynasty and its people';[32] Hatton does not situate her evocation precisely in terms of its historical period, but her depiction of the imagined world, and of the old man's role in that society, locates it as a construction which draws on medieval Wales.

The human characters in 'Hoel's Harp', introduced in lines thirteen to fifteen, are the dramatis personae of the poem. In 'Hoel's Harp' it is Hoel himself who 'speaks'. Hoel, once beloved and fêted by the great and good, having outlived his usefulness, is now cast out: 'Compell'd to seek precarious bread . . . dragg'd along with grief and pain'.[33] As so often in her oeuvre Hatton dramatizes the voice of a male character, a poet and a 'remembrancer of a dynasty and its people'; if Hoel is a male artist, however, he is also a dispossessed, peripheral figure, no longer respected by the society which spawned him. He wanders in sad exile from the hub of cultural and political life, surviving on the charity of the poor and unexalted – his creativity now confined to the occasional entertainment of these people. It is notable that the physical sustenance which Hoel gains from the poor people who take him in has the effect of reigniting his creative fire. He discovers a space in exile from which to speak as an artist when the mainstream, albeit a culture in decline itself, has abandoned him. The character of Hoel is described overwhelmingly in terms of his material and physical disadvantage:

> A wand'ring harper, old and poor,
> And sightless too, came slowly on;
> A stripling led him o'er the moor,
> Whose eye was sunk, whose cheek was wan . . .
> His harp of other days the pride
> Was feebly borne against his side,
> A load too weighty to sustain,
> Now dragg'd along in grief and pain . . .[34]

Such is the woeful level of Hoel's strength that the weight of his own body and artistic talent have become almost unbearable burdens. Hatton assumes the voice of a male poet, who, like any nineteenth-century woman with ambitions to write, is disadvantaged by the combination of his body and his creativity. She speaks, through Hoel, for the poet who yearns for a place within the authorized tradition, but who is condemned by the restrictions of physical and material weakness to exist at the outer margins of sanctioned culture. Such a characterization clearly has implications for a feminist reading of the poem, but also perhaps for an understanding of Hatton's position as an exiled poet in Wales. The character of Hoel, who is expelled to the margins of what is itself an increasingly marginal culture because he lacks the physical strength to survive there, offers a reading which incorporates the frustrations of gender-defined constraints, alongside the creative potential of life at the edge of a peripheral culture which is itself threatened by external forces. Hoel mourns the passing of his time as the remembrancer of and speaker for the culture which he still values. In stressing the importance of memory in his former role as official national bard, the poem implies that the power of such recollections as a source of communal history will be lost with Hoel's decline:

> My hand now feebly sweeps the string,
> From which no streams of rapture spring;
> Yet still to memory 'twill impart,
> When midst its chords my fingers move,
> Events recorded on my heart . . .[35]

Hoel is thus empowered as an artist by the need he experiences as an exiled poet in a colonized country; through Hoel, I would argue, Hatton is able to achieve similar creative fulfilment.

The connection between Wales and artistic production made in 'Hoel's Harp' also appears in her stanzaic poem 'Kidwelly Castle'. In 'Hoel's Harp' allusions are made to the importance but vulnerability of poetry and music as vehicles of history; in this piece explicit links are made between art and political potency. The epigraph reads: 'Princes and heroes pass away: / The minstrel too, who sang their deeds, / Sleeps in his narrow bed.'[36] The poem relates its speaker's impressions on regarding the ruins of Kidwelly Castle. The voice vacillates between high-toned rhetoric – 'Where sleeps the sounding harp, oh Cambria! tell?' – and intimate use of the personal pronoun – 'Like you . . . / I only wake at this lone hour to weep'.[37] In her aforementioned essay Bridget Orr speculates that 'gender inflects the production of colonial discourse'.[38] It is possible to interpret such fluctuations as manifestations of the process of recognition and identification experienced by the dispossessed and disenfranchised poet towards the similarly subjugated country in which she has found a home. In his 1991 book *National Identity*, Anthony D. Smith discusses the way in which national identity 'provides a powerful means of defining and locating individual selves in the world'.[39] 'Ann of Swansea' clearly underwent a process of self-identification with Wales; by adopting the pen-name Hatton consciously located herself as an 'individual in the world' belonging firmly to the Welsh nation. It is possible to read 'Kidwelly Castle' as dramatizing the poet's process of self-definition through its various phases. Tellingly, in terms of this reading, the poet's impressions in the piece centre on senses of frustration and loss at the demise of Welsh militancy against English colonialism – which she connects to the compounded anguish of the debasement of Welsh art. She begins by depicting the loss of Wales's poets as both symptom and partial cause of Wales's political decline:

> Where sleeps the sounding harp, oh, Cambria! tell? . . .
> Moulder'd to dust, alas! thy minstrels rest,
> To dark oblivion all their songs decreed;
> Whose high wrought themes with ardor fir'd the breast,
> Urg'd the bold thought, inspir'd the gen'rous deed.
>
> Vainly thy genius weeps o'er past delight,
> And listens vainly for that lofty breath,
> Which spurr'd thy hardy warriors to the fight
> And taught the glory of despising death.[40]

Hatton's identification with the colonized subject here does not preclude the use of a somewhat patronizing tone. But this note of condescension is modulated by her admission later in the poem that she is inclined towards the same political and artistic torpor:

> Oh race of heroes! all your minstrels sleep,
> Like you, inclos'd within the narrow bed
> I only wake at this lone hour to weep,
> And sadly ponder on the mighty dead.[41]

The iambic rhythm places a stress upon the word 'all' in the first line of this stanza; combined with the expansion of the semantic field in the following lines to include the speaker herself, the linguistic emphasis implies the speaker's self-identification as belonging to the ranks of politically and artistically impotent Welsh poets. Hatton's concentration in the poem on legendary and distant historical figures rather than living people – she evokes 'proud Aneurin' and 'Llewellyn's splendid banners' – enables her to exceed the non-violent dialogism between self and other which Orr argues is characteristic of Wortley Montagu's travel memoir. Wortley Montagu's account of her sojourn in Turkey focuses on the people, as well as the culture she encountered; Hatton's Welsh poetry concentrates less on immediate personal interaction than on solitary flights of fancy, often, as in 'Kidwelly Castle', focused on ancient times and ancient characters. By using poetic resources popularized in the sensibility period, such as the use of the medieval past, of Celtic heroism, of folk culture, and by capitalizing on the distance such techniques allow her from living Welsh subjects, the poet is able to move beyond the 'moments [which] suggest . . . wonder or admiration', which Orr detects in Wortley Montagu's writing. In constructing for herself the persona of a disempowered Welsh artist, the poet creates a voice which hails the Welsh cultural identity she seeks.

In her stanzaic piece 'Swansea Bay', Hatton eschews the medieval Wales of 'Hoel's Harp' and 'Kidwelly Castle' for a more contemporary place and time. Interestingly, the construction of Welsh identity in this poem is perhaps more vexed than in either of the other pieces. There is evidence that by the early years of the nineteenth century Swansea was already a highly Anglicized town;[42] the poetic resources which the contemporary urban sprawl therefore afforded Hatton for recreating the artistic and political empathy which she achieves in her archaic pieces may have been limited, paradoxically, by the very familiarity of her everyday surroundings.

Moira Dearnley refers to Hatton's notorious 'dislike of Swansea';[43] Hatton's piece 'My Father' would seem to corroborate this view. As she remembers her father, the poet laments the particularly crushing nature of her exile in the town:

> To bury me where never should survive
> The germs of talent that were budding forth –
> Where they no aid from culture might derive
> But perish as the weeds that choke the earth.[44]

This is a scathing indictment of the place from which the poet took her pen-name. Ironically, the town from which Hatton derived her poetic identity is depicted here as culturally barren and therefore suffocating to her creativity. Perhaps not surprisingly, given this attitude towards exile in Swansea, the proximity of contemporary Wales seems to offer less potential for poetic identification than the historically distanced settings of 'Hoel's Harp' and 'Kidwelly Castle'. The poem 'Swansea Bay' is constructed as a contemplative monologue as the speaker ponders her situation whilst roaming the seashore. Hatton's favoured octosyllabic pace is in evidence again; the construction of rhyming couplets is, for the most part, regular and apparently unstrained, including the refrain of 'Swansea Bay' at the end of the last line of each stanza. The first-person voice and present-tense narration are sustained throughout, giving the effect of intimacy and immediacy. 'Swansea Bay' opens in typical sentimental angst:

> In vain by various griefs opprest,
> I vagrant roam, devoid of rest,
> With aching heart, still ling'ring stray
> Around the shores of Swansea Bay.[45]

The formal regularity of the piece frames an edgy, unquiet meditation;

the repetitive quality of the verse evokes the rhythmic pattern of the waves, constant but uncontrolled; the imagery is of restive, barely contained energy: 'restless waves' , 'the tide's tumultuous roar', 'pensive moon'. The poem evokes the speaker's own sense of bondage within undefined 'griefs', as she surveys the freedom of the open sea:

> Tis not for me the snowy sail
> Swells joyous in the balmy gale;
> Nor cuts the boat with frolic play.
> For me the waves of Swansea Bay.[46]

The Welsh setting in the poem marks the boundaries which define the speaker's captivity. Swansea Bay itself represents the very edge of her emotional imprisonment; its breaking waves symbolize the narrowness of her confinement, the ocean beyond the tantalizing freedom she is denied. Interestingly, the poet's engagement with Welsh people, despite the immediacy of the context, remains impersonal. The Welsh appear only to symbolize the depth of the speaker's isolation; she imagines their unselfconscious vitality deriding her despair:

> The glow of health that tints each cheek,
> The eyes that sweet contentment speak;
> To mock my woes their charms display,
> And bid me fly from Swansea Bay.[47]

It is interesting that the poet's identification with Wales is more problematic when faced with living Welsh subjects. As a writer she is able to empathize in a profound way with Welsh artists of the distant past; she accesses communal history with relative ease. In 'Swansea Bay' everyday Welsh people are transmuted into images of her reluctant captivity in Wales.

By the time of her death in 1838 'Ann of Swansea' had apparently become accepted as a popular local literary figure. Her portrait was commissioned in 1834 by the town of Swansea and now hangs in the Glynn Vivian Art Gallery there; her obituary in *The Cambrian* spoke in glowing terms of her personal qualities: 'She was much esteemed and regarded by a numerous circle of friends, who will long regret the loss of one whose highly gifted mind and cheerful disposition conduced to render her society both intellectual and agreeable.'[48] Ironically, given her antipathetic attitude towards Swansea, Hatton had, it seems, eventually achieved in her adopted Welsh community the kind of respect and respectability which had eluded her in wider society. Whilst she obviously needed the material security which her relatively decent obscurity in Wales had brought her, she was compelled, presumably by economic expediency, but also, perhaps, by natural flamboyance, to seek celebrity in her own right, as her prolific production as a writer demonstrates. Her adoption of the pseudonym 'Ann of Swansea' indicates the degree of affection and affinity which she developed for her adopted country during her years as an exile in Wales. My readings of Hatton's Welsh poetry offer the possibility that her sense of belonging to her Welsh community may have both originated in, and been tempered by, the coercive basis of her residence there.

In her recent historical survey *Britons: Forging the Nation 1707–1837*, Linda Colley argues that it was only in the latter half of the eighteenth century, in the wake of defeat in America, and in the face of the threat from France, that the process by which Scotland, Ireland and Wales were fully incorporated in cultural terms as part of Great Britain was completed:

> The sense of identity here did not come into being . . . because of an integration and homogeneity of disparate cultures. Instead, Britishness was superimposed over an array of internal differences in response to contact with the Other, and above all in response to conflict with the Other.[49]

Colley emphasizes the retention of difference in individual Celtic cultures, despite the process of provincialization which resulted in the overarching British identity. In my readings of the poetry of Ann Julia Hatton, who wrote during the period which Colley describes, it is possible to detect evidence of both the incorporative process and the persistent difference. Hatton's Welsh poetry offers evidence of the way in which a highly marginalized woman writer, who is exiled in Wales, relates in poetic terms to her adopted country, and through it outward to the English cultural centre. Hatton finds in her dislocated experience of Welsh culture the material through which to express herself as a marginalized, dispossessed woman poet. She voices her identification with the tyrannized and disenfranchised through the use of archaic sources of Welsh history. Hatton's medieval pieces can be read to some extent as the reverse angle of the incorporative process detailed by Colley. Her strongly anti-colonial stance in them may be interpreted as the reaction of an adopted Welsh citizen to the drive towards integration by the English centre. It is significant, perhaps, that Hatton's volume was published in Waterford, Ireland, a sister Celtic nation, rather than in London or one of its provincial English satellites. It is in Hatton's more contemporary poetry that her sense of the restriction in the marginality of her exile can be discerned. In 'Swansea Bay', for example, Welsh landscape, people and culture are vehicles for expression of her experience of alienation and confinement, rather than creative and political empowerment.

★ ★ ★

The works of Jane Cave and Ann Julia Hatton, I would suggest, present an opportunity to consider the ways in which the experience of Welshness in its varying degrees was accessed by women writers of the late eighteenth century, in order to explore and articulate their relation, not merely to national identity, but also to positions of gender, class and poetic authority.

3

Felicia Hemans, empire and Welsh culture

There can be few of us who hear the opening lines of the most anthologized poem by Felicia Hemans without experiencing a degree of recognition. 'The boy stood on the burning deck' is a phrase which has power like few others in the English language to trigger spontaneous recitation in the hearer. Of the vast corpus of alternative following lines, almost none, however, could have borne retelling in the presence of the exquisitely genteel Mrs Hemans. Nevertheless, that the words of an early nineteenth-century woman poet, whose name is largely forgotten, should have impacted on the communal consciousness of succeeding generations to such an extent is testimony to the magnitude of her initial popularity. Felicia Hemans enjoyed a remarkable degree of commercial success in the course of her writing career and had for her readers an appeal which endured after her death until well into the Victorian era. Her literary output was prodigious; Hemans published her first volume of verse at the age of fourteen, and produced her last work only twenty days before her death in 1835 at the age of forty-two. In the course of her career Hemans published twenty-six volumes of poetry, a collection of prose articles on 'Foreign Literature' for the *Edinburgh Review* and two verse dramas. Interestingly, the first of these dramatic works, *The Vespers of Palermo*, was performed at Covent Garden in 1823, with Charles Kemble, brother of Ann Julia Hatton, taking the male lead; sadly the work was not a success; it was savaged by the critics and was withdrawn after the opening night.

In her book *Victorian Women Poets: Writing Against the Heart*, Angela Leighton observes that 'chronologically Hemans is a Romantic poet'. As Leighton notes, however, 'her poetry lacks the political and metaphysical speculation of those [Romantic] contemporaries, and seems, indeed, in its domestic and female concerns, to represent an early transition into the characteristic concerns of Victorian verse'.[1] 'Although Hemans died in 1835, two years before the accession of Victoria to the English throne, her work certainly remained very popular throughout the early and mid-nineteenth century and she is still regarded as the archetypal Victorian woman artist; she is cited as being 'one of the most widely read, widely published, and professionally successful poets of the nineteenth century'.[2] In recent years Felicia Hemans has been the subject of much discussion among feminist scholars. In an effort to reclaim for a feminist criticism this hugely influential nineteenth-century artist, a range of theoretical approaches have been brought to bear upon her large oeuvre of poetical works. With varying degrees of ingenuity and success, attempts have been made to interrogate Hemans's reputation as the conservative and conventional voice of English Victorian values. Amid all this critical clamour, however, little or no attention has been paid to her links with Wales. But a Welsh woman contemporary with Hemans, the Hemans enthusiast, biographer and historian, Jane Williams, Ysgafell, asserted that the poet considered herself a 'naturalized Welsh woman';[3] certainly her biographical and literary connections with Wales are extensive enough to render conspicuous their disregard in recent essays and anthologies.[4]

Hemans was born in Liverpool in 1793 and died in Dublin in 1835; but, as Peter Trinder remarks in his essay on her in the Writers of Wales series, '[she] has just title to be numbered among the writers of Wales, for here she spent all but the first and last few years of her life, and all her happy years'.[5] In 1800, at the age of seven, Hemans moved with her family to Abergele in north Wales; after her marriage in 1812 she lived for a time in Northamptonshire, but returned to her family home in Clwyd before long, when her husband was made redundant from the army. There she remained through her husband's abandonment of her and their children in 1818 and the death of her beloved mother in 1827, leaving Wales reluctantly in 1929, when the circumstances of her sons' education compelled her to do so.

Her emotional attachment to her Welsh home is evident in many of the occasional poems Hemans wrote during and after her years of residence there, and in 1822 her collection *Welsh Melodies* was published. These lyrics, designed to be set to music, draw on Welsh history and poetry and are a celebration of Welsh culture, evincing an enthusiasm for, and considerable familiarity with, the source materials. Clearly, then, Hemans's experience as a woman and her output as a poet were affected by her practical and emotional attachments to Wales. In this chapter I will make a brief survey of the range of current critical approaches to Hemans, giving attention to the usual categories of class and gender. Additionally, in the light of the growing body of theoretical material which examines women's writing in the context of post-colonial cultures, I intend to focus on analysis of hitherto neglected poems by Hemans on Welsh themes. I propose to consider whether these works yield insights into the experience of the woman artist in Victorian culture which make even more complex the 'English' feminist perspective currently available. I begin, however, with an examination of Hemans's work in relation to the issue of class.

★ ★ ★

The reputation of Hemans as instrument and embodiment of Victorian domestic ideology[6] rests on the distinctly bourgeois character of her poetic and personal sensibility. In her book *White, Male and Middle Class: Explorations in Feminism and History*, Catherine Hall details the process by which the industrial bourgeoisie emerged in Britain to political, economic and cultural pre-eminence during the period between 1780 and 1830.

Hall details the significant influence of Evangelical Christian morality on the formation of Victorian domestic ideology. The Evangelical mission to 'reform the manners and morals of the nation' entailed a preoccupation with the home as primary site of interest. As Hall notes, the domestic sphere was potentially more fruitful territory for the control of sin and corruption than the world at large. Evangelicals saw women as 'naturally' formed for a life of privacy and reticence, whereas men were 'naturally' better equipped for vigorous public activity. Despite their belief in the inherent weakness of women's nature, the Evangelicals nevertheless set great store by women's capacity for moral leverage.

At a time when the rise of bourgeois capitalism enabled its wives and daughters increasingly to abjure paid work, the Evangelical model offered a welcome solution to the problem of women's place in society. Hall argues that the dominance of domestic ideology in Victorian Britain was the result of the rapid expansion of industrial capitalism, but that 'the way that home was realized, lived in and experienced within the middle ranks was crucially mediated by Evangelicism'.[7] By the 1830s, bourgeois family life, presided over by the apparently inactive yet hugely influential wife and mother, was seen as the model for proper living.

It is clear from the evidence of many poems by Hemans that her personal spirituality was clearly influenced by the doctrines of Evangelical Christianity. It is notable, however, that unlike either Jane Cave or Ann Julia Hatton, for all her Evangelicism, Hemans remained throughout her life a devout Anglican. There is no evidence in the biographical material available, or the poems, that Hemans was influenced, negatively or positively, by Welsh Nonconformity.

It is possible to see Hemans, then, in her poetry and her conduct, as the archetype of mid-nineteenth-century bourgeois ideology, heavily influenced as she is by Evangelical models of moral respectability. At the same time, however, she would seem to present something of a problem in relation to dominant notions of class and gender-defined behaviours: for Hemans was a celebrated figure who took a conspicuous role in public life. Angela Leighton discusses the negotiation by Hemans of the contradictions inherent in her situation, referring to the poet's construction of 'a generalized story of woman's enduring domestic loyalties [as] the means by which she fended off the feared stigma of professional ambition'.[8] The success of this strategy is evidenced by the reception given to Hemans by her contemporaries and later Victorian commentators. In a telling article, published in 1847, the critic George Gilfillan waxes lyrical as he envisions Hemans the poet at work:

> You are saved the ludicrous image of a double-dyed Blue, in papers and morning wrapper, sweating at some stupendous treatise or tragedy from morn to noon, and from noon to dewy eve – you see a graceful and gifted woman, passing from the cares of her family, and the enjoyments of society, to inscribe on her tablets some fine thought or feeling, which had throughout the day existed as a still sunshine upon her countenance, or perhaps as a quiet unshed tear in her eye . . . in the transcendent sense, her life was a poem.[9]

Gilfillan's assessment of Hemans's creative process clearly entails a heavily gendered notion of woman as poet. It also assumes a leisured and implicitly monied background. In the presentation of Felicia Hemans to the world, the dominant model of bourgeois domesticity is foregrounded. Angela Leighton refers to this image as the 'long-lasting and popular myth of Hemans',[10] and indeed it is the image which endures to the present day. The poet's own class position, however, is more equivocal than this widespread impression of her allows. Hemans was born into a family of some wealth and social standing. William Michael Rossetti, in his 'Prefatory Notice' to her *Poetical Works*, describes Hemans's father as 'a merchant of considerable eminence, a native of Ireland, belonging to a branch of the Sligo [Browne] family'.[11] Financial losses which occurred soon after the birth of Felicia Hemans, however, were compounded some time later when her father debunked to Quebec, leaving his wife and children permanently to fend for themselves. When she was fourteen years old Hemans, encouraged by her mother, published a volume of verse which was intended to help the family out of financial difficulties precipitated by the father's desertion. When, in 1818, after six years of marriage and the birth of five sons, her own husband executed a similar act of abandonment, the poet's role was ratified as sole provider for herself, her mother and her children. Thus, from an early age and throughout her life, the security Hemans experienced as a member of the bourgeoisie was undermined in financial, social and emotional terms. She learned, I would argue, not only to mistrust the prevalent idealized view of the bourgeois nuclear family, but also to rely upon her own resources in order to maintain the appearance of effortless gentility. As Leighton observes: 'She clung tenaciously to the respectability which her provincial, non-intellectual background made both precious and yet precarious.'[12] It is the combination of preciousness and precariousness in representations of bourgeois ideology in verse by Hemans which has rendered her work both interesting and problematic to many of her contemporaries as well as to numerous more recent critics.

The representations Hemans makes of class in her poems are somewhat circumscribed. In his monograph on Hemans in the Writers of Wales series, Peter Trinder remarks that, despite her own narrow experience of the world at large (she never left the shores of Britain), Hemans nevertheless maintained a 'continuing enthusiasm for heroic exploits . . . [and] the choice of exotic locations for narrative'.[13] Indeed, a large proportion of the poems in her oeuvre feature excursions concerned with famous characters and events in a multitude of differing historical, biblical, mythological and cultural locations. A glance at the contents pages of any of her numerous collections evidences this interest. The preoccupation Hemans displays with distant and alien settings, incidents and figures has been discussed in terms of an understanding of her position in relation to gendered models of domesticity.[14] The poet's fixation on the heroic and the exotic is equally interesting, however, in terms of class issues.

One area of particular interest for Hemans is that of royalty. Born in 1793, her experience of living under a monarchy would have been coloured by the reign of the profligate George IV as regent and king, and later that of the almost equally reviled William IV.

Whilst George III had lost popularity in the wake of defeat in America and prolonged wars with France, and had relinquished credibility through his increasing bouts of madness, he was nevertheless seen as a decent, if uncharismatic, man. George IV, however, as regent and king, was held in general contempt for his moral degeneracy; as Linda Colley wryly observes, soon after his marriage 'the prince reverted to gluttony, architecture and mistresses'.[15] Clearly, in the context of the Evangelical campaign for national moral regeneration, the condition of a monarchy headed by such a figure was cause for public concern. Hemans herself was moved in 1820 to write a monody entitled 'Stanzas to the Memory of George III'. After nine years of his son's regency, the king's death occasioned Hemans to pen an extravagant eulogy. The epigraph consists of two Old Testament quotations; the first, from the book of Nehemiah, refers to King Solomon the wise – 'Among many nations was there no king like him' – and the second, from the Samuel I, is spoken of Abner, warrior ally of King David, murdered by a kinsman – 'Know ye not that there is a prince and a great man fallen this day in Israel?'[16] The dead monarch is thus connected from the outset of the poem with the kingly qualities of enlightenment and courage and with the concept of betrayal by those closest to him. This is a telling intimation in terms of the poet's depiction of the Hanoverian monarchy. The piece opens in histrionic tribute:

> Another warning sound! The funeral bell,
> Startling the cities of the Isle once more
> With measured tones of melancholy swell,
> Strikes on th'awakened heart from shore to shore.
> He at whose coming monarchs sink to dust,
> The chambers of our palaces hath trod.
> And the long-suffering spirit of the just,
> Pure from its ruins, hath returned to God!
> Yet may not England o'er her Father weep:
> Thoughts to her bosom crowd, too many, and too deep.
>
> Vain voice of Reason, hush! – they yet must flow,
> The unrestrained, involuntary tears;
> A thousand feelings sanctify the woe,
> Roused by the glorious shades of vanished years.
> Tell us no more 'tis not the time for grief,
> Now that the exile of the soul is past.
> And Death, blest messenger of Heaven's relief,
> Hath borne the wanderer to his rest at last;
> For Him Eternity hath tenfold day,
> We feel, we know, 'tis thus – yet Nature will have way.[17]

Interestingly the poem begins on a note of plaintive caution, symbolized in the king's death knell. In the opening quatrain, the solemn rhythm of the funeral bell is evoked through a combination of iambic metre with trochees beginning alternate lines, and regular syllable count and punctuation. The poet's warning to the nation is ostensibly that death will reward the just by despatching them straight to heaven; the unjust, by implication, should take heed and mend their ways before the converse and deeply undesirable fate overtakes them. The effect, however, is to link the old king's passing with a sense of national threat. Furthermore, this presage, the poet declares, is 'Another warning'; the suggestion is that the nation has already received admonition of foreboding before the death of the king. This may be read, I would argue, as a veiled reference to the 'ill-advised' leadership of the regent and new monarch. The poem continues over twenty-two stanzas of pious panegyric. The late king's infamous mental health problems are euphemistically elided in arch references, for example, to his experience of 'the woes of many a bitter lot'.[18] In the final stanza, however, the poet addresses the issue of the succession; her anxieties are evident:

> All else shall pass away – the thrones of kings,
> The very traces of their *tombs* depart;
> But number not with perishable things
> The holy records Virtue leaves the heart,
> Heirlooms from race to race – and oh! in days,
> When, by the yet unborn, thy deed are blest,
> When our sons learn 'as household words' thy praise,
> Still on thine offspring may thy spirit rest!
> And many a name of that imperial line,
> Father and patriot! blend in England's songs with thine![19]

Here it becomes clear that the poet warns not only the nation, but the monarchy itself. Whilst monarchs disappear in time, history remains and the conduct of kings is remembered. Her invocation that the spirit of the old king infuses his progeny for the sake of the nation would seem redundant given a popular successor; as it is, the poet's expression of such a hope implies that its fulfilment is dubious in the current context.

Any engagement by Hemans in her poems with the lower classes is extremely perfunctory. Of more than seven hundred poetical works contained in the Albion edition of her collected verse, only a very few refer to explicitly lower-class subjects.

'The Peasant Girl of the Rhone' and 'The Shepherd-Poet of the Alps' clearly depict labouring rustics from foreign countries; 'The Cottage Girl' describes an anonymous peasant child in an indeterminate region of an unspecified land. In the late 1820s, when these poems were published, the presence of the labouring poor was increasingly to the forefront of British social consciousness. A combination of the agrarian and industrial revolutions at home and the American and French Revolutions abroad created a climate ripe for class conflict.[20] The so-called Peterloo massacre had taken place in 1819, when a troop of mounted yeomanry charged a largely working-class crowd of men and women gathered to hear a speech on parliamentary reform. As David Thomson notes, 'The first reaction of the Government was repression . . . But repeatedly throughout the century reforms were effected only as concessions to extreme pressure from below, and as alternatives to riot.'[21] Given this volatile background, the reluctance Hemans shows to engage in her poems with the lower classes of her own time and place is conspicuous. Chronologically, of course, as Leighton has noted, Hemans is a Romantic. A Romantic tendency to sentimentalize the 'noble savage' is certainly part of her project in these pieces. In 'The Shepherd-Poet', for example, the eponymous protagonist is figured as a heroic revolutionary. 'The Cottage Girl' is a short and somewhat inane piece, in which the poet muses on the capacity of a child glimpsed at play to render charming an otherwise unremarkable rustic scene. Though the girl in the poem plays outside a cottage, she is otherwise classless.

Clearly, then, the divisive relationship between the upper and labouring classes, which caused considerable public alarm during the years of Hemans's writing career, is almost entirely ignored in her work. It may be useful in an analysis of her treatment of the lower classes to consider the position of Hemans in terms of her links with literary Romanticism. It is clear from the numerous epigraphs to her verse which cite work by first- and second-generation Romantic poets that Hemans was an admirer of these artists; additionally, her work resonates with many of the thematic and linguistic qualities characteristic of Romantic verse. A considerable body of feminist scholarship has explored the problematic position of women poets in relation to Romanticism, and I will return to a discussion of this material later in the chapter in an examination of Hemans and gender issues. What I want to suggest here, however, is that the subject position of Hemans as a member of the emergent bourgeoisie may have affected her creative capacity within Romanticism, compounding her already vexed perspective on the self-assertive, politically radical ethos of the movement. It is in the interstices of this complex cultural plexus, I would argue, that the poet's self-evident struggle with the depiction of lower-class experience can be located. The position Hemans holds in relation to the radical politics of the Romantic movement, inspired as it was by the revolutions in America and France, is problematic. This unease is exemplified in her dramatic poem 'Prisoners' Evening Service', published in her 1834 collection *Scenes and Hymns of Life*, which is dedicated, incidentally, to 'William Wordsworth Esq., in token of deep respect for his character, and fervent gratitude for moral and intellectual benefit derived from communion with the spirit of his poetry.'[22] 'Prisoners' Evening Service' describes, in a melodramatic style which verges on the farcical, the scene inside 'The Prison of the Luxembourg in Paris during the Reign of Terror'. The dramatis personae of the piece consist of D'Aubigné, 'an aged royalist', and his young daughter, Blanche; the narrative details the pair's anguished courage as the moment of their violent death draws inexorably near. The poem's depiction of the doomed father and daughter bewails their gory fate, without a hint of criticism of the corrupt system from which they emerge. At one point Blanche demands:

> Oh! shall we gaze again
> On the bright Loire? Will the old hamlet spire,
> And the gray turret of our own chateau,
> Look forth to greet us through the dusky elms?[23]

Hamlet and chateau are seen here in organic unity; injustice and brutality are ignored in an idealized picture of the social hierarchy whose cruel rigidity spawned the revolutionary 'Terror' of 1789.

Early nineteenth-century bourgeois ideology, heavily influenced by Evangelical values, was explicitly anti-Jacobin in character. As Catherine Hall notes, 'In the wake of the French Revolution . . . Evangelicism provided a rallying point against Jacobinism . . . That response was "in open conflict with . . . new working-class organization and conscious-ness".'[24] For Hemans, then, the elevation of 'low and rustic life' advocated by the young and radical Wordsworth in 1802 was as intract-able a difficulty as the elevation of sublime nature, for example, was appealing.[25] I suggest that her reluctance to engage with lower-class subjects is linked to this political misalignment with the literary movement, which most profoundly influenced her poetic sensibility.

★ ★ ★

Having dwelt at some length on the subject of representations by Hemans of class identity, I turn now to a consideration of her poetry in relation to early nineteenth-century gender issues. It is in this area that the majority of recent critical work on Hemans has concentrated, and it is here, I would suggest, that re-evaluation of her reputation as 'the undisputed representative poet of Victorian imperial and domestic ideology' is most compelling.[26]

In his 1835 poem, 'Extempore Effusion on the Death of James Hogg', Wordsworth, with whom she was acquainted, was moved to sing her praises: Wordsworth includes Hemans as the only woman, among such luminaries as Scott, Coleridge and Charles Lamb, in a list of poets. In 'As if but yesterday departed', Elizabeth Barrett Browning composed an elegy in her honour in which she acclaims 'that mystic breath which breathed in all her breathing'.[27] Interestingly, however, both these apparent enthusiasts also expressed private reservations about the limitations of Hemans's rather ladylike approach; Barrett Browning complains in correspondence that Hemans was 'too conventionally a lady to be a great poetess';[28] Wordsworth privately dilutes his earlier fulsome praise by describing her approach as 'too elaborate and studied'.[29]

It was this 'womanly' quality in her verse which had endeared Hemans to critics and the public at the height of her fame. She was described variously as 'infinitely sweet, elegant, and tender',[30] 'exquisitely feminine',[31] 'the spirit of romance in female form'.[32] As the century progressed, however, the moment for appreciation of such qualities passed, and opinions about the excessive delicacy of Hemans's sensibility were no longer confined to private correspondence; in the 'Prefatory Notice' to his 1879 edition of her *Poetical Works*, for example, William Michael Rossetti remarks of her poetry: 'besides exhibiting the fineness and charm of womanhood, it has also the monotone of mere sex'.[33] The general prescriptiveness of such critics, and Rossetti's extreme arrogance in particular, are grating; a cursory glance at the collected poetical works of Hemans, however, seems to bear out complaints of her acquiescence to, and idealization of, nineteenth-century female gender roles. In her tellingly entitled 1812 piece 'The Domestic Affections', for example, Hemans extols the virtues of that place 'far from life's tumultuous road, / [where] Domestic bliss has fixed her calm abode'. The poem centres on the image of the home as a site of nurturing serenity in the midst of a world of physical and, more importantly, moral danger:

> Whence are those tranquil joys in mercy given,
> To light the wilderness with beams of Heaven?
> To soothe our cares, and through the cloud diffuse
> Their tempered sunshine and celestial hues? . . .

Say, do they grace Ambition's regal throne,
When kneeling myriads call the world his own? . . .
Or dwell with luxury in the enchanted bowers,
Where taste and wealth exert *creative* powers.
Favoured of Heaven! O Genius! are they thine?
When round thy brow the wreaths of glory shine; . . .
No, sacred joys, 'tis yours to dwell enshrined,
Most fondly cherished in the purest mind;
Nursed on the lap of solitude and shade,
The violet smiles emblossomed in the glade;
There sheds her spirit on the lonely gale,
Gem of seclusion! treasure of the vale!
Thus far from life's tumultuous road,
Domestic bliss has fixed her calm abode.[34]

The poet promotes the domestic ideal in terms which apparently reject the worldly alternatives presented by ambition, wealth, creativity and genius. Her italicized emphasis on 'creative', however, is interesting; as wife, mother and poet, the irony of her own position in renouncing the creative impulse is clearly not lost on the speaker of the piece. Domestic bliss in all its halcyon purity is characterized as an unambiguously female state; maternity is used as a metaphor for the soothing nurture offered to the world by such fireside perfection:

As when dread thunder shakes the troubled sky
The cherub, infancy, can close its eye,
And sweetly smile, unconscious of a tear,
While viewless angels wave their pinions near;
Thus, while around the storms of discord roll,
Borne on resistless wing, from pole to pole;
While war's red lightnings desolate the ball,
And thrones and empires in destruction fall;
Then, calm as an evening on the silvery wave,
When the wind slumbers in the ocean cave,
She dwells unruffled, in her bower of rest,
Her empire, home! – her throne, affection's breast![35]

Hemans deploys the discourse of secular male domination in describing the private domain prescribed by society as woman's sphere. The use of feminine pronouns, combined with rhetorical syntax, exclamatory punctuation and italicized emphasis renders the tone of the extract energetically celebratory of the qualities it describes. The poem continues in the same eulogizing mood for some three hundred lines, depicting the range of dangerous worldly pursuits from which 'Domestic bliss' provides the male adventurer with precious refuge. The sailor 'Midst the dead calm, the vigil of the deep', the soldier 'In hostile climes', 'the shipwrecked wanderer . . . on the barren coast',[36] are all shown to benefit from contemplation of this highly gendered vision of domesticity; it is what enables them to undertake their journeys, and what precipitates their psychological, if not physical, survival. It is significant, however, that by the end of the piece, the poet is weighing the advantages offered to the – implicitly male – world against the physical and spiritual cost to the female figure in providing it. The metaphor of maternity, previously used in the poem as a symbol of all-bounteous creativity, is inverted here to evoke the sacrifice and waste involved in sustaining the domestic ideal; the mother-figure, previously characterized as the provider of protection for her infant who remained 'unconscious of a tear',[37] is now depicted, in heavily sentimental detail, watching her child die:

> There, bending still, with fixed and sleepless eye,
> There, from her child the mother learns to die.
> Explores, with fearful gaze each mournful trace
> Of lingering sickness in the faded face;
> Through the sad night when every hope is fled,
> Keeps her lone vigil by the sufferer's bed.
> And starts each morn as deeper marks declare
> The spoiler's hand – the blight of death is there.[38]

The sentimental tone borders on the melodramatic, and clearly provides ammunition for detractors who accuse Herman of clichéd puerility. It seems to me, however, that in terms of semantics, the connotations of the poem offer possibilities for reading it as a subversion, rather than a celebration, of early nineteenth-century gender values. The ideology of separate spheres may be read as redefined by the poet here; she depicts the doctrine as lifegiving and enabling to the men who rely upon it to fuel their forays into the world at large, but ultimately draining and destructive to the women who are its source. The woman's sphere unproblematically glorified earlier in the poem as her 'empire . . . throne . . . unruffled bower of rest'[39] is transmuted now into the deathbed of youth, the site of atrophied promise:

> Lo! by the couch, where pain and chill disease,
> In every vein the ebbing life blood freeze . . .[40]

It may well be, of course, that the rebellion by Hemans here is an act of unconscious rather than deliberate defiance; clearly it is impossible to overlook the poem's inherent conservatism. I am not suggesting that Felicia Hemans should be read as an unruly early nineteenth-century woman; what I propose, however, is that her reputation as the embodiment of ladylike comportment – intended as a compliment by her immediate reading public, and interpreted pejoratively by many of her literary successors – is perhaps more problematic a concept than it at first appears.

Arch-conservative or otherwise, by the end of the nineteenth century the reputation of Hemans as a poet had been severely eroded; her name survived only in connection with a few of her more heavily anthologized pieces, among them, of course, the above-mentioned 'Casabianca' and her other much-parodied standard 'The Homes of England'.

The Anglo-American feminist imperative to establish a tradition of women's writing has meant that since the 1970s the work of Hemans has been subject to renewed scrutiny. Her poetry has been analysed in terms of its reception: Elizabeth Helsinger, Robin Lauterbach Sheets and William Veeder, for example, are interested in the way 'responses to her work reveal the climate of thought in which the major women poets defined themselves and sought their audience'.[41] It has been examined with reference to its conditions of production: Norma Clarke and Cora Kaplan, for example, both explore the extent of the complicity by Hemans in and her resistance to the nineteenth-century ideology of gender-defined separate spheres.[42] None of these writers finds in Hemans's work very much to recommend it either in terms of artistic merit or gender-political radicalism. The traits of consummate femininity which endeared her to her earliest readers, and alienated those who followed, clearly rankle with many late twentieth-century commentators. Her poetry is seen as having 'little artistic significance',[43] for all that its popularity attests to her position as 'the undisputed representative poet of Victorian imperial and domestic ideology'.[44]

More recently, though, a number of critics have attempted to problematize the dismissal of Hemans on these grounds. In her book, *Victorian Women Poets: Writing Against the Heart*, Angela Leighton, whilst acknowledging the 'troubling limitations' of Hemans's work, nevertheless recognizes that her poetry 'came to focus on the woman artist, however misunderstood and tragic, however much pining to be a wife and mother instead. As a result, the thematic tension in her work shifts from external gender difference to internalised self-division.'[45] Susan Wolfson, in her essay '"Domestic Affections" and "The Spear of Minerva": Felicia

Hemans and the Dilemma of Gender', considers the ways in which poems by Hemans may be read as dramatizing the conflicts experienced by the early nineteenth-century woman writer between domesticity and artistic creativity. Wolfson sees the work of Hemans as making a very positive contribution to a feminist account of early nineteenth-century British culture.[46]

Through numerous examples, Wolfson argues that poetry by Hemans should not be dismissed as merely clichéd and sentimental; she proposes that, far from endorsing and promoting the dominant patriarchal ideology, the work may be read as interrogating its moral authority. Wolfson's reading of Hemans approaches her writing in the light of a number of post-modernist critical perspectives, applying to the text Marxist and psychoanalytic theories through which she is able to achieve insights, obscured to the commentators on Hemans already mentioned, into the experience of the woman poet in early nineteenth-century Britain. These, then, are more promising approaches to reclaiming this most 'published of nineteenth-century poets' for a feminist criticism. I now intend to examine the Welsh poems by Hemans in order to assess the importance of the poet's links with Wales for an understanding of her position in terms of Victorian literary culture.

★ ★ ★

Tricia Lootens, in her essay 'Hemans and Home: Victorianism, Feminine "Internal Enemies", and the Domestication of National Identity', dismisses the significance of Hemans's Welsh poems in the construction of the poet's sense of national identity. Lootens acknowledges that whilst tensions may exist beneath the surface of the apparent celebration by Hemans of English imperialism, this is a result of the poet's gendered subject position, rather than any ambivalence arising out of her Welsh background.[47] Given the apparent contradiction between the jingoistic reputation of Hemans and her claims to naturalized Welsh status, it seems important to give serious attention to her poems on Welsh themes. In doing so I will refer to an enterprising recent essay by Jerome J. McGann entitled 'Literary History, Romanticism, and Felicia Hemans'.

McGann's essay is imaginatively and unusually constructed in the form of a discussion between three interlocutors, 'Anne Mack', 'J. J. Rome' and 'George Mannejc'; as such, it does away with the possibility of providing any single authoritative reading. Indeed, the tone of the piece is self-consciously playful in its dealings with the concepts of authorship and literary theory, as McGann, through his fictional personae, interrupts and contradicts himself throughout. Through the formal properties of his essay McGann thus alerts the reader to the viability of his thesis, which is that, providing the reader suspends acquiescence to dominant notions of canonicity and authority, even the most apparently transparent of literary texts has the potential to generate a range of readings allowing critics access to the untold stories of British culture. In a sense, McGann's choice of Hemans as site for the exposition of his theory is evidence of the extreme unlikeliness of her candidature for such a task. There is a sense of scientific detachment as McGann demonstrates the efficacy of his theory on a work by Hemans, in the mode of a doctor trying out an experimental cure upon a last-hope patient. He chooses her 'The Homes of England' and proposes that this anthem to the durability of ancient ideologies of class, gender and colonialism may be reimagined as an interrogation of the myth of cultural endurance. Through the contradictory and often sardonic contributions of the three interlocutors, McGann discusses the possibility that 'The Homes of England' may be read not as clichéd and sentimental, but rather as a revelation of the ideological significance of such cultural conventions as cliché and sentimentality. He explores the idea that the apparent elevation by Hemans of the values of nineteenth-century British imperialist culture is 'actually a celebration not of those ideological reference points but of the images and forms the ideology requires for its sustenance'.[48]

McGann suggests that 'The Homes of England' ought not to be written off as a safe and syrupy glorification of its subject matter, but acknowledged rather as a very deliberate attempt to problematize Victorian assumptions about the power, durability and, by implication, divinely appointed authority of the British imperial project. This, of course, goes further than Wolfson's psychoanalytic interpretation of poetry by Hemans as a manifestation of unconscious female defiance. The various 'voices' through which McGann's essay is articulated enable him to anticipate the incredulity of his readers, and the self-parody acts as an intellectual cop-out of sorts.

What I propose is that an examination of Hemans's Welsh poetry, bearing in mind the ideas with which McGann's essay is working, may add to an understanding of her practice in 'representing England to the English' by taking into account her experience as an artist writing from the geographic and political margins of the dominant patriarchal and imperialist culture. McGann's thesis attempts to demonstrate the ambivalence inherent in even the apparently most transparent panegyric by Hemans of dominant nineteenth-century British ideology, and thus provides an ingenious and potentially useful platform for a 'reimagining' of Hemans as a Welsh poet. To this end, and using McGann's model of superficiality and substantiality as a starting-point, an examination of one of Hemans's *Welsh Melodies*, 'The Hall of Cynddylan', which is her rendering of the ninth-century anonymous verse 'The Elegy on Cynddylan', promises a new perspective on Hemans's experience of home.[49]

Welsh Melodies, the collection in which this poem appears, was published in 1822, some five years before 'The Homes of England'. In contrast with 'The Homes of England' it describes an architectural signifying system whose moment has already passed. The 'Hall of Cynddylan' is 'lonely and bare', whereas in the 'Homes of England . . . gladsome looks of household love / Meet in the ruddy light!'; the 'Hall of Cynddylan is voiceless and still / The sound of its harpings hath died on the hill',[50] whereas in the 'Homes of England' 'woman's voice flows forth in song / Or childhood's tale is told'.[51] If, as McGann argues, Hemans evokes in her celebration of 'The Homes of England' a prophecy of the destruction of that same social order which the homes themselves represent, it ought to be possible to invert the equation in relation to 'The Hall of Cynddylan'. According to McGann, 'The Homes of England', in all their apparently thriving glory, stand for a moral and political system, the days of whose ascendancy are numbered. By the same token it might be suggested that the deserted and desolate 'Hall of Cynddylan' functions as a mesh of quotations of signifying signs inherited from ancient and legendary Welsh culture, and, further, may be read as symbolizing ideas whose moral and creative potential remains for the poet substantial and enduring. Clearly the poem is a rendering by Hemans of an ancient Welsh work, and the original remains recognizable in her version. Even given the inherited origin of the material, however, Hemans's adaptation is potentially interesting in terms of testing McGann's thesis.

Though its setting is ancient Wales, and its tone rhetorical, there is a quality of immediacy about the poem. It opens: 'The Hall of Cynddylan is gloomy tonight / I weep, for the grave has extinguished its light'; present tense and first person are sustained throughout, as the speaker declaims in high and dramatic style her grief at contemplating the empty building:

> The beam of the lamp from its summit is o'er,
> The blaze of its hearth shall give welcome no more!
>
> The Hall of Cynddylan is voiceless and still,
> The sound of its harpings hath died on the hill!

> Be silent for ever, thou desolate scene,
> Nor let e'en an echo recall what hath been.[52]

Here the poet utilizes the material of Welsh legend, material which has survived to fuel the imagination of poets long after its visible architectural signs have decayed into rubble. The poem ends with the speaker, last of her line after defeat in battle, vowing to follow her tribal chief and kinsfolk to the grave:

> The Hall of Cynddylan is loveless tonight,
> Since he is departed whose smile made it bright!
> I mourn; but the sigh of my soul shall be brief,
> The pathway is short to the grave of my chief![53]

Heroic martyrdom is always impressive; though oozing pathos, the final lines ring with a splendid and defiant theatricality. Whilst Hemans depicts a culture ravaged by war or pogrom, the external evidence of whose existence lies abandoned and decaying, her appropriation of its legendary resources nevertheless seems to attest to the durability of that culture's moral potency and generative artistic potential.

'Quotation', to use McGann's term, from the inheritance of her Welsh upbringing recurs frequently throughout Hemans's large oeuvre of poetical works, and by no means always refers to the resources of ancient Welsh culture and history. As Rossetti observed, a great many of her poems are inspired by the contemporary physical and emotional landscape of her Welsh childhood. When Hemans reflects upon 'The Sound of the Sea' she remembers the waters around her north Wales home; when she describes 'Our Lady's Well' it is 'a beautiful spring in the woods near St Asaph' to which she refers.[54] The motif of home, central to so much work by Hemans is connected in a profound way to her experience in the north Wales countryside. McGann seizes upon use by Hemans of home as a poetic device to advance his theory of subversion through apparent celebration; in his reading, the poet's preoccupation with the nature of domesticity 'probes painfully for the truth of her own most cherished fiction, the fiction of the stable and love-founded hearth'.[55] Susan Wolfson similarly makes a great deal of the ambivalence of Hemans towards images of home, arguing that her work 'intermittently exposes discrepancies of domestic experience and domestic ideal'.[56] In the poems which relate to her Welsh experience, it seems to me that the idea of home is represented in terms which render even more complex the relationship between Hemans and the dominant culture of her time. In many of her explicitly Welsh pieces, she focuses on the ancient Wales of history and legend; many, like 'The Hall of Cynddylan', are translations of classical Welsh poems. Hemans was clearly influenced by the late eighteenth-century proto-Romantic cult of sensibility with its character-istic preoccupation with Celtic culture.[57] What I want to examine here, however, is the possibility that the Welsh connections also provide additional resources through which the poet may explore and articulate her experience as woman and artist in early nineteenth-century Britain.

'The Cambrian in America' is unique among the *Welsh Melodies* in that it does not refer to ancient Welsh culture. In setting and tone the piece evokes a far more immediate experience, as the exiled speaker dreams of his homeland. This is an interesting site on which to base an examination of the poet's attitudes in relation to issues of conformity and resistance, marginality and canonicity, for it dramatizes ideas about physical and spiritual freedom. The title defines the context: the Welsh speaker, identified as male in the last line, is an immigrant a long way from home. Gwyn A. Williams discusses what he sees as the myth of the exile in Welsh consciousness:

> The *Cymry ar wasgar* (the 'exiles') are cherished in Welsh emotional life; they have their special day at the National Eisteddfod . . . But this truth registers so powerfully on the Welsh imagination precisely because the Welsh . . . remained in objective terms a small people . . . By any objective measurement, their emigrants were only a handful.[58]

The dedication by Hemans of a poem to 'The Cambrian in America' testifies to the impact of the idea. Her poem uses the figure of the exile as a trope expressing a range of emotions connected with her favourite 'home' motif. The opening lines construct in vividly sensual terms an exotic transatlantic world of limitless possibility:

> When the last flush of eve is dying
> On boundless lakes afar that shine;
> When winds amidst the palms are sighing,
> And fragrance breathes from every pine:
> When stars through cypress boughs are gleaming,
> And fireflies wander bright and free . . . [59]

There is a sense of constant movement in these lines, with the repeated use of present participles at the ends of lines one, three and four, which adds to the impression of freedom and wide possibility the words convey.

The verbs used, however, are all intransitive – to die, to shine, to sigh, to breathe, to gleam, to wander; the impression of potentiality is therefore undermined by a sense of aimless, unfulfilled movement. At line seven the speaker declares an emotional rejection of these apparently tantalizing prospects when he identifies as his addressee the place he has left behind:

> Still of thy harps, thy mountains dreaming,
> My thoughts, wild Cambria! dwell with thee!

The contrast is marked between the lushness of detail in the opening lines, and the lack of specificity in the reference to Wales. The American vista offers a spectrum of physical pleasure, the Cambrian dream only memory and death. But the speaker, whilst acknowledging the starkness of the opposition, is nevertheless 'wearied' by contemplating life in the New World, preferring to dwell in his memories of 'wild' Wales. His restless isolation stems from the beauty and serenity of the surroundings he surveys. The shifting horizons he describes in such sensual terms are always tranquil, but it is a harmony which fails to soothe his sense of nomadic desolation. The wildness of the Welsh mountains represents the spiritual ease which, paradoxically, physical freedom fails to deliver. 'Home' for this speaker is not his immediate physical location, but the home of his soul, in Wales. Home is shown to offer emotional and spiritual nurture, but it is 'wild' and for the speaker it is also associated with physical death:

> Sweet land, whence memory ne'er hath parted!
> To thee on sleep's light wing I fly;
> But happier could the weary-hearted
> Look on his own blue hills and die.[60]

Post-colonial critics have discussed the conjunction of place and displacement in the position of the settler colonist in the New World. Bill Ashcroft, Gareth Griffiths and Helen Tiffin, for example, refer to the settler's drive to establish 'a transplanted civilization . . . Having no ancestral contact with the land, they dealt with their sense of displacement by unquestioningly clinging to a belief in the adequacy of the imported language.'[61] For the 'Cambrian in America', himself driven from home by the industrial imperialism of a conquering power, and who may have suffered the imposition of an 'imported language' whilst still on native soil, the experience of settling in the New World was inevitably less clear-cut than this model allows. Hemans's poem may be read as demonstrating an awareness of the contradiction inherent in the Welsh exile's perspective. For him, the colonial impulse is fuelled by the instinct for physical survival yet smothered by the threat of spiritual extinction, given that it is unlikely that he will, in the long term, be able to sustain any attempt to recreate the linguistic and cultural conditions of home in the new context.

But the construction of 'home' during this early nineteenth-century period was not only a problem for the colonizers forced into emigration in order to survive materially. Disguised beneath a fictionalized account of one man's experience of emigration, I would argue, is a dramatization of the conflict between the nineteenth-century woman writer's impulse to conform to the widely propagated ideal of domesticity and her aspirations to wider worldly encounters. For this woman writer the domestic is the site of a comfort which is purchased at enormous cost. Its attractions for her are rooted not in material but in emotional security, and are won at the expense of the potential wide horizons of her creativity. It is suggested here that the early nineteenth-century duality which idealized domesticity as a woman's true place, whatever her ambitions may have been to experience other worlds, in binding her to the narrow horizons of her 'own blue hills' also bound her to her death. Hemans in her poetry embraces that death, just as the 'Cambrian in America' yearns for his distant home, which would have entailed his own impoverishment had he stayed in it. But it is the imperialistic aspirations of England during this time which have both impoverished his Welsh homeland and uprooted him to the colonial site. In 1822 Hemans complains with exasperated good humour of the constrictions inherent in her own experience of the 'domestic ideal':

> I am actually in the melancholy situation of Lord Byron's 'scorpion girt by fire – Her circle narrowing as she goes,' for I have been pursued by the household troops through every room successively, and begin to think of establishing my *métier* in the cellar.[62]

Letters written by Hemans later in life, however, testify with greater seriousness to the extent of her frustration at the encroachment of domestic responsibilities upon her own creativity:

> It has ever been one of my regrets that the constant necessity of providing sums of money to meet the exigencies of the boys' education, has obliged me to waste my mind in what I consider mere desultory effusions . . . My wish ever was to concentrate all my mental energy in the production of some more noble and complete work.[63]

Such insights support what the Welsh poems suggest, which is that, whilst in her poetry generally Hemans may appear to be celebrating the domestic and the feminine sphere, she is keenly aware of the pain and desolation of the woman's lot, as constructed by the ideology of the period. Although she stays at home, she too is as painfully self-divided as the Cambrian on American plains. In her famous poem 'Evening Prayer at a Girls' School', for example, Hemans describes to the girls at prayer the burden of womanhood which will soon be theirs to carry:

> Her lot is on you! – silent tears to weep,
> And patient smiles to wear through suffering's hour,
>
> . . .
>
> Meekly to bear with wrong, to cheer decay,
> And, oh! to love through all things. Therefore pray![64]

It could be suggested that the position of Hemans as a Welsh writer, whose sense of home is complicated by the geographic and political marginality of her experience, enables this multi-layered rendering of the domestic.

I have brought to bear a range of critical perspectives upon Hemans's Welsh poems, and in doing so I would argue that these pieces offer useful new perspectives on the poet's position in relation to the highly gendered ideology of her time. It is important to note, however, that in attempting to read Felicia Hemans as a Welsh writer one is faced with a plethora of impediments arising out of the evidence of the poet's oeuvre.

Regardless of her biographical credentials and poetic claims to Welsh identity, a glance at the range of her work reveals that the reputation of Hemans as a major poet of Victorian imperialist jingoism is fully deserved. Her general endorsement of colonial aggression is evident in many of her poems. Hemans's volume *Records of Women with Other Poems*, published in 1828, includes her poem 'Edith', which is subtitled 'A Tale of the Woods'. In this piece the poet narrates the tragic tale of Edith, a newly-wed English emigrant to America, who, having been widowed in an Indian attack on the convoy in which she travelled, is adopted by a kindly and childless Indian chief and his wife. Despite her grief and her 'streaming wound', Edith manages to stay alive just long enough to convert her rescuers to Christianity. The flimsy pretext of this indulgent sentimentality does not detract from its promotion of ethnic and religious colonialism. Catherine Hall discusses the complex intersections of class, gender and ethnicity which underpin bourgeois Evangelical Christian attitudes to colonial activities in the period. She argues that:

> religion provided one of the key discursive terrains for . . . the construction of a national identity . . . Religious beliefs provided a vocabulary of right – the right to know and to speak that knowledge, with the moral power that was attached to the speaking of God's word. One of the issues on which they spoke was what it meant to be English.[65]

Hall suggests that through the Christian mission to convert the colonies, and its representation, the English were able to define themselves as rightfully dominant in their relation to others, specifically their colonized and converted subjects. She further argues that, in order to achieve conversion, 'active Christian manliness' was necessary: 'For Evangelical Christians the action of combating sin, of enlisting in the army of God, provided a worthy arena within which they could prove their manhood.'[66] In Hemans's poem 'Edith', Englishness is seen through the religious conversion of the Indian couple; it is depicted as patient and self-sacrificing, as educative and civilizing; it is also effected by the ministry of the young English woman. Tellingly, however, in her act of conversion, Edith's strength is spent, and she dies almost immediately after her 'foster parents' have declared their new-found Christian faith. The virility understood to be essential to missionary activity is thus seen to be impossible to sustain in a woman. Clearly, the attempt to identify with the authentically English project of religious colonialism is mitigated for the poet by the effects of gendered difference. There is, however, no indication in the poem that the experience of Hemans as a 'naturalized Welsh woman' inflects her identification with the English colonial enterprise.

Further signs of the identification of Hemans with English colonialism may be found throughout her oeuvre. In addition to the famous 'Homes of England', the Albion edition of her collected works is littered with verses which celebrate the English imperial project, poems such as 'England's Dead', 'English Soldier's Song of Memory', 'The Crusader's Return', 'Curfew Song of England', 'The English Boy', 'The Name of England'. In 'England's Dead', Hemans glorifies the imperial drive which has resulted in the burial of its dead throughout the global empire. The poem moves through fourteen stanzas which list the numerous foreign sites where Englishmen have fallen in establishing and extending the empire. Hemans figures the empire 'on which the Sun never sets' in a gruesome image of sacrificial bloodshed; there is nowhere in the world,

Hemans proudly boasts, which is not a final resting-place for the corpses of English colonizers:

> The warlike of the isles,
> The men of field and wave!
> Are not the rocks their funeral piles,
> The seas and shores their graves?
>
> Go stranger! track the deep,
> Free, free the white sail spread!
> Wave may not foam, nor wild wind sweep,
> Where rest not England's dead.[67]

There is no sense of irony in the poet's tone as she reverences not the dead themselves, but the explicitly English imperial enterprise in which their sacrifice was made. The rhetorical dismissal 'Go stranger!', addressed to the non-English of the world, and repeated in the second and final stanzas, reads as a chilling indication of arrogant and aggressive colonialism.

In 'The Name of England' the poet claims this bellicose and exclusive national pride as her own:

> The trumpet of the battle
> Hath a high and thrilling tone;
> And the first, deep gun of ocean-fight,
> Dread music all its own.
>
> But a mightier power, my England!
> Is in that name of thine,
> To strike the fire from every heart
> Along the bannered line.[68]

The poet's proprietorial 'my England' indicates an endorsement of, and an identification with, the imperial drive. Her claim, that the name of England has the power to extinguish 'the fire from every heart' that resists it, suggests a smugness which defies moral interrogation, and which is at odds with the poet's celebration of Celtic heroism against colonial oppression in poems such as 'The Harp of Wales'.

I cannot help but admire the theoretical pyrotechnics with which Jerome J. McGann illuminates 'The Homes of England'; I have also found his thesis stimulating in terms of reading the Welsh poems of Hemans. I would defy even McGann, however, to generate readings of 'England's Dead' and 'The Name of England' which refuse the poet's position as arch-English imperialist. Whilst the 'superficiality' of 'The Homes of England', it may be argued, refers to architectural symbols of an imperial culture doomed to decline, the two poems discussed above figure human sacrifices to empire as symbolic tokens of arrogant territorial aggression.

In 1826 Hemans published a collection of poems entitled *Lays of Many Lands*. The volume contains twenty-one works which draw on the traditions and legends of countries ranging from north Africa to the Indian sub-continent, from Scandinavia to the Deep South of America, and several continents in between. In all of these poems Hemans depicts heroic scenes and characters in glowingly sentimental terms. In these works she deploys the resources of folk culture in order to explore a range of issues such as freedom, death, loyalty and tradition. Hemans prefaces the collection with an explanatory note: 'The following pieces may so far be considered a series, as each is intended to be commemorative of some national recollection, popular custom or tradition.'[69]

★ ★ ★

Having considered Hemans's work in some depth in relation to the concept of national identity, I am ultimately convinced that her Welsh poems represent no more than another parasitic deployment of 'local colour' material. I am persuaded that a knowledge of Welsh culture provided Hemans with useful additional resources for explorations of gendered marginality within the constrictive literary and social canons of her time. I am also satisfied, however, that her experience of Welshness by no means diluted her sense of herself as a member, and, more importantly, a promoter of the English imperial establishment.

4

Maria James, Cambrian poet in America

Little is known about Maria James; even the dates of her birth and death are unconfirmed. One volume of her poetry and the biographical introduction which prefixes it represent the full extent of material available on this nineteenth-century Welsh woman poet. An examination of these meagre resources, however, indicates rich and hitherto unexplored territory with which to supplement an understanding of the experience of the woman artist in the context of nineteenth-century Western society. For Maria James was a Welsh emigrant to America; she and her family were part of the wave of working-class settlers who set out in the first quarter of the nineteenth century from Wales, and, indeed, from all over the British Isles, for the shores of the United States. According to her own account of her experiences, supplied, it is claimed, only under pressure from her editor, James left an unspecified region in the north of Wales at the age of seven, a monoglot Welsh-speaker. Her family joined a community of Welsh quarry-workers in New York State, where her father later qualified as a 'professor of religion',[1] and where her mother held community prayer meetings in the Welsh language. At the age of ten James joined the household of the Garretson family in nearby Rhinebeck as housemaid and companion to the young daughter, Mary. James remained with the Garretson family for the next five years, shared the educational opportunities available to Mary, and began to write poetry for her own satisfaction. Mary Garretson describes in a letter to the same editor how her family were extremely impressed with James's intelligence and her aptitude for learning and self-expression. Thus, when she was fifteen years old her employers sent her to a position as apprentice to 'an excellent mantua-maker' in New York City, where it was thought she might better fulfil her potential.[2] James was away from Rhinebeck for a period of approximately nine years, returning eventually to take up her previous position as well-loved servant to the Garretson family. According to Mary Garretson, James returned a much changed figure, accompanied by 'many sad feelings', and though always having 'the fear of God before her eyes . . . she became decidedly pious'.[3] On her return James wrote more frequently than ever and, presumably through the agency of her well-intentioned employers, her work began to appear in local newspapers and literary magazines. In 1838 the Garretson family showed one of her poems to a visiting friend, Mrs Potter of New York City; Mrs Potter in turn showed it to her husband, A. D. Potter, DD, of Union College New York. In 1839 Dr Potter published a volume of verse by James entitled *Wales and Other Poems*, for which he wrote an introduction. After the publication of this material nothing further is known about Maria James. It is upon Potter's collection and the early biographical material supplied to him by Maria James and Mary Garretson that I base this study.

Sadly, from the evidence of *Wales and Other Poems*, it seems that the enthusiasm of the Garretsons and the Potters for James's verse was misplaced. Whilst James was clearly an intelligent woman with a certain ingenuity for making lines rhyme, it is impossible to share her patron's fervour for the quality of her work. Formally, the verse is varied but pedestrian, ranging from roughly iambic couplets to less regular patterns, but remains, throughout, driven by the poet's compulsion to achieve rhymed line endings. In terms of thematic composition, the poems tend, generally, to lack complexity. The poet is a somewhat self-absorbed artist whose writing, for the most part, reflects her circumscribed vision. I do not, therefore, propose my readings of the work of Maria James on the basis of its literary merit. What I do contend, however, is that this poetry presents a rare and potentially useful opportunity to supplement an understanding of the experience of the nineteenth-century woman writer at a range of theoretical levels.

Recent anthologies and studies of nineteenth-century women's writing have given space to literary output by working-class artists.[4] Carol Shiner Wilson, for instance, has observed that 'economic dependence, emotional starvation, social displacement and the denial of the pleasures of the imagination' pervade the world of the less privileged nineteenth-century woman writer.[5] Joel Haefner discusses the heightened sense of restricted creativity which is encoded in the poetry of working-class women of the period.[6] The value of such studies to a feminist history of the period is widely recognized; an examination of class identities clearly adds to the complexity of a range of issues surrounding the 'othering' of the female subject.

In their 1989 work *The Empire Writes Back: Theory and Practice in Post-colonial Literatures*, Bill Ashcroft, Gareth Griffiths and Helen Tiffin consider the position of what they term 'settler colonies'; the experiences of the settler colonists are examined in the text in addition and contradistinction to those of indigenous colonized peoples. Ashcroft, Griffiths and Tiffin remark upon the urge which propels the settlers to 'establish a literature separate from that of the metropolitan centre'.[7] They note the vast range of anthologies and literary histories which emerge out of such colonial societies as that in the United States, for example, in order to define and redefine the shifting parameters of national literary identity.[8]

As Ashcroft et al. acknowledge, these are different problems of identity from those encountered by the colonized peoples of the world. These are difficulties which arise as much out of sameness as of difference. The colonists found themselves compelled to forge a literature which distinguished itself from that of the imperial centre; at the same time, however, in the act of claiming parity, the settlers were reasserting the values of the centre and, by implication, its authority to define authenticity in moral and aesthetic terms. Ashcroft et al. cite Renata Wasserman in locating language as an important element in this conflict:

> the early writers had both to legitimize the American and differentiate it from the European, stressing 'the difference in nature and equivalence in value' between the New World and the Old. The task was made easier by the fact that they were writing in English, but at the same time it was rendered problematic by the fact that the language of the metropolis came with its own 'connotational and ideational baggage'.[9]

In their *Post-colonial Studies Reader*, Ashcroft, Griffiths and Tiffin describe the convergence and intersection of post-colonial and feminist discourses:

> [Women] share with colonized races and cultures an intimate experience of the politics of oppression and repression . . . In the last ten years, however . . . feminism has highlighted a number of the unexamined assumptions within post-colonial discourse, just as post-colonialism's interrogations of western feminist scholarship have provided timely warnings and led to new directions.[10]

What the work of a writer such as Maria James seems to offer is greater insight into such issues. I would posit that, as a working-class Welsh woman living in a 'settler colony' and writing in English, Maria James is a figure whose position is displaced geographically, politically and linguistically to a far deeper intensity than that of the subjects with which post-colonial and feminist scholars have concerned themselves to date. In the course of this chapter I intend to examine poetry by James in the light of recent feminist and post-colonial scholarship. I intend to test the potential of her contribution to providing 'timely warnings' to both discourses of their limitations in addressing a comprehensive range of subject positions; and I hope to begin to explore whichever 'new directions' poetry by James seems to indicate for a more inclusive approach to nineteenth-century women's studies.

★ ★ ★

I turn first to the question of class. Maria James's consciousness of her status as domestic servant, placed as such in childhood and subject always to the wishes of her employers, is a thread which is woven throughout her poetry. In their 1981 study, *Victorian Women: A Documentary Account of Women's Lives in Nineteenth-Century England, France and the United States,* Erna Olafson Hellerstein, Leslie Parker Hume and Karen M. Offen reproduce extracts from the diary of a nineteenth-century middle-class New England housewife which attest to the difficulties of obtaining and retaining suitable girls for domestic service, who are, the diarist declares, 'as scarce [*sic*] as gold dust'.[11] Clearly, in such a climate, the prospect of a servant-poet, inflated with ideas which might cause her at worst to desert her position for the lure of literary success, and at best result in a deterioration of her standard of work, was one which might have caused alarm among the middle-class readership of James's work. In his introduction to the volume, A. D. Potter takes great pains to acknowledge and allay the potential anxiety of his readers at his promotion of poetry by a servant-woman. He pre-empts the range of criticism he anticipates will be levelled at him for his efforts on James's behalf:

> Many persons, I apprehend, will be inclined to doubt the wisdom of drawing from their obscurity, poems written under such circumstances. By some, the position of the authoress will be assumed as of itself sufficient evidence that they want merit. Others may hold, that even if not deficient in this respect, they ought still to be suppressed, since their publication can be of little service to her, and may do positive harm to others in similar situations. If not successful with the public, this volume, which has been to

its writer the source of so much innocent pleasure, will become (it is said) the occasion of intense mortification and pain; while, on the other hand, should it prove eminently popular, it will be but too apt to impair the implicity of her character, and awaken aspirations which, in such a case, must be doomed to disappointment. At best it will be thought to hold out to domestics, and those who lead lives of labour, an example of doubtful import, and one which is as likely to mislead as to profit.[12]

Potter's defence of James as a poet implies an absolutely rigid social structure in which, regardless of her success, the servant-woman's poetry 'can be of little service to her'. It is this underlying assumption which Potter employs to soothe whatever threat James's volume might have seemed to present to the social status quo of its middle-class American target-readership. For he reassures the reader, at great lengths, of the wisdom of her employers in their encouragement of her writing which 'abstained from any appeals to her ambition';[13] and of James herself who 'feels less solicitude in regard to the reception of these pieces, than is felt by many of the friends who have interested themselves in procuring subscribers'.[14] Indeed, in her letter to Mrs Potter, which is included in the introduction to the volume, James herself demonstrates the admirable qualities of self-abnegation and lack of ambition claimed on her behalf: 'As I advanced towards womanhood, I shrunk from the nickname of poet which had been awarded me: the very idea seemed the height of presumption.'[15] The consensus then, among friends and patrons of James, on the impossibility of her entertaining unhealthy aspirations, is absolute; and, ostensibly at least, the poet dutifully concurs. The poetry itself, however, suggests a more problematic reality. The 'Motto' with which James opens her collection is an interesting early indication of the tensions masked by her apparent acquiescence to her designated role; the humble servant whose talents exist only in order to reflect well upon her 'betters' does not entirely succeed in disguising her restlessness:

> I would not ask, – for that were vain, –
> To mingle with the reaper train, –
> Who gayly sing, as hast'ning by
> To pile their golden sheaves on high;
> But with the group who meet the view,
> In kerchief red and apron blue,
> I crave the scatter'd ears they yield,
> To bless the gleaner of the field.[16]

The poet dramatizes a life of servitude here through the rural metaphor of the harvest. The conditional tense in the opening line connotes a hesitancy which, I would argue, can be read as grounded equally in resentment and in modesty. The poet refrains from demanding an active part in the life of the world; not, it is implied, because she does not desire it, but because she knows that to ask would be futile. Her role is prescribed in the piece as passive observer, benefiting only vicariously from life's generative processes, but regarding, with longing, discarded remnants of the crop. The reapers' vitality is celebrated in descriptions of golden colour and constant hectic motion: those who take an active part in the world are perceived, not as individuals, but as a large, ever-progressing entity, 'the reaper train'; the verbs used in connection with the reapers imply animated energy, 'gayly sing', 'hast'ning by', 'To pile . . . on high'. The depiction of the group to which the speaker belongs is, by contrast, less homogenized and far more subdued. The speaker describes herself in a uniform defining her as part of a group which lacks the joyful unison of the reaper train: she wears the livery of domestic servitude. The speaker is clearly of this nexus, but retains a first-person voice, unable to 'mingle' in the way she desires; the sense is of unfulfilled isolation within the group. The verbs used here are supine in quality, 'meet', 'crave', 'bless'; and, whilst the speaker claims these ancillary attributes as her own, the tone is disaffected, desperate even, as she describes her longing to gather what scraps the reapers leave behind.

As an opening epigram, the 'Motto', I would suggest, undercuts much of the painstaking reassurance on grounds of class hierarchy which precedes it in the introductory passages of the volume; it may also portend a collection of poems which represent a more useful index of the experience of a working-class woman writer than the heavily guarded initial comments would indicate. James's concern with ideas about social position and personal aspiration is central to the collection. In Mary Garretson's introductory comments, the reader is informed that as a child the poet's sympathies gravitated towards the ruling classes: 'She was . . . very aristocratic in her notions. Her pictures of the noble and grand were perfectly unreal; and I well recollect that, in our little disputes as children she always took the aristocratic . . . side of the argument.'[17] The poetry written in adulthood evidences this fascination with the pre-eminent ranks of society; however, by this point the poet's sympathy is transmuted into a more self-centred perspective. In her piece 'Napoleon's Tomb', composed, as the head note explains, 'on seeing a little marble representation of the tomb of Napoleon Buonaparte',[18] James meditates, over twenty-one stanzas on the compelling folly of worldly ambition. She begins:

> In St Helena's lonely isle,
> Begirt by ocean's wave,
> The warrior-monarch laid him down,
> To slumber in his grave.
>
> But ere the icy hand of death
> Had closed that restless eye,
> Ambition call'd her numerous sons
> To see their brother die . . . [19]

The pretext of the poem is to illustrate that the rewards of Napoleon's megalomania are hollow and fleeting when 'A captive on a lonely rock / The mighty conqueror dies'. In the final stanza the poet, having considered Napoleon's fate, prays for her own serenity of soul:

> Thou source of pure, unbounded love!
> Bestow this gift on me:
> A calm contentment with my lot,
> Whate'er that lot may be.[20]

Such an entreaty, however, suggests a certain restlessness on the part of the speaker; she begs the divinity for 'calm contentment'; the implication is that she currently lacks this state of grace. Moreover, the body of the poem is devoted to describing Napoleon's overweening ambition in terms of ostentatious eulogy:

> Thy fame shall shine a polar star, –
> Thy deeds a beacon light.
>
> Alone among the souls of men,
> A wonder of the age, –
> The glory of thy bright career
> Shall swell th'historic page.[21]

The speaker's homage to Napoleon's temporal achievements is so complete that her claim to repudiate the lure of earthly ambition is rendered somewhat hollow. It is possible to read the poem as a warning against the dangers of overreaching from one who has herself fallen victim to a hunger for more than her birthright allows. Despite its pretence to endorse the precepts of submission to social rigidity as emphasized in the introduction, the piece offers evidence of a poet whose struggle with her own experience of thwarted ambition is intense and ongoing.

In another piece, 'The Broom', James makes an enterprising case for the positive aspects of life as a domestic servant. The poem propounds the virtues of the humble broom in securing the material security of she who wields it. It begins with an imaginative and rather lyrical description of the implement itself:

> Give me a broom, one neatly made
> In Niscayuna's distant shade;
> Or bearing full its staff upon
> The well-known impress 'Lebanon'.
> A handle slender, smooth and light,
> Of bass-wood, or of cedar white;
> Where softest palm from point to heel
> Might ne'er a grain of roughness feel –
> So trim a fix, the stalks confine;
> So tightly drawn the hempen line;
> Then fan-like spread the divided wove,
> As fingers in a lady's glove –
> To crown the whole, (and save beside),
> The loop, the buckskin loop is tied.[22]

The rhetorical imperative 'Give me a broom . . .', combined with the lively nursery-rhyme and -rhythm patterning, suggest a cheerful and conversational tone; the poet is self-consciously lighthearted here in her attitude towards the subject of her role in life. This sensual and minutely detailed description connotes the speaker's intimate acquaintance with the apparatus of her domestic employment. It suggests her capacity for a species of epicurean pleasure in the functional simplicity of the object. Mention is made of exotic locations, a recurring theme in James's oeuvre to which I will return. In this poem, allusions to 'Niscayuna' and 'Lebanon' seem incongruously fanciful in relation to the humble broom. These references add a wistful note to the apparently enthusiastic celebration of domestic service, as if the speaker's imagination roams far from the present moment in an effort to relish the pleasing qualities of the broom. There is a poignant contrast between the far-flung and exotic countries the speaker mentions, with which she is clearly fascinated, and the circumscribed context in which she is constrained. The comparison constituted here between the broom's 'fan-like' spread and the 'fingers in a lady's glove' also suggests that Maria James is yearning to associate herself, in a similarly whimsical ironic fashion, with a class position more privileged than her own. As a servant her opportunity to wear gloves would have been limited. Much as she extols its inherent pleasures, the broom thus symbolizes the speaker's confinement rather than her unequivocal delight. In the second section the speaker relates the satisfaction to be found in humble obscurity, untroubled by events in the wider world:

> With this in hand, small need to care
> If C . . . y or J . . . n fill their chair –
> What in the banks is said or done –
> The game at Texas lost or won –
> How city belles collect their rings,
> And hie to Saratoga Springs; –
> To Erie's or Ontario's shore,
> To hear Niagara's thunders roar –
> While undisturb'd my course I keep,
> Cheer'd by the sound of sweep, sweep, sweep.[23]

Ostensibly these lines espouse the advantages of a quiet life; but once again the speaker lingers over the names of far-off places. The listing of place-names begins carelessly enough, with reference to 'the game at Texas'. Women's supposed lack of interest in sporting events is an enduring cultural commonplace; at this point the reader can believe in the speaker's lack of concern with worldly matters. As the litany of places builds, however, the tone shifts to one of mounting emotion. The speaker's imagination is captivated by the idea of the freedom enjoyed by 'city belles'; the catalogue of possible destinations becomes overlong, syntactically and semantically, as the speaker dwells on the extent of physical possibility enjoyed by others. When the speaker imagines 'Niagara's thunders roar', it is impossible to accept her claims happily to reject the opportunity of hearing it at first hand. The final couplet of the section evokes the repetitive sound and motion of the broom as the speaker sublimates her agitation in the regular 'sweep, sweep, sweep'.

Later in the piece the speaker locates the importance of the broom to her material survival:

> Nor is this all; in very deed
> The broom may prove a friend in need;
> On this I lean, – on this depend;
> With such a surety, such a friend,
> There's not a merchant in the place

> Who would refuse me silk or lace;
> Or linen fine, or broad–cloth dear,
> Or e'en a shawl of fam'd Cashmere,
> Though prudence whispering, still would say,
> 'Remember, there's a rainy day.'[24]

This is a subtle depiction of the frustrations of life as a servant. The speaker indicates the potential for income in her ability to wield a broom; at the same time, however, she hints at the dire implications for her represented by a loss of that capacity. The detailed description of possible purchases appears at first to be a frivolous celebration of conspicuous consumption. This sense, however, is undercut at the end of the section when the speaker is reminded by 'prudence' of the imperative to provide for a 'rainy day'. The speaker cannot enjoy the fantasy of luxury becaue she is too painfully aware of the threat contained in a future where she is unable to work. If the broom has saved her from poverty in the present, what will become of her when she is unable to wield it with vigour?

'The Broom' is evidence of attempts by James to make the best of her lot, but in these efforts, I suggest, it is possible to discern evidence of her protesting too much an acceptance of her fate. Despite its apparently cheerful approach to class structures, this poem indicates much of the same sense of frustration and anxiety as that expressed in the more obviously gloomy pieces.

In his book, *Passage to America*, Terry Coleman remarks upon the perception of America in the popular imagination of the British public during the first half of the nineteenth century:

> Since independence, the United States had welcomed emigrants . . . the policy . . . towards immigrants was stated in 1817 by John Quincy Adams, when he was Secretary of State . . . He said America invited none to come, but would not keep out those who had the courage to cross the Atlantic. They would suffer no disabilities as aliens but could expect no advantages. Both immigrants and Americans would have the same opportunities, and their success would depend on their activity and good fortune.[25]

Coleman cites an enthusiastic contemporary source who declares that 'The heavens of America appear infinitely higher – the sky is bluer – the clouds are whiter – the air is fresher – the cold is intenser – the moon looks larger – the stars are brighter'.[26] In his 1960 study, *American Immigration*, Maldwyn Allen Jones speculates on the causes of mass immigration to America from the beginning of the nineteenth century; whilst acknowledging 'the push and pull of impersonal economic forces',[27] Jones asserts that 'no less important were the hopes, fears, and dreams of millions of individual immigrants'.[28] In her biographical introduction to her volume, James describes her feelings when making the journey to America: 'my imagination was revelling among the fruits and flowers which I expected to find in the land to which we were bound'.[29]

Maria James and her family were part of the impulse to 'cross the Atlantic'; whether compelled by economic expediency or by dreams fuelled by popular mythology of American promise, it can be assumed that, like five million or so fellow immigrants, the James family undertook their journey in a spirit of optimism. I would suggest that the textual evidence of such poems as 'Motto' and 'Napoleon's Tomb' indicates tensions between the idealized fantasy and the lived experience. As a woman and a writer, James evidently discovered that, although she was prepared to contribute ample hard work, the extent of the required good fortune fell short of being sufficient to fulfil her own early vision of American promise: the New World was not, after all, for her, a land teeming with 'fruits and flowers' ripe for the plucking. All she received were the 'gleanings' from richer tables.

★ ★ ★

Linked to and often overlapping her preoccupation with disappointed ambition on the basis of class is the way in which James handles the issue of gender. In nineteenth-century America, as in Britain, the act of writing for public consumption was, for a woman, fraught with problems at both practical and conceptual levels. For the middle-class American woman, like her British counterpart, the urge to write and be read, whether from the need for self-expression or for economic reward, could be tempered with shame born of transgressing dominant codes of feminine decorum; many stories and verses by American women of the period reflect these tensions.[30] For the working-class woman who would write, the physical and cultural pressures against her achieving expression were intensified, as evidenced by the material by James already discussed. Much of what women were writing in the period, on both sides of the Atlantic, is concerned with what Angela Leighton has termed the 'ethic of home';[31] at a time when popular consciousness conceived of the domestic in idealized and heavily gendered terms, women writers were understandably interested in exploring the complexities indicated by their own lived experience of home. For a poet such as James, whose status in terms of both gender and class was defined by the parameters of the domestic space, the issues inevitably became blurred.

Interestingly, Maria James's attitudes towards class hierarchy, although viewed from different social, geographic, chronological and linguistic perspectives, can be seen to link closely with those of her predecessor and fellow native Welshwoman, Jane Cave. Like Cave, James is highly critical of the rigid class system which fails adequately to value or reward either virtue or talent in those unfortunate enough to have been born poor. Clearly her point of view on inequalities of class is more intensely subjective than that of Cave. James has suffered from the material effects of the system to a far greater degree than Cave's more academic moral criticism implies. Nevertheless, the congruence between the respective approaches to class issues of Cave and James is notable, particularly when viewed in the light of the very different attitudes of the other poets already discussed. Ann Julia Hatton is clearly an eccentric case in terms of class status, but Felicia Hemans is a useful point of comparison. From her very middle-class viewpoint, the preservation of the status quo is vital. Despite some apparent reservations about the conduct of individual monarchs, Hemans in her poems is concerned to promote the stability which ensures the interests of her own bourgeois class grouping. It is significant that Cave should share a more radical political vision with her working-class compatriot than with her middle-ranking peer. The connection between Cave and James, I would argue, stems in part from the fact that they share the same religious roots – Welsh Calvinistic Methodism. As Ieuan Gwynedd Jones observes in his book, *Mid-Victorian Wales: The Observers and the Observed*, during the early part of the nineteenth century 'a Welsh Nonconformist radical view of society was formed, expressed and [eventually] absorbed into the consciousness of the industrial working class'.[32]

In the United States Methodism was not so strongly associated with the working class; it appears to have been the religion of a range of class groups (certainly the Garretsons, who employed James, shared her Methodist faith). Nevertheless, Cave's radical tendencies may certainly be accounted for by reference to her Welsh Nonconformist upbringing. The pattern which begins to emerge through an exploration of these women poets suggests that religion may have been for the Welsh a stronger marker of cultural difference than either class or linguistic identity. In terms of gender, the orthodoxies of Nonconformity recognized a woman's spiritual equality with men, even though they often reinforced her subordination to male authority.[33]

Biographical claims made in the introductory passages by James herself and by her patrons, suggest that her relationships with other women were central to the poet's experience as woman and writer. James acknowledges the influence of her own mother in somewhat formal tones: 'My mother was an upright, conscientious Christian: – how often have I heard her voice in prayer for the souls of her children, so fervent, so sincere.'[34] This seems a less than warm recommendation. Additionally, however, the mistress of the house which employed James, Mrs Garretson, her daughter Mary and Mrs Potter, the house guest whose interest in James's work precipitated *Wales and Other Poems*, all appear to have been important in various ways, none of which are sentimentalized by the poet herself.[35] Her declared literary foremothers all emerge out of the conservative mainstream of early nineteenth-century gender ideology in Britain and America; James refers in her biographical note to having read Hannah More's *Cheap Repository Tracts* as a young woman;[36] she also dedicates an elegy occasioned by More's death which is included in *Wales and Other Poems*; in it she laments the passing of this 'friend of my youth', noting, in somewhat monotonous detail, the large number of More's works with which James has been familiar.[37] Interestingly, however, her epitaph to More's memory attaches utilitarian rather than aesthetic value to her heroine's literary production:

> Her valued life has pass'd away,
> Like one long, useful, summer's day . . .[38]

The piece reads as if the technical demands of the rhyming couplet may have represented the central concerns in the formation of these sentiments. In her reference to other female writers, however, James seems equally restrained in her praise. In her poem 'The Album', for example, she dismisses the work of Hemans and Sigourney as less inspirational than nature itself, symbolized here by the clover flower.[39]

Despite her obvious interest in ideas about her own creativity, and despite the derivative nature of much of her verse, James appears, then, to have been unprepared fully to acknowledge her debt to the work of other, more successful, women writers. What, then, of her personal relationships with women? Perhaps her friendships, rather than her literary antecedents, empowered her as a writer and a woman. Three poems in the volume are addressed to young women who seem to have been known to James. 'To Winnifred', 'To Harriet' and 'To Constance' are positioned consecutively in *Wales and Other Poems*, to form a short series of pieces with a number of thematic and tonal features in common. All three poems signal a greater degree of emotional investment than is demonstrated in the poet's introductory references to the women in her

life, or in her poem 'To Mrs Hannah More'. In 'To Winnifred' the
address is intimate and affectionate:

> May every good thy steps attend,
> My child, my sister, and my friend; –
> Here on the earth may'st thou be bless'd,
> And lastly find eternal rest.[40]

Already, in the first stanza, good wishes for the young subject do not
preclude reference to her death. True to her own form, the poet goes on
to warn Winnifred of the dangers inherent in youthful optimism, and, in
apparently unwitting self-contradiction, persists with her doom-laden
prophecy:

> Would my experience nought avail,
> But just to tell that hope may fail,
> I would not cloud thy youthful mind,
> But choose to leave thee deaf and blind.[41]

Winnifred may have wished that her poetic friend had remained faithful
to her rhetorical promise, and refrained from uttering such depressing
benediction. Leaving aside the tautological mechanics of the stanza,
however, James's familiar preoccupation with thwarted hope is central to
this item of motherly, sisterly and friendly advice.

In 'To Harriet' the poet's mood is more celebratory, if rather plaintive
in its evocation of feminine youth: she seems to recall her own girlhood as
she declares:

> I love the sweet geranium's smell,
> Its scollop'd leaves and crimson flower;
> Of days long past it seems to tell,
> And memory owns its magic power.
> But lovelier, sweeter far the maid
> Whose breast with feeling glows, and truth,
> Whose hopes on heaven are early stay'd,
> To guide and guard her wayward youth.[42]

By the time James arrives at dispensing counsel 'To Constance', however,
poignancy is replaced once more with prognostication on corruption and
decay:

> There's blight on earthly joys, my love;
> There's blight on earthly joys . . .
>
> The fairest flowers will soonest fade, −
> will soonest fade and die . . .[43]

If James is unable to rejoice wholeheartedly in the beauty of girlish potential in 'To Harriet', her position in 'To Constance' rejects any pretence towards the celebration of womanhood. The flower motif, used in 'To Harriet' to evoke the sensual promise of the young woman, is transmuted here into images of contamination and atrophied life force. This series of poems offers no hope on earth for the young woman, whose potentiality, however vibrant, is fated only to perish and die. The promise of eternal life, the pieces imply, remains unconvincing when compared with the visions of death and disappointment with which they are juxtaposed:

> There's a change on all below, my love, −
> There's a change on all below;
> Time speeds us on toward the tomb, −
> Speeds on through weal and wo [sic].[44]

An examination of James's poetry in terms of gender issues seems to me to offer evidence of a woman writer's experience of domesticity which is more intensely problematic than that of many of her contemporaries. Her position as domestic servant saw James's confined to a home over which she could exercise less control or influence than the 'Angel in the House' of any class, who was at least mistress of her own household. She was compelled to experience the world as woman and artist through the well-meaning mediation of her masters and mistresses.[45] The verse James wrote, I would argue, resonates with the difficulties of such a position. Ideas about artistic and physical freedom, about creativity and frustration, and about hope and thwarted ambition are dramatized through a range of rhetorical strategies. But whether framed in a meditation on the song of a bird, or in a lecture to a young friend, discussion by James of women's status is always demoralized and embittered; it is also inextricable from notions of servitude and domesticity created by the poet's experience of social class.

★ ★ ★

The question of the poet's sense of national identity remains to be addressed. In the introduction to her recent volume, *Nineteenth-century*

American Women Writers: An Anthology, Karen L. Kilcup remarks upon the way in which 'Cultural crossings, which mesh with constructions of identity based on class, ethnicity, ability, age, and other features, form an important strand in the fabric of nineteenth-century American women's writing'.[46] The notion of 'cultural crossings' in this context seems to me to be a useful perspective from which to explore James's verse in terms of her national identity. For, as a child emigrant, James spent most of her life, and all of her writing career, at great distance from Wales; her work might easily qualify for inclusion in a collection such as Kilcup's. Only the title poem in *Wales and Other Poems* relates specifically to the country of her birth; in addition to an examination of 'Wales', I propose, therefore, to adopt Kilcup's concept of cultural crossing in order to analyse the extent to which the sense James had of herself as a Welsh woman intersects with her experience in an immigrant community and later as servant to a second- or third-generation American household.

It is impossible to determine the reasons for the choice of 'Wales' as the title piece in the volume. Its position as title and opening verse, however, lends some importance to both poem and subject matter. Regardless of whether 'Wales' was selected by the editor solely in order to capitalize on the local audience of Welsh emigrants, or whether the title reflects a preference on the part of the poet herself, the prominence of 'Wales' in a collection published for the American market, clearly identifies James's work with her native community.[47] By announcing its marginality in this way, the title of the volume already suggests some form of cultural zigzagging.

'Wales' itself presents a useful index of the approach James has to her own national identity, for in the poem she refers to her homeland in relation to the themes of landscape, religion, creativity and language, all of which represent points of cultural intersection with her American experience, arising in others of her works in the collection.

In her introductory passages James refers to 'Wales' as having been written from memories to which she ascribes the force of absolute veracity: ' "Wales' is a kind of retrospect of the days of childhood; if it has any merit, it must be owing to one particular, namely, that it is the truth from end to end.'[48] Given that she left Wales before the end of '[her] eleventh year', the claims James makes for her own powers of recollection and description seem somewhat optimistic; what is clear, though, through her assertion of 'truth', is the strength of her feeling for her Welsh roots. She depicts Wales in the poem as a land of mystery; its geographic distance from her readership and herself is used in order to establish its enigmatic difference. The poem opens:

> Beyond the dark blue sea,
> Beyond the path of storms,
> Where wave with wave, in converse loud,
> Uprear their forms, –
>
> Westward, on Britain's isle,
> The rocky cliffs are seen,
> With cities fair, and ruin'd towers,
> And meadows green.[49]

The poet's reminiscence of Wales admits nothing of the hardships which compelled her family to seek its fortune, and risk its safety in the journey across the Atlantic. This, then, is the idealized 'truth' of childhood memory. In her imagination Wales appears as a magical Utopian country, and as such it functions as the symbolic repository of her youthful optimism and creative exuberance. The Welsh landscape James describes is a strange synthesis of the fairytale spires which the opening stanzas connote, of sweet rural meadows and of an organic form of countryside development:

> But cities fair, or towers,
> Are not so dear to me
> As one lone cot that stood beside
> A spreading tree.
>
> Yet well I mind the fields
> Where best I lov'd to roam,
> Or meet my father when at night
> Returning home.
>
> And well I mind the path
> That led towards the spring,
> And how I listened when the birds
> Were carolling.
>
> And well I mind the flowers,
> In gay profusion spread
> O'er hill and dale, and how I deck'd
> My garden bed.[50]

In this rendering of home, there is no hint of the bitter regret which so often characterizes James's constructions of the domestic space. Here, the sense is of growth and positive activity: nature luxuriates in the form of a 'spreading tree', and spreads her riches in 'gay profusion' in Wales; the child in Wales 'roams' at liberty, and lives at 'home' in the security of a primal bond with nature and her immediate family. When, in stanza nine, the mountains appear it is in personified form and with the same sense of benign movement:

> There Snowdon lifts his head
> To greet the rising day,
> Whose latest glories linger round
> The summits gray.[51]

This is not the sublime majesty of Wordsworth's Snowdon, which implies awesome threat with its extreme beauty;[52] it is a kindly, domesticated mountain which conspires with meadow and garden to form a nurturing place of safety for the childhood memories of the young poet; and it is this mountain which the poet constructs as the site of Welsh artistic power:

> There sleep her sons of fame;
> There rest her bards of yore:
> And shall the Cambrian lyre
> Awake no more?[53]

The poet is clearly drawing upon the vogue for ancient Celtic culture and her depiction of Wales's sleeping poetic giants is a well-worn trope of early nineteenth-century verse;[54] but equally, I suggest, the emigrant is locating her homeland as the source of her own artistic imagination. More interesting still is the way in which she goes on to link mother-tongue with poetry:

> *Cymry*, thou wert of old
> A land renown'd for song;
> But where is now thy soul of fire, –
> Thy melting tongue?[55]

In her biographical note, James describes her first experience of the English language:

Towards the end of my seventh year, I found myself on shipboard, surrounded by men, women, and children, whose faces were unknown to me . . . I also had an opportunity to learn a little English during the voyage, as 'take care', and 'get out of the way', seemed reiterated from land's-end to land's-end.[56]

Her acquisition of English clearly occurred during a period of physical isolation, on a ship at sea, and of psychological alienation from most of the people around her; the first words James learned were harsh imperatives of caution and admonition. The contrast is stark between this and her memory of the 'melting' Welsh tongue. In the poet's imagination Welsh is a language made for poetry; in her memory English is rooted in danger, obedience and the control of self by others. The inadequacy of language fully to express emotion is a recurrent theme in James's poetry, and I want to explore the possibility that this concern is linked with the tensions between her contrasting experiences of Welsh and English linguistic culture. A large body of post-colonial theory has concerned itself, in recent decades, with the problem of language as the 'fundamental site of struggle'.[57] Some scholars have posited the potential of English as a tool for the task of subverting the imperialist project. Chinua Achebe, for example, is confident of expressing himself as an African in English: 'I feel that the English language will be able to carry the weight of my African experience. But it will have to be a new English, still in full communion with its ancestral home but altered to suit new African surroundings.'[58] Conversely, however, theorists such as Ngugi Wa Thiong'o have noted 'the fatalistic logic of the unassailable position of English in our [African] literature'.[59] Ngugi describes the richly suggestive nature of his native language, and its eminent suitability, in his view, for the production of literature; he argues that the enforced dominance of the imperial language through education and indoctrination has resulted in destructive disharmony, for the colonized subject, between culture, communication and community. Maria James was compelled to come to terms with the language of the colonizer – not on native soil, with native topography and community available as terms of reference – but during a dislocated, transitional period where all familiar cultural markers were absent. I would suggest that her perspective on her native tongue as the language of poetry in 'Wales' dramatizes the tension between these opposing schools of post-colonial thought. In 'Wales' James has attempted to express her Welsh experience in an English which is tempered with Welsh vocabulary and illustrated with motifs from ancient Welsh culture. The product of this 'altered' English, however, is literature which speaks of its own inadequacy, and of the poet's regret at circumstances which have meant the passing of that 'melting tongue' as a vehicle for the poetry of her homeland and herself.

In her introductory letter, Mary Garretson refers to the importance of religious experience in the life of the young Maria James, noting, in particular, the piety of James's mother:

> Her mother was an excellent woman, and had just moved to the slate quarries, in Clinton, about 7 miles off. I remember her constantly at the church; the whole distance to which she walked. She was at that time the only professing Christian in the little settlement; the rest she used to assemble at her house, to read for them, and pray with them in her own language.[60]

The centrality of religion in James's world-view is clear on even a cursory perusal of her work. A glance at any one of the poems in *Wales and Other Poems* reveals the poet's ritual reliance upon Christian doctrines of suffering and redemption. In 'Wales' the poet links the issue of religion explicitly to that of the Welsh language and Wales itself:

> 'Twas in that tongue that first
> I heard the Book Divine,
> The guide through life's bewildering maze, –
> A light to shine.
>
> . . .
>
> I heard Jehovah's praise
> In *Cymry's* native tongue,
> And hung upon those artless strains, –
> In rapture hung.[61]

If Christian religion forms the focus of the poet's experience as a woman and a writer, this identification of Wales and the Welsh language as a source of faith, as well as of poetry, adds weight to the proposition that, for this writer, English is ultimately an ineffectual vehicle for the expression of self for which she strives. In stanza fifteen the poet attempts to describe the fusion between language and religious experience which her early Welsh recollections conjure:

> 'Twas like the gushing streams
> In dry and thirsty land,
> Or soul-dissolving melody
> Of some full band.[62]

In endeavouring to express the force of her emotional response to the memories, the poet resorts to cliché; in her haste to conform to regular versification patterns, the rhyme is forced. Despite the technical gaucherie, however, I would argue that visible in the imagery of the stanza are traces of the poet's struggle to articulate her sense of self in a language which, for her, is inimical to the task. The simile of drought and water refers to the poet's awakening to Christianity through hearing the Bible read in Welsh. In the poet's imagination there is thus a fundamental connectedness between the faith which shapes and sustains her conscious processes and the language of her homeland; both, I would suggest, are part of the same lifegiving, energizing system of psychological self-support upon which she relies for survival in a world which has disappointed her. Mention of 'soul-dissolving melody' in this stanza establishes a clear semantic link between the 'melting tongue' of Wales, artistic creativity, and the spiritual rapture of religious faith and practice. In the poem 'Despondency', James deploys the same blended image of Welshness, spirituality and music; at her lowest ebb, the poet's mood of depression is tempered by her awareness of God's beneficence, as she imagines psychic communication from the country of her physical and spiritual birth:

> When sudden o'er those waters
> The sound of music stole, –
> Low whisper'd, from a 'still small voice,'
> That reach'd the inmost soul . . .[63]

The imagery suggests a diffuse, heterogeneous experience – both linguistic and spiritual; the match between language and religion, when applied to the Welsh model in these poems, is perfect and complete. The contrast could not be stronger between this vision of absolute harmony of experience and expression and the poet's earliest memories of the English language, abrupt, harsh and rigid. Ngugi argues that:

> Language as communication and as culture are . . . products of each other. Communication creates culture: culture is a means of communication. Language carries culture, and culture carries, particularly through orature and literature, the entire body of values by which we come to perceive ourselves in the world.[64]

Ngugi's thesis presupposes the colonized subject's position within her native community, and with a degree of access to literature, oratory and readership in her native tongue. I am suggesting that James's poem 'Wales' demonstrates the difficulties experienced by a writer dislocated from her native culture, community and language; unhappy in her perception of the world from the alienated position in which she finds herself, ungainly in her attempts to communicate its essence in the language of the colonizer.

James closes 'Wales' with a heartfelt declaration of her own Welshness:

> Land of my fathers! ne'er
> Shall I forget thy name, –
> Oh ne'er while in this bosom glows
> Life's transient flame![65]

The poet's sense of loyalty to the country of her birth is clearly earnest and deep-rooted. I have already referred, however, to the proportion of her life spent in America. It is important to consider the ways in which this allegiance converges or intersects with how James understands herself as an American citizen. For this purpose I intend to adopt Kilcup's concept of 'cultural crossings'.

The first piece by James to draw the attention of her editor, the Reverend Potter, was 'An Ode, written for the 4th of July, 1833'. This is a triumphant celebration of American unity which promises to complicate the notion of James as a self-declared Welsh poet:

> I see that banner proudly wave, –
> Yes, proudly waving yet,
> Not a stripe is torn from the broad array, –
> Not a single star is set;
> And the eagle, with unruffled plume,
> Is soaring aloft in the welkin dome.[66]

Throughout the poem, however, the poet remains apart from the spectacle she describes. Whilst she praises the general 'peace and plenty' around her, and acknowledges the 'joy' of the festival, the poet never implicates herself in the collective prosperity or in the carnival of the day. The first-person speaker appears only once, in the opening line of the piece; thereafter the scene is described by a distanced, formal voice which appears to have no personal investment in that which it depicts. Interestingly, the poet also remarks upon the inadequacy of language to express the emotion she observes:

> How feeble is language, – how cold is the lay, –
> Compar'd to the joy of this festival day . . . [67]

English is failing her in the attempt to render the passion of others, just as it fails her in expressing her own. The poem, then, presents evidence that by 1833, twenty years or so after her arrival in America, James was prepared to bear witness to her observation of the American ethos of freedom and stability. It contains little to suggest, however, that she felt any sense of belonging within that language or community.

In 'A Town in Dutchess County', written the following year, James takes a more playful approach to the idea of home in America. The poem is constructed as a riddle in verse, and demonstrates, better than most of her work, the wit which her patrons claim on her behalf. In this piece the poet acknowledges the benefits of life in America, and by implication the problems of surviving elsewhere:

> My whole, is a spot on the face of creation,
> Where industry banishes want from the door;
> Where the axe, and the plough, and the mill-wheel in motion,
> Bring fulness of bread to the poorest of poor.[68]

In this place, the poet observes, hard work results in freedom from physical hunger; connoting, thus, that she knows of a place where no amount of exertion will guarantee 'fulness of bread'. Here, then, is an encoded recognition, missing from the eulogistic 'Wales', of the material hardships which caused the poet's uprooting from the emotional nurture of her homeland. Tellingly, however, she refers only to freedom from physical hunger, and only to manual occupations; there is no mention of the availability of emotional or psychological elevation, nor of the possibility for success through intellectual pursuits. In these areas, home in America offers little potential.

★ ★ ★

My readings of poetry by Maria James presents interesting material with which to supplement available accounts of nineteenth-century women's experience. Her status as domestic servant invests work by James, I would argue, with opportunities to make existing perspectives on gender and class identities more complex. Her position as an emigrant who has undergone economic and linguistic colonization away from her native soil opens her writing to interpretations which problematize current post-colonial thought. I have argued that a consideration of poetry by James, in particular 'Wales', problematizes the position of those post-colonial theorists, such as Chinua Achebe, who argue for the viability of post-colonial writers' adopting the colonizer's tongue. The work of Ngugi Wa Thiong'o, by contrast, rejects the possibility of authentic expression of post-colonial culture through the medium of the colonizing language.

What I read in these poems tends to endorse Ngugi's position: I have proposed that the poetry indicates an unease on the part of the poet with the English language as a satisfactory vehicle for her self-expression; this is visible in her self-conscious exploration of the issue of language, and in the textual fabric of the verse. I would suggest, however, that James's work adds a further dimension to Ngugi's interpretation of post-colonial experience. In the case of Welsh immigrants, unlike that of indigenous colonized peoples, there is often no existing community which they can address in the mother tongue. Such linguistic dislocation may well render more deeply profound the sense of alienation from the colonizer's language which Ngugi notes in describing his own creative process.

Maria James was exiled linguistically twice over, from Wales at the age of seven, and then from her family when she was ten years old; her move to the Garretsons' home was the first time the poet was completely immersed in the English language. The sudden and lasting separation from her Welsh-speaking home at this young age, I would argue, was a traumatic and formative experience in her emotional and poetic development. Given that the transition also coincided with the beginning of her life as a maid, it also entailed for James her loss of freedom and independence as well as of childhood and Welsh. It seems to me that the poems dramatize a close connection between the poet's experiences of alienation, confinement and loss of cultural identity. I would further argue that the work demonstrates the loss of linguistic and national identity to be at least as formative in Maria James's particular subject position as are her class or gender roles. This is remarkable in view of her acutely problematic experience of gender identity. My readings suggest that, even given a sense of the domestic space as disempowering prison, such as that of the maidservant Maria James, national identity, or rather the loss of it, can be more crucial in the formation of poetic voice than other social factors already well rehearsed by feminist historians.

5

Death and identity in the poetry of Sarah Williams

Details of the life of Sarah Williams are scant. Prefacing the volume *Twilight Hours: A Legacy of Verse*, a collection of poems by Williams which was published posthumously in 1868, is a 'Memoir' written by E. H. Plumptre, the poet's former headmaster in a London school for girls. The 'Memoir' contains a number of revealing insights into the character of the poet, but very few solid facts about the dates, places and people in her life. It is clear from Plumptre's account that Williams died after a long illness in the spring of 1863, 'in her thirtieth year'.[1] Welsh on her father's side, Williams is known to have regularly visited Wales. From the evidence of a number of poems on Welsh themes it is clear that the poet retained some emotional connection with the country of her father's birth, but lived and died in London.

In a letter to her publisher, Williams discusses the scope of her own literary field, and offers an intriguing insight into her poetic philosophy:

> It is one of my few deep convictions that the supernatural is natural, that in the moral world, as in the physical, lightnings, volcanoes, avalanches, are as truly natural as fish-ponds and croquet grounds. Nature includes all. Art should include all, only let each artist take the department that suits him. The *supernatural* needs a man's strength and depth; the *exceptionally natural* is the ground I mean to take and work, God helping me.[2]

Interestingly, then, the sense Williams has of her poetic identity is explicitly gendered. Elaine Showalter, in her 1993 volume *Daughters of Decadence: Women Writers of the Fin-de-Siècle*, discusses the position of the woman writer in relation to the aesthetic tradition: 'The decadent artist was invariably male, and decadence . . . defined itself against the feminine.[3] Williams implicitly acknowledges this bias; she is, however, no New Woman writer, intent on purging 'aestheticism and decadence of their misogyny' and rewriting 'the myths of art that denigrated women'.[4] Instead of contesting the jurisdiction of men over the emotional excesses of what she terms the moral 'supernatural', Williams claims for herself an adjacent territory defined as the 'exceptionally natural'. The term implies a species of creativity which arises out of an intense connection with the minutiae of women's lived experience; this is achieved whilst suggesting in the word 'exceptional' a certain significance, even distinction, in the specificity of women's writing.

For Williams, this definition of the 'exceptionally natural' is in practice rather elastic. Her oeuvre extends across a variety of poetic forms, encompassing folk ballad, children's doggerel, Gothic melodrama, historical re-enactment, religious, reflection – both philosophical and satirical – and meditations on nature. In common with many mid-Victorian poets, the work includes considerable technical variation; however, the execution of diversity is not always accomplished with aplomb.

E. H. Plumptre is ambivalent in his pronouncements on the qualitative value of Williams's work: 'Less than most poetry by young writers did it present the echoes of the greater poets of our time. It had neither the excellences nor the defects of imitative verse . . . its being the utterance of one who sang "as the birds do".'[5] The relative significance of the capacity to sing 'as the birds do' is not elaborated upon by the poet's erstwhile pedagogue. The unknown author of the obituary of Williams in the periodical *Good Words* is even more patronizing in his/her faint praises:

> Death puts a subtle finishing touch on the poet's work . . . What seemed weakest and faultiest before often leaps into radiant meaning under the new lights thrown on it by the knowledge of sorrows bravely borne, sufferings as bravely hidden, and the revelation of secrets which make life sacred in the keeping of theirs; and death sacred in the knowledge of them.[6]

Williams herself is realistic in assessing her own talent; having set out to her publisher her poetic intentions as discussed above, she is pessimistic in gauging her capacity for artistic realization: 'Now you have my confession of faith artistic. Only you and I know the chasm between the endeavour and the result. It would be ludicrous, if it were not pathetic to compare purpose and production.'[7] This self-assessment by Williams is brutally honest, and I do not propose to attempt an elevation of her work to canonical status. It is clear, however, that Williams is an engaging figure whose ideas, opinions and attitudes hint at potentially interesting rewards which may be gained from more thorough reading of her poetry and correspondence.

The circumstances of the poet's death are related in terms of glowing esteem by both Plumptre and the anonymous obituary writer of *Good Words*, to which Williams had been a regular contributor. Williams died as a result of the surgical procedure which had been 'her one chance of life'.[8] Plumptre describes the painful decision with which the poet was finally confronted:

> she had to make the choice, so often forced upon sufferers, between the certainty of long lingering agony and the possibility of deliverance from it, accompanied by the risk of a more immediate close. Acting on the counsel of friends and medical advisers, she embraced the latter alternative, with apparently a foreboding clear to herself, though not disclosed to others, of what the end would be. And so that end came; and she slept and was at rest.[9]

The extent of her suffering and of what must have been considerable personal courage on her part, is evidenced by the decision taken by Williams to undergo surgery at a time when post-operative mortality rates were high, and the practices of surgery and anaesthesiology were at best experimental.[10] A fellow woman poet and contemporary of Williams, the working-class writer Eliza Cook, expresses the general sense of dread experienced by the Victorian public at the prospect of surgery:

> There are hearts – stout hearts – that own no fear
> At the whirling sword or the darting spear, –
> That are ready alike to bleed in the dust,
> 'Neath the sabre's cut or the bayonet's thrust;
> They heed not the blows that Fate may deal,
> From the murderer's dirk or the soldier's steel:
> But lips that laugh at the dagger of strife
> Turn silent and white from the surgeon's knife.[11]

Cook continues, over four gory stanzas, concluding succinctly with an image of the terrifying species of decision faced by the Victorian sufferer: 'And a dread of the grave and a hope of life / That rest on the work of the surgeon's knife'.[12]

The experience of unremitting pain and the anticipation of death which caused the poet to choose the fearsome 'surgeon's knife' is evident throughout Williams's oeuvre in an inevitable preoccupation with mortality. A high proportion of the poems included in *Twilight Hours* demonstrate a concern with death and dying; an equally large number meditate upon humanity's fitness for heaven and the tribulations of its preparatory journey through life's vale of tears. In her works Williams evidences a strong Christian faith, but one which does not preclude expression of anger and bitterness at life's suffering, or a questioning of the deity's purpose. In her short piece 'Faint Heart', for example, the self-absorbed speaker questions the value of her life of pain:

> Why was I born, ye angels? was it well?
> Ye might have killed me, such a little thing!
> And I have been in Heaven all this while,
> And missed mine heritage of suffering.
> Would it have been a loss? I cannot tell:
> God knows.[13]

The rhetorical structure of the stanza, through a series of melodramatic demands and declarations, lends it an almost suicidal urgency. The rhythm of the piece is irregular; lines one and five begin with a trochee, lines two, three and four with an iambus; if line six is read with the stress on the second syllable, the bald response 'God knows' may be construed as the speaker's sudden resignation through religious faith. If the stress falls on the word 'God', however, it is possible to read this line as a modulation in tone from self-pity to anger at a divinity whose design remains cruelly unfathomable. The poem continues in the same ambiguous tenor, as the speaker broods on the pointlessness of resistance:

> Why cry and moan? what matters anything?
> Why vex the quiet air with vain complaints?
> The army of immortals marches on,
> And must not tarry, though one, footsore, faints:
> Would it be better if another stayed?
> God knows.[14]

This may be interpreted as a fairly conventional representation of the Christian doctrine of spiritual surrender to the all-knowing and merciful father in Heaven. Alternatively, a case can be made for reading the interrogatory and rhetorical form replicated here as amplifying the speaker's bitter frustration at the futility of her own anger. The reprised 'God knows' may be read as veneration at the mystery of godhead or, equally, as an expression of doubt and confusion over the divine purpose.

Plumptre refers to the spiritual development of Williams as influenced by '"pious stragglers from the Church", but not imbued in any degree with the antagonism of Nonconformity, nor even with its characteristic theology'.[15] Plumptre seems acutely concerned to exonerate his former pupil from the rebellious taint implied by what were presumably her father's religious allegiances. There is evidence in the poet's writings, however, that her approaches towards Christianity favoured dissenting rather than established Church practice. One short poem included in *Twilight Hours*, 'The Roundhead's Chaunt', eulogizes the faith of the Puritan warrior:

> Though the way may be long,
> Though the wicked may be strong,
> God is stronger and eternity longer.
> Though great Cromwell be dead,
> And with him our mighty head,
> Wise and tender is the Lord, our one Defender.[16]

The piece continues through three equally awkward stanzas. The technical demands of military chant and readable verse are clearly irreconcilable for Williams here; the tone of her panegyric, however, is without irony. The poem endorses wholeheartedly the spiritual and political ethos of Cromwell's mission, and subverts Plumptre's attempts to homogenize its author's secessionist spiritual disposition. However, despite this spirited defence of the Puritan ethos, much work by Williams indicates a degree of cynicism towards organized religion of all varieties. In her humorous piece 'Yeoman Service', for example, the poet dramatizes the deathbed thoughts of a lapsed Nonconformist family man, anxious to reconcile himself with the Almighty in advance of the impending moment of reckoning:

> When the minister came from Bethesda after my soul,
> He declared I was Pagan in strength, it grieved him to say.
> 'Are the Christians all weak then?' I asked: 'if so none for me';
> Let the women be meek, but the men must stand till they die.
> Holy Father, forgive me! I am but sore angered with these;
> I am Thine, as Thou knowest, Thine alone, never bended my knees
> To the Pope, nor the Saints, nor the Virgin; nor cowered to please
> The young parson in yellow, whose moans fit the Chapel of Ease.[17]

The speaker goes on to detail and demonstrate the extent of his sins and hypocrisies:

I am great against liars myself; yet I lied to the squire
When I met him, along with the rest at his coming of age,
And hurra'd for 'Our noble young master' – he, mean as a hound!

And again, when the parson I spoke of came here t'other day,
Out of church he is gentle, and pure as a woman, and poor,
And the poverty is such a kinship, becomes him so well,
That I called him 'Your Reverence' humbly: I doubt it was wrong.

There's another sin, too, on my conscience when we were first wed,
I was jealous with Janet, miscalled her a sinner one day,
And I struck her! She lives with the angels this many a year;
But I'll scarce dare to meet her till Thou, Lord, hast spoken to her first.[18]

The irony is clearly directed against the decidedly impious speaker; his frantic eleventh-hour attempts to indemnify his afterlife through direct address to God constitute caustically funny censure of this familiar brand of insurance Christianity. The satire is also achieved, however, at the expense of the agents of organized religion. The bedside manner of the 'minister from Bethesda' is hopelessly inept; he churns out meaningless platitudes which serve only to confuse and further alienate the dying man. The speaker equates his own dishonesty in addressing the parson as 'Your Reverence' with the hypocrisy of cheering the squire on his birthday – 'he, mean as a hound!' The implications of this are fraught with danger for a clergy which would take for granted the respect and commitment of the community it serves, for the speaker is not an evil man, indeed he is characterized in the poem as a rather likeable Everyman figure, struggling to summon his own negligible good deeds to accompany him on the imminent journey to death. 'Yeoman Service' indicates familiarity with, and, I would argue, a certain affection for the tenets and practice of Welsh Nonconformity. As a moral fable the poem, whilst light-hearted and humorous, remains cynical about the impact and value of institutional religion, rather than about Nonconformity itself.

The 'Memoir' includes a number of extracts from the poet's letters to her publishers; these fragments provide additional insights into her attitudes to the world around her: Williams emerges as a shrewdly opinionated woman with a sharp, often irreverent wit. In one extract her unorthodox view of religious practice is glimpsed: 'I had a sabbath feast yesterday in the "Unspoken Sermons". It is not much to say they are above any of the spoken ones that I ever heard. My experience of sermons has been unhappy.'[19] This reinforces the impressions gained from

Williams's poems of a deeply religious woman whose instincts lean towards Nonconformist practice, but whose most fulfilling religious experience is solitary and intensely personal. The poet is clearly influenced by Nonconformist approaches to Christian spirituality, a leaning which links her with a number of the other Welsh poets examined in this book.

I have discussed the ways in which, for Williams, her Christian faith is inflected by her personal experience of physical pain and impending death. There is another problematic facet to her spiritual disposition as it emerges through her poetry and letters, one which distances Williams further from the devotional piety of some of her more fastidiously religious 'sister' Welsh poets. This exists in the tension she appears to have felt between her inclination towards the more severe forms of Protestantism and the sensual pull of aesthetic poetry, specifically that of Algernon Charles Swinburne. In a letter to her publishers Williams rationalizes, in some detail, her attraction to Swinburne's work:

> As to Swinburne, I believe that he has so much power over me that he will not let me read his bad things; in the *Poems and Ballads*, the pages turned over as though some one else was turning them, till at the wonderful Litany the invisible presence said 'Halt!' I began and ended with that. One such poem is enough for a morning's reading.[20]

The publication of Swinburne's *Poems and Ballads* in 1866 had attracted a barrage of abuse from a number of prominent critics on the grounds of its decadent immorality; most notable among these attacks was Robert Buchanan's satirical piece 'The Fleshly School of Poetry', which appeared in *The Contemporary Review* in 1871.[21] Williams acknowledges in this extract the magnetic force of Swinburne's 'power' over her, thus attesting to exactly that dubious potency about which his detractors expressed such fear. Williams, the Nonconformist Christian, is clearly mindful of these anxieties. She deploys the ingenious strategy of abdicating to the mysterious presence of Swinburne himself the responsibility for her reading; amusingly, she endues the infamous degenerate with exquisite qualities of moral discernment in judging for her the appropriate reading matter. As Williams continues to avow her own innocence, it is difficult to read her assiduous protestations without injecting a note of irony:

> I find no reason why I should not read Swinburne's poems: certainly I had little more than an hour, and so perhaps had only time to get the good in them. And of course it is possible that I may have read something very bad

without knowing it: in which case it cannot have done me much harm
. . . Surely such music cannot be destined for Satan's palaces.[22]

Williams includes in her letter a stanza dedicated 'To A. C. Swinburne'
which demonstrates the extent of her devotion to his work, and the depth
of the unease entailed in this allegiance:

> I dare not rhyme within the poet's court,
> Nor shake my jingling bells against his harp;
> But if my greeting can but solace him,
> If all unconsciously he hear my voice
> Cry 'Elder brother, hail! God comfort thee,
> And give to thee a golden harp one day';
> If he can feel a friend's hand in the dark,
> Then I am glad: if not, I am content
> To reverence in silence.[23]

Appreciation of Swinburne's art is unmistakable; Williams is concerned to
solace her idol, and by implication defend his position against those who
criticize him. Paradoxically, what is also clear is the poet's desire that
Swinburne should be 'saved', thus implying the sinfulness of the
perspective she seeks to defend. For Swinburne to receive a golden harp
from God, as Williams hopes, would require, according to the Christian
doctrines to which Williams adheres, sincere repentance of his sins and
acceptance of Jesus Christ as saviour. Such salvation seems unlikely, but
Williams, the devout Christian with a proclivity for Puritan precepts, is
unable to resist the voluptuous lure of Swinburne's verse. There is
ambiguity inherent, then, in her spiritual formation: Williams is fervently
committed to the idea of Jesus Christ as saviour, favouring unadorned and
keenly individual codes of practice identified with Welsh Nonconformist
denominations; she is also, however, drawn to the celebration of heavily
sensual experience contained in the poetic art of the aesthetic movement,
particularly that of Swinburne. Her taste for the decadent in poetry is also
at odds, therefore, with her choice of religious form, but implies also a
degree of divergence from the moral mainstream of the mid-Victorian
period. In her stanzaic poem 'Nazarene Thou Hast Conquered' Williams
employs further strategies for negotiating these tensions, engaging directly
with Swinburne's rejection of Christian dogma. The poem refers to the
purported last words of Julian the Apostate, a Roman emperor who
attempted to restore paganism to post-Christian Rome,[24] but it is also,
tellingly, an allusion to Swinburne's lines from 'Hymn to Proserpine':

'Thou hast conquered, O pale Galilean: / The world has grown grey from thy breath!'[25] Williams writes in the form of a first-person declaration of regret for having deserted Christ the saviour:

> In my haste I cried against Him,
> Faithful God and tender friend;
> I let fall the hand that held me,
> And I would myself defend.[26]

The speaker goes on to describe the futility of self-reliance, whose punishment is far worse than anything God could devise:

> Then for chastisement came scourging,
> When mine own hand held the rod,
> And I found myself more cruel
> Than ever seemed my God.[27]

In dramatizing the death throes of the defeated pagan, Williams also enacts the salvation she imagines for her literary hero. If the poem is read as the repentant voice of Swinburne, the final two stanzas attempt to redress his accusation that Christianity has clothed the world in drabness:

> But a flash of tender sunshine
> Came and smote upon mine eyes;
> Then I swooned upon the pathway,
> And I dared not stir nor rise.

> He of Nazareth had conquered,
> And I bathed in His smile;
> Then he shewed me a cord of crimson –
> He had held me, all the while.[28]

The contrast is dramatic between Swinburne's account of Christ's insidious grey breath and Williams's depiction of 'sunshine', 'smile' and 'crimson cord'. Williams characterizes her speaker as subject to a dynamic conversion experience involving a range of extreme physical responses. The model of Christian revelation constructed here is one of luminous, passionate ecstasy, in direct contrast with Swinburne's depiction of vapid enervation, but in line with the more enthusiastic practice of Calvinistic Methodism.[29] The image of the crimson cord, connecting the speaker with Christ, even through periods of repudiation, carries a range of meanings: it may represent a visceral and fundamental link, through its connotations of the umbilical cord – the throbbing channel of vital blood which sustains all human life through the gestative period. The image functions, then, to establish the primacy of the human relationship with Christ; it also has the effect of implying that what the speaker has experienced is an aspect of the process which that relationship entails. Doubt, even rejection of Christ need not, therefore, be seen as insurmountable obstructions to redemption. The poet is thus able to reclaim her literary hero, to rationalize her devotion to his work, and to reassure herself, at the same time, about her own fitness for heaven. Additionally, the image resonates with the approaches to Christian devotion espoused by Welsh Nonconformist Christianity as practised by Williams's Welsh father. Jane Aaron has explored the ways in which the doctrines of Calvinistic Methodism in the period lent themselves to an understanding of the conversion experience as essentially a female-centred process:

> Christ is the bridegroom and the convert the bride, whatever the sex of the sinner . . . It was men rather than women who had traditionally functioned as the constructors and primary users of rationalist systems of thought, but these organizing human structures only featured in conversion as arrogant and wrong-headed obstacles to the truth, to be incinerated in the incandescent moment of revelation.[30]

In analyses of poetry by Ann Griffiths, Aaron links this gendered view of spirituality with women's poetic creativity, noting that her poems 'served . . . as a private . . . record that gave the relief of expressive form to the pressure of inward experience'.[31] The use by Williams of the 'crimson cord' image in 'Nazarene Thou Hast Conquered', with its connotations of pregnancy and birth, suggests what may be an unconscious acquiescence on her part to the gendered understanding of communion with Christ which Aaron observes. It seems to me that, in her representation of Christian spirituality in this piece, the poet may be influenced by the sensibility of Calvinism which allows for the transcendental force of women's, as of men's, spiritual creativity. Thus, in arguing for the salvation of Swinburne's soul, Williams not only establishes permission to enjoy the work of her idol, but also recognizes and asserts her own capacity for spiritual and, arguably, poetic fulfilment.

Williams, then, like Jane Cave and Maria James, can be seen to draw from her Welsh lineage a religious sensibility which is a significant factor in her perception and negotiation of the world. Like those two poets, Williams, I would argue, gains from her Welsh Nonconformist background resources through which to express herself as a woman and a poet. It is interesting that her Nonconformist tendencies remain, in her poems, somewhat equivocally defined; whilst conspicuous enough to have caused Plumptre's defensive reference in the 'Memoir', Williams's religious allegiances are nevertheless to some extent obscured in the verse, hidden behind the intimate and often poignant relationship which is depicted between the poet and her God, and behind her paradoxical attraction to decadent aesthetics. She shares with Jane Cave – herself, of course, a fellow London-based Welsh poet – a proneness towards ambiguous religious representation. Cave, too, attempted to reconcile herself to Anglican worship whilst retaining loyalty to the doctrines and practice of her father's Welsh faith. It is notable that in the case of Maria James, however, there is no sense of defensiveness with regard to her Nonconformist religious orientation. James, living in America, was free of the influence of established Anglican Church prejudice and was clearly able to express her Methodist devotion without inhibition. It seems to me that a consideration of poetry by Sarah Williams supports the proposition, already suggested in earlier chapters, that religious orientation is a significant element in these women's sense of themselves as poets. It is a factor which, I would argue, informs their experience and understanding of other aspects of their subject positions, such as those of class, gender and particularly national identity.

★ ★ ★

Having dwelt at some length on the general religious and literary background to the poetic output of Sarah Williams, I now consider the issues of class, gender and national identity, beginning with her approach to notions of class.

From the little biographical material available it is possible to conjecture that Williams belonged to the burgeoning merchant class of mid-Victorian Britain. Gareth Stedman Jones has described the 'social domination of London by non-industrial forms of capital',[32] noting the ascendancy of the social group of which Robert Williams appears to have been a part: 'The true aristocracy of Victorian London was composed, not of those whose income derived from industry, but those whose income derived from rent, banking and commerce.'[33] At any rate, the Welshman Robert Williams was clearly successful enough in London life to send his daughter to the establishment presided over by E. H. Plumptre MA, a man sufficiently confident in his social seniority to edit and publish

Twilight Hours, and to pen in supremely confident tones the 'Memoir' to which I refer. From this position of bourgeois economic ease, the class view held by Sarah Williams emerges as somewhat circumscribed. Her approach to the aristocratic classes in her writing is, for the most part, to ignore them. There are no references to the nobility in the available extracts from her letters. In the poem 'The Dauphin in the Temple Prison', however, Williams dramatizes the tragic plight of the young son of Marie Antoinette, who, as the reader is informed in a footnote, 'From the time he was told that some admissions of his had been used to condemn his mother to death . . . never spoke until shortly before he died, eighteen months after, in the eleventh year of his age.'[34] The poem resonates with the often sentimental approach of Felicia Hemans to distant monarchy.[35] 'The Dauphin in the Temple Prison' is comprised of a rhetorical direct address from the prince to his dead mother, in thirty-six lines of rhyming couplets. It depicts in mawkishly sentimental terms a figure of tragic nobility, losing no opportunity for heightened pathos:

> O mother keep me till I come to thee,
> Until I from this darkened world shall flee:
> So darken'd for so long a time it seems
> That I can scarcely picture in my dreams
> The life we led before the shadows fell
> Which blotted out the face we loved so well![36]

Like Hemans, Williams does not subscribe here to the political views of her Romantic predecessors. The poem not only attempts to depict the human cost of the 1793 'Terror', but canonizes the notion of kingship:

> The lips kept mute for so long for her dear sake
> Unclosed at length; it was her name they spake:
> Then, closed in sculptured beauty, were at rest;
> The captive king was crown'd among the blest.[37]

There is clearly a contradiction between this implicit condemnation of the murder of a monarch and the celebration of Cromwell's spiritual mission in 'The Roundhead's Chaunt'. I would argue, however, that, given the poet's general lack of interest in the aristocracy (and in this Williams differs from Hemans), it is not possible to read this piece as serious evidence of her political allegiances. It seems to me that Williams is taken by the poetic potential of the Dauphin episode, and develops it as a histrionic saga of universal sentimental appeal, which is intended to transcend, in its tragic fascination, the boundaries of class and nationality.

Writing by Williams, both epistolary and poetic, issues overwhelmingly from the perspective of her middle-class position, and is implicitly addressed to an audience of the same milieu. Certainly there emanates from the text an assumption of common cultural competence and shared experience between poet and reader. In one letter, for example, Williams demonstrates the depth of her class-bound assumptions:

> In this delicious weather one must keep out all day; this afternoon the sunset colours on the sea were exquisite . . . Of course it is utterly impossible to describe this sort of thing; but I suppose one's instinct of speech is ineradicable. Talking of instincts, I fancy the desire for some kind of audience or public is one almost universal.[38]

The use by Williams of the universal pronoun in discussing firstly what was, to many Britons in the period, the unimaginable luxury of leisure, and, further, the premise of a general human desire for publicity, is extremely telling. To take the issue of leisure first: much recent feminist scholarship has been concerned with challenging the gendered stereotype of the Victorian bourgeois 'lady of leisure'.[39] Given the problematic nature of women's relationship to leisure arising out of the invisibility of much female work in the period, the development of leisure time through the Victorian period has been identified as a bourgeois concept and linked to, among other factors, the increased profitability of the capitalist firm which allowed for some release of the labour of family members.[40] It is possible that Williams was part of a family which had 'progressed' to this stage of social development. At any rate, the middle-class Victorian's enjoyment of recreation, as illustrated by Williams in her letter, was by no means universal among the general population of Britain. In the light of middle-class privilege in access to leisure, the second assumption made by Williams in the extract, relating to the desire for audience, is an even more extravagant claim. The remark is, however, as much a useful marker in gauging the sense Williams had of herself as woman and poet as an indicator of her class identity, and as such I will return to this extract later in the chapter in a discussion of gender.

Williams makes as little explicit reference in her verse to issues of class as she does to the question of rank and the aristocracy. What does preoccupy her, however, is the idea of the city, and this is certainly linked to her perceptions of prevalent social conditions. Marxist critics have produced a large corpus of material which focuses on the Victorian realist novel as profoundly influenced by historical economic and social forces; Raymond Williams, notably, has explored representation of the city in Victorian fiction.[41] I intend to analyse Sarah Williams's city poems on the same basis. Matthew Arnold, writing in 1868, the year of her death, referred to the inhabitants of East London as 'those vast, miserable, unmanageable masses of sunken people'.[42] Arnold's view of the London working class is symptomatic of bourgeois anxieties about the wretched and, more significantly, threatening condition of the city's poor. Gareth Stedman Jones describes the growing alarm of the bourgeoisie throughout the 1860s:

> At their most immediate these fears centred upon the maintenance of order and stability. There had already been premonitions of disorder at the beginning of the decade . . . some social tension remained, and . . . the middle-class population . . . continued to express considerable anxiety . . . London was visited by a 'plague of beggars'. 'No-one who lived in the suburbs', wrote Thomas Beggs, 'could help feeling that they were in circumstances of considerable peril'.[43]

Jones cites a range of sources in evidencing this general climate of middle-class social insecurity. What emerges from these extracts is the extent to which what was seen as the dangerous 'demoralization' of the London poor threatened bourgeois confidence. Jones notes that one of the causes of this demoralization was perceived to be the operation of public and private charity, in particular the 'indiscriminate giver': 'As Trevelyan put it "labour is the great antidote to crime . . . The effect of modern charity has been to suspend this primeval law".'[44] In her poem 'The Song of the City of Sparrows' Williams depicts the city street in winter. The speaking voice of the piece is that of the sparrow itself, declaring its stoicism in the face of hunger, cold and city grime:

> . . . although we're plain and songless,
> And poor city birds are we,
> Yet, before the days of darkness
> We, the sparrows, never flee;
>
> . . .
>
> Then we glide among the housetops,
> And we track the murky waste,
> And we go about our business
> With a cheerful earnest haste;

> Not as though our food were plenty,
> Or no dangers we might meet;
> But as though the work of living
> Was a healthy work, and sweet.[45]

Plumptre cites this poem as evidence of the poets 'naturalness and spontaneity'.[46] I want to suggest that the piece may be read symbolically as an expression of the anxieties to which Gareth Stedman Jones refers. The sparrows are clearly inhabitants of the city, the most drab, the least individually mighty and the greatest in number. It seems to me, then, that it is possible to read the lowly sparrows as symbolic of the city's poor. In the *Manifesto of the Communist Party*, published in 1848, Marx and Engels foretell the fall of the bourgeoisie to working-class revolution: 'What the bourgeoisie . . . produces, above all, are its own gravediggers. Its fall and the victory of the proletariat are equally inevitable.'[47] In her poem, by contrast, Williams depicts a benign, cheerful horde. The generally regular *ABAB* rhyme scheme, the scrupulously rhythmic alternation of eight- and seven-syllable lines, and equally symmetrical punctuation, establish a chirpy, upbeat pace. The repeated assertion of phrases in the semantic field of productive occupation – 'go about our business', 'the work of living', 'healthy work, and sweet' – add to the impression of a docile, unthreatening community of the poor. Those poor are not demoralized through the lack of motivation to work; on the contrary, they define themselves in terms of their capacity for contented labour through times of hardship. If Williams, like so many of her middle-class contemporaries, perceived a sense of menace from the London poor, this type of verse may represent an attempt to defuse her own anxieties through self-reassurance, and, perhaps, serve as a somewhat sanguine didactic exemplar directed at the poor themselves.

Regardless of the degree of the poet's anodyne intentions, what also emerges from the piece is a strong sense of the collective strength of the city's poor. The description of the sparrows as 'songless' is particularly interesting; if the sparrows are read as the city poor, this reference to their lack of voice may connote the political disenfranchisement of the mid-Victorian working class. Of course, this also applied at the time to women of all classes. Angela Leighton's hypothesis that 'The low legal status of women from all classes probably gave them a natural sense of identity with other dispossessed creatures under the rule of "man"'[48] may hold true for Williams, and the poet's reminder that 'we, the sparrows, never flee' perhaps indicates an identification on her part with her fellow voiceless occupants of the city. This is particularly persuasive in view of her declared personal imperative to be heard in a public arena. In any case, the poem suggests a warning to the holders of power that the drab, impoverished city-dwellers, like women, perhaps, endure to 'hover round the window, / And peck against the pane'.[49]

In one of the few poems by Williams which deals with explicitly Welsh themes – and one which uniquely in her work has a Welsh-language title, 'O Fy Hen Gymraeg' – Williams depicts a bleak London cityscape which functions as a metaphor for the emotional and material poverty of England in the eyes of the Welsh characters who live there. Although there is no specific reference made to class in the poem, the poet's familiar preoccupation with the city recurs; in this piece the urban is encoded as explicitly negative. The male Welsh speaker addresses his London-born daughter on the subject of their metropolitan home:

> The people are frozen hard here –
> Not you, my darling, not you! –
> And the air is thick with its yellow fog,
> And the streets have slime for dew.
> There is never a line of beauty
> In all the weary rows,
> And the saddest thing of the whole is this,
> That the bareness no one knows;
> They are quite contented, and think it fine.
> O fy hen Gymraeg![50]

This stanza echoes that symbolic representation by Charles Dickens of oppressive London life at the opening of *Bleak House*, published in 1852.[51] Like that depiction of the rancid London atmosphere, Williams's detail of thick yellow fog suggests an aura of insidious decay and disease. The image of 'slime for dew' is a vivid one which evokes a species of pestilent and pervasive oppression. Dew-fall, conventionally seen as a refreshing and supremely natural phenomenon, is transmuted in the poem into a threatening and manufactured occurrence. The idea of this noxious and glutinous substance descending daily, unbidden, and adhering to all surfaces suggests inhibition of movement and the enforced use of energy in unpleasant and dangerous activity. The city is thus seen by the speaker to corrupt the natural, to enslave its inhabitants and to expose them to the threat of poisonous taint. This stanza also seems to quote William Blake's 1793 poem 'London'.[52] Blake's political leanings were, of course, progressive to say the least: his so-called revolutionary poems, 'The French Revolution', 'America: A Prophecy' and 'Visions of Albion' indicate the extent of his Jacobin tendencies. Given her firmly middle-class position, the way in which Williams treats the city seems unlikely to involve more than a cosmetic similarity to that of Blake. The image of 'weary rows' of city buildings, recalls the 'charter'd streets' of Blake's piece; similarly, the reference by Williams, in the penultimate line of the stanza, to the city inhabitants' obliviousness to their plight strongly suggests Blake's famous notion of 'mind-forg'd manacles'. Where Blake's poem implies the potential for revolution, were the city-dwellers to shrug off the psychological chains which enslave them, the speaker of 'O Fy Hen Gymraeg' declares that the people of the city are 'quite contented and think it fine'. I would argue that this may be read as symptomatic of the anxieties Jones notes. In her exploration of an apparently classless city, Williams gives expression to the potential threat represented by the rising urban squalor she observes; at the same time she attempts to repress those fears in the rather hackneyed axiom that those most affected know no better. In the logic of the poem, humanitarian intervention is therefore redundant and futile. The problem of the 'indiscriminate almsgiver', which, as Jones asserts, was an influential concept in mid-Victorian perceptions of the city, is thus resolved in the poem: the city-dwellers are 'quite contented', and it would be wrong, therefore, to attempt philanthropy on their behalf. Tellingly, unlike Blake's observer, Williams's speaker does not 'wander thro' each charter'd street'; rather, he pronounces on the state of the inhabitants from the position of his own fireside. But, interestingly, this is no safe vantage point, a fact which becomes clear as the speaker describes the impact of city life on his own well-being:

> You may put the candle by;
> There is light enough to die in,
> And the dawning draweth nigh.
> Only the want remaineth,
> Gnawing my heart away:
> Oh for a word of my mother's tongue,
> And a prayer she used to pray . . .[53]

My readings of her poems indicate that Williams holds a perspective on class issues, which, whilst ostensibly altruistic, is nevertheless heavily influenced by the concerns of her own bourgeois milieu to ensure survival and growth in the face of the increasingly troubling presence of a fast-expanding working class.

★ ★ ★

Both E. H. Plumptre and the *Good Words* journalist write of Sarah Williams in terms which celebrate the conventional virtues of Victorian womanhood, emphasizing her piety, her fortitude, her self-deprecation: 'No one could have been warmer, more considerate, or have shown more *womanly wile* in her ways of giving sympathy' (my emphasis).[54] Both writers also praise the poet's intelligence, but it is acclaimed as 'brilliant, sparkling, vivacious',[55] adjectives which suggest an entertaining feminine accomplishment, a valuable addition to drawing-room society. The impression of Sarah Williams which emerges out of the extracts from her letters is, by contrast, of an assertive, even strident thinker. Plumptre notes that her publishers soon 'recognized, both of them, that they had a correspondent who was an exception to the common run of letter-writers'. He adds that Williams 'appears to have welcomed the opening thus given, and uttered herself more freely to them because there were not in their case the restraints of previous acquaintance'.[56]

In view of the content and tenor of the letters, Plumptre's observations seem amusingly understated. The remark by Williams, for instance, that it is 'a dreadful piece of bosh that "an honest man's the noblest work of God!" To say nothing of the angels – a good woman is infinitely higher'[57] renders rather dubious her patron's claims for her proclivities towards consideration and 'womanly wiles'. Such outspoken disparagement of both received wisdom and male virtue seems to demolish Plumptre's affirmations of feminine self-deprecation and coyness.

Her views on the work of some of her male contemporaries are equally incisive; they also are often scathing, and are expressed with supreme confidence. The anonymous male victim of one of Williams's informal reviews, for example, fares rather badly: 'I am afraid the author of ★ ★ ★ would not approve of my criticisms. Novices are always Draconian, you know, and my first impulse would be to pitch the whole thing into the fire.'[58] Clearly no acquiescent subscriber to the theory of male supremacy in the field of literature, neither is she daunted by the prospect of commenting on work by as distinguished an author as G. H. Lewes:

> I have read some capital papers of Lewes' in the 'Fortnightly Review' . . . rather heathenish, – I think he has a tendency that way; but solid, original and thoughtful. Oddly enough, the paper on 'Style' concluded with, I believe, two (of course unintentional) examples of tautology . . . What never-ending comfort any kind of art is.[59]

This illustrates not only the depth of Williams's interest in literary studies, but also her perspicacity as a reader. The drily ironic concluding remark acknowledges the poet's own shortcomings as a writer, but it also demonstrates her irreverent approach to notions of authority and canon.

Letters by Williams are strewn with witty aphorisms on a wide range of subjects. One such remark hints at her attitude towards gender-political issues: 'Don't you like political women? I do – they scold so.'[60] This was presumably made in response to a comment by her male correspondent. Williams manages to challenge her publisher's antipathetic approach to women with political views, to assert her own opposition to this opinion, and through humour to escape from any taint of suspicion that she herself may deserve the epithet 'political'. With tongue firmly in cheek, what Williams also achieves is to scold her publisher and hence intimate her own credential as just the kind of woman he has attempted to deride. Little wonder that the recipients of her letters considered them to be 'exceptional'.

I have already identified in Williams a preoccupation with the concept of self-expression, and a need in particular for an audience. Elizabeth Barrett Browning's Aurora Leigh describes her reasons for writing thus:

> I . . .
> Will write my story for my better self,
> As when you paint your portrait for a friend,
> Who keeps it in a drawer and looks at it
> Long after he has ceased to love you, just
> To hold together what he was and is.[61]

Williams reveals that her own imperative to write is connected with the need for the recognition of self by others. Her assumption that the instinct for audience is universal suggests the force of the drive she experienced to write and be read. In order to 'hold together' what she 'was and is' Williams craves, not merely the exploration and articulation of the inner self described by Barrett Browning's Aurora, but also public acknowledgement of her existence as a speaking subject. Aurora professes herself as satisfied to keep her voice enclosed in the confines of the drawer and thus of the domestic sphere, but Sarah Williams states her need for a larger, more public context. The concept of female authorship during the Victorian period as a subversive, even defiant, mode of entry into a public sphere prohibited to women is one which has been frequently discussed by twentieth-century feminist theorists.[62]

In one of her letters Williams discusses the issue of her public identity in reference to her pen-name 'Sadie':

> I am willing to appear quite anonymously, and I would yield altogether to your reasoning were 'Sadie' only a *nom de plume*; but the name, self-given they say in baby days, has so grown with me, has become so literally a part of me, that I could lose both the others with less sacrifice of identity. In fact I am Sadie or nobody, which it shall be I leave to you.[63]

Presumably the 'other' names referred to here are 'Sarah Williams' or 'Miss Williams'; it is telling that the poet rejects these appellations on the grounds that her preferred alternative was 'self-given'. Although this extract was no doubt included to illustrate her self-effacing modesty, it provides additional evidence, if such be needed, of the determined and feisty nature of the poet, who, whilst claiming willingness to submit, doggedly resists her publishers' wishes to the point of issuing a threat of withdrawal if pushed. Further, in the light of the urgency of the desire Williams expresses for audience, this fragment seems to me to assert a far more complex response than self-effacement. The pseudonym, traditional masking device of the Victorian woman writer, is deployed by this poet in order to assert what she sees as her true identity. In another letter Williams expands on her attachment to the nickname:

> I suppose most of us have two or three titles and characters to match. At home and with my friends I have always been Sadie, so self-named, they say before I could speak plain. Sarah is my grim, business signature, which at first used to make me feel as if I had been starched. Miss Williams belongs to me, as never having had a sister, nor, for that matter, a brother.[64]

The given name of Sarah is described as uncomfortable and imposed; the inherited name, Miss Williams, is seen as applied to her by default in the absence of another candidate; only the self-chosen 'Sadie' represents what Barrett Browning terms the 'better self', the identity which must be written, read and acknowledged. It is interesting that her sense of her poetic identity is so closely linked with the intimacy of the personal world Williams inhabits. In Barrett Browning's declaration of poetic intent, there is a sense of separation between the personal self and the writing self. For Williams, an understanding of the compulsion to write involves a fusion between persona and poetic identity. Separation occurs at the level of the identity over which she has no control, the imposed identity which is seen by the world at large, and which allows for no independent 'voice' to emerge.

The centrality of issues of identity and voice in women's poetry from the Victorian period has been discussed by numerous critics.[65] Clearly, these were key issues in Williams's writing project. For exploration of the ways in which the preoccupations impacted on her literary practice, I turn now to the poems themselves.

'A Clever Woman' is a piece which appears for the first time in the 1872 edition of *Twilight Hours*, in a section entitled 'Questionings'. It is the only work in the collection which engages overtly with the so-called 'woman question'. Significantly, perhaps, the poem was recuperated by Plumptre from Williams's papers after her death, and may not have been intended for publication. The piece is worth quoting in its entirety:

> If I knew a clever woman
> I would ask her this:
> Are the clever women happy?
> Are there things they miss –
> Knowing sadly that they miss them,
> Seeing far off bliss?
>
> If I knew a clever woman
> I would still inquire:
> Is it sighing to breathe strongly?
> Panting to aspire?
> Are they dizzy looking upwards,
> Burnt with Heaven's fire?
>
> Once I saw a clever woman
> In a picture frame;
> All alone I had my lady,
> But no question came.
> I just knelt and said 'I love you',
> Echo knows her name.[66]

The nursery-rhyme rhythm of the piece belies the seriousness afforded the subject matter. The first-person speaking voice, though not identified directly, is implicitly female: the series of questions planned for the clever woman become increasingly heartfelt as the poem progresses. The first stanza refers to the view of women's intellectual and, particularly, literary development, commonly expressed in written material from the period and summed up by G. H. Lewes in the *Westminster Review* in 1852: 'Almost all literature has some remote connexion with suffering . . . The happy wife and busy mother are only forced into literature by some hereditary organic tendency, stronger even than the domestic.'[67] Williams articulates the idea that intellectual activity is incompatible with women's happiness. The notion is framed in a question whose rhetorical essence is inescapable. Any question so framed is understood in the colloquial English idiom to assume the response 'No'. It is possible, however, with minimal reordering of emphasis, to read the line as rather less pre-emptive. If stress is placed on the first syllable of 'happy', the question reads as genuinely musing. The second stanza lists the possible symptoms of the unhappy clever woman. It is a litany which implies doubt of the value system which defines the clever woman as unfulfilled. The poem literally interrogates the assumption that intellectual ambition in a woman is unhealthy. Having listed the supposed emotional symptoms of the clever woman in the first stanza, the speaker now recites those of the physical variety: sighing, panting and dizziness.[68] The final stanza deploys the device of the picture frame, and, again, the speaker seeks to establish communion with her object. The expression of love for the clever woman makes clear the speaker's and thus the poet's identification with the desire for intellectual achievement. The reference to 'Echo' in the final line is particularly interesting. Echo is represented in Greek mythology as a nymph who, having rejected the amorous advances of the god Pan, was punished by being torn to pieces, only her voice surviving.[69] Thus the figure of Echo symbolizes Victorian society's fears for a woman who in rejecting the possibility of fulfilment through love becomes only a voice. Williams, however, asserts her love for the clever woman, despite the hazards she has described. This seems to me to dramatize the poet's declared need to become a 'voice' which is heard. In 1865 Charlotte M. Yonge had published her novel, *The Clever Woman of the Family*, in which the clever woman is demonstrated to be entirely misguided in her pursuit of intellectual fulfilment, and ultimately inferior to men. It is not possible precisely to date this piece by Williams, but it is likely that the poem, possibly not destined for publication, was written in response to the reactionary conclusion of Yonge's novel. 'A Clever Woman' also represents a striking contrast to the construction by Felicia Hemans of female intellect and creativity in, for instance, her poem 'Woman and Fame'. 'Woman and Fame' has received significant critical attention in recent years from feminist scholars concerned with its ambivalent vision of female artistic creativity.[70] The poem, unlike 'A Clever Woman' by Sarah Williams, emphasizes the inevitable misery which is the lot of the intellectual woman who seeks an audience for her creative expression:

> Fame, Fame! Thou canst not be the stay
> Unto the drooping reed,
> The cool fresh fountain in the day
> Of the soul's feverish need:
> Where must the lone one turn or flee?
> Not unto thee – Oh not to thee![71]

In 'A Clever Woman', the speaker is drawn to the clever woman with an intensity which carries a strong homoerotic charge. In 'Woman and Fame' Hemans demonstrates no such loving warmth towards the woman who would seek intellectual success. 'A Clever Woman' suggests, then, a lively approach to gender-political issues which re-inforces the impression gained of Williams through examination of her correspondence.

In many other of her poems, however, progressive views on gender issues are not consistently indicated. The unity of personal and poetic, which Williams projects through her adherence to the pen-name 'Sadie', for example, is not fully borne out by an examination of the poems. Williams, like many mid-Victorian poets of both sexes, deploys a diverse range of perspectives and speaking voices in her verse. For the woman poet in the post-Romantic period, the need to experiment with a range of possible speaking positions was a pressing one.[72] In many poems by Williams the persona or perspective tested is that of a male speaker or central protagonist – in 'Yeoman Service', 'The Roundhead's Chaunt' and 'Nazarene Thou Hast Conquered', for example, already discussed, and in others such as 'The Coastguard's Story', 'Omar and the Persian', 'O Fy Hen Gymraeg' and 'Snowdon to Vesuvius', the latter a poem in which two mountains are personified as brothers in dialogue across the miles. It can be argued that Williams attempts to occupy in her poems the position of 'other' by assuming 'his' speaking voice. In his Preface to the 1872 edition of *Twilight Hours*, Plumptre publishes fragments of the unfinished piece 'The Poet's Wooing', in which Williams describes the influence of love and suffering on the development of the poet; tellingly, unlike Barrett Browning's description of the same process in *Aurora Leigh*, in this piece the poet speaker is male:

> I had thought I had no heart except to sing about.
> Softly the twilight days went on and on,

With here and there a scent of faded flowers,
Or dash of rain against the window-panes.

Whereat my soul looked out upon the world.
And now behold I had a heart new-born;
Trembling it put on life and felt for light . . .[73]

Sentiment and expression are rather clichéd. Williams dramatizes the experience of the poet in terms of safe sentimentality; the issues of self-assertion and self-representation encountered by Williams in the course of her own creative development are ignored. I have proposed that Williams's need to write may proceed from the impulse to claim for herself some measure of control over power and meaning which she recognizes in the 'other', in this case, the figure of the poet. What her assumption of male personae in her poems, and in particular in this piece, provides is evidence of the extent of problems of identity and authorship faced by the woman poet of the period. Williams does not depict a woman poet, and her attempts to establish a space to speak through the 'voices' of this and a range of other male figures results in verse which is derivative in form and content. Tellingly, she is more successful when the speakers of the poems are implicitly female.

In the poem 'A Face Seen at the Window', for example, issues of gendered identity are explored through the first-person and implicitly female speaker's address to the figure of a woman framed in a window. Angela Leighton describes the image of the picture as one of the recurring strategies employed by Victorian women poets in 'identifying themselves as poets in a society which, on the one hand, casts them in an unremittingly sentimental mould, and, on the other, was astonished at their mere existence'.[74] Williams uses the framing device here to identify herself primarily in terms of the agony of her lived experience, for the face at the window is that of a lonely, suffering woman:

Hope writhing in the tyrant grasp of Fear,
The wail of woe that never turns nor ends.
Only a woman suffering alone
Only the rain for common company
Only my prayer for thee, sister unknown,
For Christ's dear sake the good God comfort thee!
Meeting a moment, meeting nevermore,
Till we shall smile at all our sorrows o'er.[75]

The image of hope as a contorted prisoner of fear is immediate and striking; the semantic linking of this with the phrase 'Only a woman suffering alone', and the direct address to 'thee, sister unknown' which breaks the 'frame', implies an emotional connection between speaker and protagonist. Leighton describes the ways in which women poets' deployment of the picture device subverted patriarchal notions of woman as muse and art object. She suggests that poems which describe a picture thus remain twice removed from the reality 'or present pictured tableaux of women in heroic or tragic poses'.[76] Williams uses the device in 'A Face Seen at the Window' in order to negotiate the difficulties inherent in patriarchal theories of poetry by establishing, not distance, but proximity between the speaker and the 'face'. The female object of the poem thus becomes synthesized with its speaking subject. It seems to me that in this poem the perennial consciousness in Williams of pain and imminent death becomes a resource which opens for her a poetic space from which to speak in a voice which is authentically hers; it is a space which is unavailable to her within the canonical field of patriarchal literary conventions.

With the exception of 'A Clever Woman', and in contrast to the hints of spirited heterodoxy glimpsed in the extracts from her letters, the overt attention paid by Williams to gender issues in her verse is disappointingly underdeveloped. Generally the picture which emerges from an examination of Williams's poetry is one of a woman whose sense of herself as a woman and a poet is circumscribed by her experience of living with pain and death. Her conscious approaches to issues of gender politics are limited. There are hints, however, that Williams's identity as a Welsh poet may manifest itself in her verse in terms of a more problematic relationship with Victorian patriarchal society than that resulting from either class or gender positionality. In order to explore this proposition more fully, I now begin a consideration of poems by Williams on Welsh themes.

★ ★ ★

There is no evidence that Williams ever lived in Wales, although the 'Memoir' refers to what appear to have been fairly regular visits there. There is no mention of Wales in any of the available extracts from her letters, but the obituary in *Good Words* remarks upon her 'warm Welsh temperament'.[77] What is clear from her work is that the poet experienced some sense of herself as Welsh, for several poems in the *Twilight Hours* collection are on Welsh themes.

'*O Fy Hen Gymraeg*' is footnoted: '"O for [a word of] mine own dear Welsh!" The proverbial longing of the Welsh in London'.[78] The poem enacts the deathbed moments of an exiled Welshman, presumably the poet's father. The piece is spoken by the dying man, who is sentimental in his attachment to his homeland:

> Yes, there is nothing I want, dear,
> You may put the candle by;
> There is light enough to die in,
> And the dawning draweth nigh.
> Only the want remaineth,
> Gnawing my heart away:
> Oh for a word of my mother's tongue,
> And a prayer she used to pray!
> *O fy hen Gymraeg!*[79]

The speaker's nostalgia centres on his yearning for his native tongue, and he expresses regret that he has not passed on the Welsh language to his daughter:

> I wish I had taught you to speak it
> While the light was on my brain;
> It has vanished now with the thousand things
> That will never come back again.[80]

The loss of Welsh is linked here to the powers of youth. The speaker's grief at its passing is representative, therefore, of physical as well as emotional death. The fond intimacy of the depiction implicates the speaker's addressee, by analogy the poet herself, in a shared regret at her lack of access to the language. In stanza three, the speaker makes explicit the symbolic distinction between his perceptions of London and Wales. As previously noted, the stanza depicts London as a stagnant morass, its air 'thick with yellow fog' and its streets with 'slime for dew'.

Raymond Williams traces changes in nineteenth-century representations of London, and cites the version expressed by Charles Dickens of vision of 'obscurity, the darkness, the fog that keep [people] from seeing each other clearly' as a manifestation of the paradox inherent in the idea of London. London, Raymond Williams claims, represents a system which is at the same time random, miscellaneous, rigid and determining. It is a system which is seen to sustain a complex economy at the cost of dislocating human beings from each other.[81] This is a useful proposition in examining the perspective of London presented by Sarah Williams in this poem. '*O Fy Hen Gymraeg*' may be read as evidence of the contradictory perception of the city which Raymond Williams describes. The poet depicts a subject who, like her own father, has made his fortune from the London economy, and whose social position, like her own, is sustained by the system which he (and therefore also she) nevertheless perceives as polluting, dead and deadening.

There is a mingling in the poem of contempt and pity for the inhabitants of London, which is the result of the speaker's self-elevation above the pathetic mass. Tellingly, the poet extricates herself from the taint of the same wretched condition by having the speaker interrupt his description of London with the absolution of his daughter: 'Not you, my darling, not you!' The speaker's daughter, by implication the poet herself, clearly identifies with the father's superior Welsh perspective.

In the final two stanzas, Wales and the Welsh language are depicted as the source of spiritual enlightenment. The speaker experiences a vision of his childhood in the 'place where of old we used to play, / On the edge of the mountain's brow'. The dying man's hallucination of Welsh child-hood involves the appearance upon the mountain of a Christ-like figure who 'talked to us in gentle words / That hallowed and blessed our play'. The final stanza ends with the exclamatory '*Gorphwysfa! O Gorphwysfa!/ Gogoniant!* Amen.' The lines are footnoted: 'Gorphwysfa: The name of his home, common in Wales, – meaning a resting place. Gogoniant!: Glory! The old rallying shout at the open-air preachings; said to have first suggested to Handel the idea of his Halleluja Chorus.'[82] Wales is thus presented as the resting place of the speaker's soul, a place where Christ himself may have walked, and as the inspirational home of music to boot.

From details related in Plumptre's 'Memoir' it is clear that the poet's father died a matter of months before Sarah Williams herself succumbed to the surgeon's knife. It is possible to conjecture, then, that in drama-tizing her father's death, the poet is preoccupied with the prospect of her own. Certainly, there is no sense of irony or criticism about her depiction of the speaker in '*O Fy Hen Gymraeg*'. Williams may be seen, therefore, as metaphorizing Wales and the Welsh language as the fountainhead of youth, energy, vision and possibility, and as depicting Wales as the landscape of her soul and the imaginary source of emotional, spiritual and creative nurture. Despite the positive encoding of Welsh culture here, however, the shadow of death, so often present in Williams's work, looms over her depiction of Welshness in the poem. The speaker, like the poet, is dying; his Welsh identity, for all its emotional, spiritual and creative resource, dies with him, incapable of surviving in a changing world.

'The Doom of the Prynnes' is the longest poem in Williams's published oeuvre, and, like 'O Fy Hen Gymraeg', connects Welshness with the spectres of death and destruction. The three-part poem is a bizarre Gothic melodrama consisting of approximately six hundred lines of blank verse. The speaker of the piece recalls the traumatic events of her childhood as part of a once-mighty London-Welsh family fallen upon hard times. The narrative involves the doomed love affair between the speaker's two cousins, Mark and Agnes, whose relationship is the catalyst which precipitates and symbolizes the final downfall of the Prynne family.

The poem opens with a description of the Prynne family's precarious situation prior to the enactment of its final doom:

> We dwelt together in a strange old house,
> That, like the fortunes of our family,
> Had shrunk and withered to pathetic age;
> Until men said we should some day be crushed,
> A nest of eagles 'neath a crumbling rock;
> And yet there was a certain charm in this,
> Like living on some cracked volcano side,
> That any day might yawn and let us in,
> United in the bridal of one death.[83]

The sense of impending disaster is established immediately through images of natural catastrophe: 'volcano' and 'crumbling rock'. The Prynnes are depicted as proud, a 'nest of eagles', but also self-destructive, seeing a 'certain charm' in the danger of their situation. Their family pride, conventionally a heroic quality, is negatively encoded here as a death drive.

The Prynnes live in the 'dark tumultuous heart of London town'. The description of their home is constructed in terms of incongruity:

> The room we used was once the banquet hall,
> With many coloured windows looking east,
> Across a little quaint, old-fashioned street,
> That scarcely suited its locality . . .
> The walls were oaken, wrought in deep device
> Of pomegranates and acorns once our shield;
> While underneath the mantel one had carved,
> With mingled vanity and insolence
> 'Here dined with Owain Prynne, King James the Small'.[84]

The space in which the family lives is ill-fitted to its purpose; the street on which the house is built is described as out of step with its surroundings. Prynne family pride is explicitly figured here as arrogant and futile. The Prynnes are depicted, then, as doggedly pursuing an isolated existence in an inorganic and inhospitable environment.

The speaker's father and uncle are depicted as completely absorbed in scientific activities, but both characters study the universe through distorting and ultimately limiting glasses; the father gazes at the sky through a telescope, the uncle at minutiae through a microscope. The activities of these elder Prynnes are encoded as introspective and unproductive. Mark Prynne is forced to write political editorials for money:

> Mark wrote too much and hated what he wrote,
> Till Agnes said 'I must pen leaders too'
> Whereat he answered, 'here is my receipt,
> Sneer at the Emperor, Cobden and John Bright;
> Declare that Gladstone is too eloquent,
> And that the peril of the land demands a jocund premier'.[85]

The Prynnes' one point of contact with the outside world is, therefore, a source of bitter self-contempt. Mark despises himself for prostituting his skills in order that the family may survive.

The family is depicted as isolated and insular, and the relationship between Mark and Agnes is the ultimate symbol of its destructive self-absorption. The two are protagonists in an intense and highly sexually charged communion. The danger and inevitability of their reciprocal obsession is woven into the textual fabric of the verse:

> I shivered, Agnes drew me to her side.
> 'The child is shaken with our stormy winds.'
> 'The child!' Mark cried, ' 'tis evermore the child:
> If I were dying, you would moan "The child" . . .
> She bent to kiss me, but between our lips
> There fell a crystal tear that parted them,
> And held them parted like a magician's spell;
> And then I knew, as children know such things,
> That not my life, nor love, nor deathless soul,
> Could weigh, with her, against a hair of his . . .[86]

The unhealthy, incestuous attraction between the cousins is depicted in terms of harmful magic which works to exclude even those closest and most dear. As if the impending destruction of the Prynnes were not signalled clearly enough, there appears in Part II a harbinger of disaster in the form of Mark's deranged mother, who spells out the doom of the Prynnes:

> 'A Prynne can only love a Prynne:
> Doom one.
>
> The Prynne who weds a Prynne, weds Death:
> Doom two.
>
> The Prynne who weds not Death goes mad, like me:
> Doom three.'[87]

Inevitably, as Mark and Agnes are drawn together, the prophecy reaches its ultimate violent resolution:

> Like two pure souls that on their way to earth
> Had met in vacuous space, and recognized
> Their kinship with a mythic deep delight
> And silence eloquent, so these two pierced
> Into the spirit depths of either heart,
> With solemn joy, wonderment and peace,
> Unsatisfied with sight yet gazing still;
> Until a sudden shadow dimmed Mark's eyes.
> And Agnes, reading it, saw what he feared
> For her, and in her; and she shrank, like one
> All wrongfully accused of leprosy . . .[88]

It would seem that her lover sees in Agnes's eyes shades of the madness that had condemned her aunt to misery. But before 'Doom three' can divide the lovers they are united by a cataclysmically destructive event:

> All this while a ceaseless moaning had gone round the house
> A sighing like the sighing of the sea.
> A distant gale, Mark said, but as he spoke
> It neared, and crashed against the window frames . . .
>
> And then the floor curved upward, so it seemed,
> Towards the ceiling, that, on swaying walls,
> Went round and round in dizzying circle dim.
> 'Love!' 'Love!' my cousins cried, with outstretched arms,

And flowed together, like two parted streams . . .
Then all was dark.[89]

The depiction by Williams of Welshness here is very different from that of 'O Fy Hen Gymraeg'. The Prynnes are an alienated Welsh community who are bound by the curse of their race to pursue a futile and eventually catastrophic destiny. Unlike the speaker of 'O Fy Hen Gymraeg', the London Welsh in this poem are unable to adapt to the city's system of 'negative indifference and positive differentiation'.[90] They are consequently denied access to either the material salvation promised by positive intercourse with the city's cultural and commercial economy, or the emotional redemption available through the regenerative imaginary powers of Wales as spiritual home. The Prynnes' final brutal doom is symbolized in the poem in terms of an uprooted Welsh tree:

> Before the house stood a mountain ash,
> Which some far-distant Prynne had brought to share
> The changes in the family estate.
> Though bent and scarred wih age and evil times,
> It still upreared its wand-like spears of leaves . . .

The storm, returning, had seized hold of this:

> 'Twas bowed and quivering like a foundering ship,
> With mutinous leaves, that whispered cheek on cheek,
> How they would help the wrecking wind this night.
> E'en as we looked 'twas done: the old tree fell,
> Shaking the near foundations of the house . . .[91]

The tree is symbolic of the hopelessly insular race of London Welsh, uprooted from the homeland, surviving in a 'bent and scarred' condition, only to be wrenched in the end from the inhospitable soil. The tree, like the Prynnes, is depicted as contributing to its own demise, its 'mutinous leaves' conspiring to 'help the wind this night'.

My readings of the two Welsh poems by Williams indicates an understanding of Welsh heritage as an inevitably ill-fated 'doom'. 'Sadie' depicts the Welsh as a condemned race, living in the past and unable to adapt to the modern world. In her vision, Welshness is a valuable resource in terms of her personal spirituality and creativity, but the modern Welshman is doomed either to lose his identity, and always mourn its loss, or to die. According to Williams, Welsh identity is not something to be passed on in a healthy condition to future generations. Though the poet depicts her own Welshness in 'O Fy Hen Gymraeg' as a valuable spiritual and creative resource, in 'The Doom of the Prynnes' Williams labours over the dangers of failure to accommodate one's marginality to the dominant system of bourgeois capitalism. In the economy of her verse, as in the wider Victorian economy epitomized by England's capital city, diversity is permitted, and even celebrated; in order to survive, however, all forms of miscellany must submit to the demands of the system.

★ ★ ★

In summation, then, close examination of writings by Sarah Williams reveals a woman of sharp intelligence and considerable wit. The extracts from her letters to her publishers demonstrate the poet's capacity for incisive and eloquent discussion. The poems themselves are dominated by her acute awareness of her impending death: her handling of the issues of class, gender and national identity in her poems are all informed by this perspective. Williams is a woman writer, but she is primarily a woman writer who is dying in agony. Her experience of constant suffering and impending death inflect the poet's consciousness in ways which determine not only the literary tropes at her command, but also her perspectives on a number of aspects of Victorian bourgeois culture. Whilst Williams addresses the English middle-class reader from a position of understanding and some complicity, her poems indicate doubts on a number of issues central to the value system of nineteenth-century society. Her personal ordeal provides the resources with which both to recognize and to give expression to concerns about the position of the disenfranchised, the dispossessed and those who suffer in terms of class, gender and national identities. In doing so the poet demonstrates ambivalence about the moral rightness of her own class, its social systems and its imperial aspirations.

6

Emily Jane Pfeiffer and the dilemma of progress

The writing of Emily Pfeiffer, who was born in 1827 and died in 1890, spanned the Victorian period. Pfeiffer's poetry offers an opportunity, therefore, to consider the responses of a woman writer to an era of rapid scientific and material progress, of imperial expansion, and above all of middle-class domination. This is an era which has been characterized by many historians as one of widespread triumphalism and complacency in the British upper and middle classes.[1] In this chapter I will examine Pfeiffer's work in terms of its contribution to an understanding of this period of unrivalled British prosperity. In Pfeiffer's sonnet 'A Chrysalis', published in 1880, the poet refers to the 'ebb and flow', the 'flux and reflux' of 'progress'; her use of tidal imagery connotes, I suggest, a sense of loss as well as gain, of effluent as well as production, of circularity, perhaps, rather than advancement. My analyses of Pfeiffer's poems will consider this apparent ambivalence towards the forces of economic, political and social amelioration taking place in mid-Victorian Britain. I will explore the ways in which Pfeiffer's subject position as a middle-class Welsh woman may mediate her experience and expression of these developments.

Born in Montgomeryshire, Emily Pfeiffer was Welsh on her mother's side; she was the daughter of an army officer named Davis with a passion for the arts, who had married into the wealthy Tilsley family of Milford Haven. At the time of Pfeiffer's birth, Davis was landowning and prosperous; however, during his daughter's childhood the bank in which Davis's money was invested collapsed, and the family found itself penniless. One consequence of this reversal of fortune was that Pfeiffer received no formal education; although encouraged to read, write and paint by both parents, this lack of prescribed erudition continued to influence her attitudes and actions as a woman and a writer throughout her life. When, at the age of sixteen, Pfeiffer published a volume of poetry entitled *The Holly Branch: An Album for 1843*, she was acutely conscious of the limitations imposed upon her by her family's predicament, prefacing the poems with an apologetic vindication of her own shortcomings based on the 'severe family affliction' which had hampered the progress of her work.[2] There is evidence to suggest that the young poet's self-abnegation was more significant than many such prefatory protestations, for she published nothing more for fourteen years until, after an exacting programme of self-tuition, *Valisnera: Or a Midsummer Day's Dream. A Tale* appeared in 1857. Later in life Pfeiffer became a fervent advocate for women's education, publishing a number of furious essays on the subject; and in her will she left £70,000 in trust for the advancement of women's higher education; the then University of South Wales and Monmouthshire applied successfully to the Pfeiffer Trust for funds to support the building of Aberdare Hall in Cardiff for the accommodation of women students.[3]

In 1853 the poet married a wealthy Anglo-German merchant, Jürgen Edward Pfeiffer. The marriage was apparently very happy, Pfeiffer's husband providing the financial and emotional support necessary to palliate the consequences of her childhood deprivations, and so to enable the relaunch of her writing career. Together the couple, though based in London, travelled widely; they also interested themselves in and supported a range of philanthropic concerns, including the aforesaid provision for women's education in Wales. Pfeiffer was devastated by her husband's death in 1889; she died a year later at the age of sixty-three. In the course of her writing career Pfeiffer published eleven volumes of poetry, a play in verse, two long essays on the position of women in education and work, and a number of shorter but similarly polemical contributions to the *Contemporary Review*. Pfeiffer's poetry met with considerable popular success and some favourable reviews. Some contemporary critics tended to damn her with the kind of faint and patronizing praise accorded to so many of her Victorian sisters, *The Times*, for example, allowing that 'Mrs Pfeiffer has shown that it is quite possible for a woman to write verse that shall be agreeable'.[4] The *Liverpool Albion*, by contrast, was more enthusiastic, declaring that '*Gerard's Monument* bears a closer resemblance to the greatest and most truly imaginative of Coleridge's poems than to the work of any more recent singers'.[5] Her work has received relatively little critical attention since then, although interest has revived more recently with the inclusion of a short selection of her poems in the collection edited by Angela Leighton and Margaret Reynolds in 1995, *Victorian Women Poets: An Anthology*.[6]

In her book *White, Male and Middle Class: Explorations in Feminism and History* Catherine Hall notes the ideological function of gender, in mid-to late nineteenth-century Britain, in the formation of middle-class claims to social power: 'the proper role of women was increasingly seen to be at home. The family was at the centre of Victorian middle-class social life and the fulcrum for the complex set of social values which comprised middle-class respectability.'[7]

As part of her project of examining this 'complex set of social values', and in constructing a feminist history of the nineteenth-century middle class, Hall devotes a chapter of her volume to a discussion of the importance of 'Race, Ethnicity and Difference'. She describes the mid- to late nineteenth century as 'the time when England could securely claim to lead the world in empire-building', and asserts that

> national identity was powerfully articulated by middle-class men in this period: men who claimed to speak for the nation and on behalf of others. Those men, however, lived in a society cross-cut by complex social and political antagonisms, not only those of class . . . but also of gender (which they silenced) and of race and ethnicity.[8]

Emily Pfeiffer's experience of prosperity and poverty, her declared feminism, and her support of women's causes suggest that readings of her poetry may generate useful material for a consideration of class and gender issues in the context of nineteenth-century women's writing. A number of poems in her oeuvre, however, are verse works which draw upon Welsh culture and use Welsh settings and characters, and these remain neglected by critics. Emily Pfeiffer is a woman writer whose biography suggests a strong emotional and moral commitment to the country of her birth, but who, nevertheless, lived much of her life in the English metropolis and who wrote for a predominantly English market during the heyday of nineteenth-century British imperial culture. An examination of Pfeiffer's Welsh poetry may, I suggest, allow analysis of the process of representation of the 'interrelations between class, gender and ethnicity' proposed by Catherine Hall, but one which is made more complex by a physical and psychological geography which places it at once within and beyond the dominant imperial culture.

★ ★ ★

In order to place Pfeiffer in relation to other women writers of the period, I begin by addressing her work in terms of the more familiar concerns of, first, gender and then class.

In their 1995 volume, *Victorian Women Poets: An Anthology*, Angela Leighton and Margaret Reynolds offer a brief selection from Pfeiffer's oeuvre, including her twin sonnets 'Peace to the Odalisque', in which the poet explores the slavery to which women have historically been subjected, and 'The Lost Light', her eulogy to George Eliot as 'Lost queen and captain, Pallas of our band'. Leighton and Reynolds highlight Pfeiffer's 'sceptical attitude towards the conduct of relations between the sexes'.[9] I offer my readings of Pfeiffer's poems, a number of which do not appear in the above-mentioned anthology, in order to add detail to this assertion by Leighton and Reynolds.

A number of recent feminist scholars have concerned themselves with exploring ways in which Victorian women writers have attempted to represent themselves as 'subjects of their own discourse' rather than objects of another's. Angela Leighton, for example examines the difficulties faced by the Victorian woman poet in articulating concerns about female subjectivity: 'Certainly, the many forms of self-encounter in Victorian women's poetry suggest a deep-rooted split in the very nature of the female self, as the poem tries to put together what the age has ideologically simplified or fragmented.'[10] In 'Longing and Asking', which appears in *Gerard's Monument and Other Poems*, Pfeiffer explores the idea of woman's divided self in terms of the draining demands of motherhood. The poem is constructed as a direct address to the speaker's dead mother. It opens:

> Mother, when we meet upon that shore,
> Where I too may hope to be at rest,
> Shall mine eyes behold me evermore,
> As my heart must ever love me best?
> Wilt thou claim me as I stand amaz'd
> While the veil still clogs my spirit-feet –
> Claim me with the mother-love that gaz'd
> From thy mortal eyes with such mild heat?
> Shall I owe thee sweet obedience then?
> Shall I pay thee back each foregone due?
> Shall I grow a child beneath thy ken?
> Or appear such haply in thy view?[11]

The first-person voice and rhetorical structure of these opening lines establish an emotional immediacy in the poem. The series of questions imitates the persistent rhythm of a child's litany of curiosity to her mother. The poet deploys the discourse of ownership in order to construct a female economy where selfless love accrues in the currency of the soul. The scheme of debt and repayment envisioned by the speaker in considering her mother's devotion is characterized as the mother's entitlement to the spirit of the child. The repetition of 'Wilt thou claim me . . . / Claim me with the mother love . . .', however, reads as an entreaty as much as a question; the speaker does not chafe over her mother's dominion, but rather craves its comfort. Later in the poem a contrast to this benign form of ownership is offered, as the speaker contemplates briefly, for the only occasion in the piece, the father figure: 'Oh, how short a time he thus possess'd thee – / He, the widow'd!'[12] The refusal to name the man, however, even as father, suggests the speaker's lack of emotional identification with this figure or his tragedy. The transient nature of the husband's possession is a marked counterpoint to the earlier depiction of the mother's eternal title over her child.

The speaker then focuses explicitly on the fragmented nature of a mother's experience:

> Could the heart within the mother's breast
> Keep on beating in one fix'd place?
> All day long she hears her children's voices, –
> Day or night they will not let her sleep;
> Far away with this one she rejoices, –
> Farther still with that one she must weep.
> Surely it were better she should go,
> Than live on with such divided life . . .[13]

Here the cost is detailed of the maternal empire of the soul, so celebrated in the opening lines. The woman whose body has given birth, it is suggested, cannot attain the spiritual wholeness necessary for worldly survival. It is the fragmented sense of self, engendered by the experience of mothering, which exhausts the woman to the point of death. This is clearly a challenge to the Victorian discourse of idealized motherhood, which defined maternal instinct as the essence of female nature and the ultimate goal of her self-fulfilment.[14] The speaker's consciousness of the inherent injustice and waste of this situation is clear; as in 'Martha Mary Melville', Pfeiffer repudiates the ethic of self-sacrifice of wifehood and, most radically, of motherhood itself, as viable life models. The speaker goes on to make a maudlin excursion of guilt, recognizing her own demands as contributing to the mother's demise:

> Ah, we too much wrong'd thee with our woe,
> Standing by, sweet mother, and true wife,

When the struggle which so rent thy frame,
God, in pity, made at last to cease.[15]

It seems to me that, although Pfeiffer may be justly accused here of the Victorian vice of oversentimentality, she is also making an important point about the way in which women internalize social definitions of gender roles. The speaker acknowledges her own complicity in the depletion of her mother's energies. The speaker is unable to suggest a solution to the paradox she has identified, namely that she loves and values her mother exactly because of the sacrifice the mother has made on her behalf. Both mother and daughter are shown to be trapped as objects and agents of the discourse which defines and destroys them. This act of recognition on the part of a daughter who is at once grateful to her mother and fearful of her own fate, however, may be read as an attempt to subvert the 'natural' status of social structures which condemn women to lives of physical and emotional subjugation.

But the Victorian ideal of motherhood, as of wifehood, was a product of class as well as gender ideology. I will now consider Pfeiffer's poetry in relation to class issues.

★ ★ ★

A number of feminist historians have examined the complex interplay between structures of class and gender in Victorian ideology. In her detailed study, *Uneven Developments: The Ideological Work of Gender in Mid-Victorian England*, Mary Poovey demonstrates how the constitution of gender relations 'helped depoliticize class relations at mid-century'.[16] In the mid-nineteenth century, middle-class dominance was at its height in British society; the middle class defined itself in opposition to the burgeoning working class, the landed gentry and the aristocracy. By the 1860s the entire political, economic and ideological system in Britain was defined in terms of middle-class wealth and general middle-class values; the queen, the aristocracy and Parliament all identified themselves with the bourgeois outlook.[17] Poovey offers readings of a range of literary and non-literary texts produced in the mid-nineteenth century, in order to examine the ways in which cultural representations of women supported both the middle class's economic power and its legitimation of this position.[18] In her study of the dominance of middle-class values in the period, Catherine Hall discusses the 'class-specific nature of masculinity and femininity' in Victorian ideology; she notes the way 'the limitations of middle-class femininity . . . leave very little space for the possibility of cross-class alliance'. Emily Pfeiffer's treatment of class relations in her poems provides useful exemplary material on which to base an examination of representations at the intersection of class and gender with which Poovey and Hall are concerned. In some cases the subversive potential of Pfeiffer's vision, significant, as I have argued, in the area of gender representation, is rather more ambivalent in her depiction of class identity.

Pfeiffer's work illustrates the divisive effects observed by Hall, for markedly few of the poems in Pfeiffer's oeuvre deal explicitly with relations between and among class groups. The poet shares with many of her contemporaries an interest in the distant past as literary resource. This may constitute an escapism on her part from contemporary tensions and power struggles, and an attempt to romanticize issues of social rank; the combination of her own privileged birth and luckless youth seems to have engendered in the poet a somewhat mawkish sensibility to class distinctions. In her historical pieces the poet's focus tends towards the experiences of the nobility, and her depictions of these characters is predominantly sentimental. In 'Martha Mary Melville', for example, the ancient and noble line of the Melvilles is emphasized, as is the family's honourable conduct towards its dependants. In this poem, however, although the immaculate bloodline of the Melvilles is reverenced throughout, it is a sad and lonely Mary who is left with her father, 'two Melvilles . . . / Content by their award to stand or fall'.[19] The limitations of noble birth and material wealth are highlighted in the poem; for Mary, growing old alone because of her honourable sacrifice, the privilege of her family line is shown to be cold comfort. In her shorter piece, 'The Love that Dares to Wait', to which I shall return in considering Pfeiffer's position as a Welsh writer, the poet also portrays an ancient and noble family, and, as in 'Martha Mary Melville', the poet depicts the price in human terms of inherited honour. Helen Mortimer, the high-born heroine, surrenders her lover in the name of duty. Having demonstrated the appropriate level of dignity under duress, and therefore having proved herself worthy of her bloodline in the only public manner available to her as a female Mortimer, Helen is rewarded when her father relents and calls the lover back. Both poems celebrate the chivalric code in heavily sentimentalized fashion; both construct the code as founded on the innate moral strength of its subjects; and both emphasize the personal sacrifice entailed in maintaining the burden of inherited nobility. Both poems also focus on the position of the female subject within the framework of this economy, formulated, as it is in both cases, by, and integral to the maintenance of, a fiercely patriarchal system. In 'Martha Mary Melville' women are shown to be commodities in the marriage market upon which the concept of inherited nobility depends. The character of Martha Mary exerts 'moral influence' upon her father by persuading him to secure Cissy's financial value in marriage, thus perpetuating the corrupt taxonomy which has destroyed her, and which is demonstrated to offer little emotional satisfaction to any of its subjects. In 'The Love that Dares to Wait', Helen Mortimer is similarly depicted as at the mercy of the aggressive and posturing patriarchal system which defines her and which, paradoxically, her experience is deployed to support and represent. Mary Poovey discusses the process by which bourgeois power was reinforced in the nineteenth century, noting that instead 'of being articulated upon inherited class position in the form of noblesse oblige, virtue was increasingly articulated upon gender'.[20]

Consolidation of middle-class ascendancy in the period required that the qualities of rectitude and integrity must be predicated upon factors the bourgeoisie could convincingly assert as its own. Virtue was thus relocated to the domestic sphere where middle-class women were seen as its source of nurture, preservation and, ultimately, representation. The influential work *Woman's Mission*, by Sarah Lewis, exemplifies the dominant Victorian concept of woman's moral power in society, asserting that 'it seems to be particularly a part of women's mission to exhibit Christianity in its beauty and purity, and to disseminate it by example and culture'.[21]

I have already analysed Pfeiffer's work in terms of her resistance to dominant representations of woman. I would argue that Pfeiffer's historical poems 'Martha Mary Melville' and 'The Love that Dares to Wait', in depicting a social organization which relies upon the separation of gender roles, also evidence the convergence within the ideology of sexual difference of the concepts of honour and that of woman's 'moral mission'. These pieces may be read, therefore, as, on the one hand, contributing to the process of bourgeois consolidation taking place in the period, and, at the same time, contesting the gendered foundation upon which that hegemony is based, and through which it is represented.

In her long poem 'From Out of the Night', Pfeiffer shifts her focus away from historical scenes of feudal society to a more contemporary setting; she also examines, more explicitly, the tensions inherent between sexual differentiation and class specificity during the Victorian period.

The speaker of 'From Out of the Night' is a young working-class woman who is seduced then deserted by her lover, a charming but feckless undergraduate. Whilst the exact class position of the lover's family is not specified, they are depicted as wealthy but ignoble; there is no suggestion in the piece that their status derives from true gentility, such as that of the Melvilles or the Mortimers. Lynda Nead has detailed the Victorian preoccupation with various forms of female sexual deviancy, particularly the prostitute and the fallen woman.[22] Nead discusses the 'narrative of the fallen woman as a pitiful social victim' which functioned in Victorian society as a mechanism for deconstructing the threat of her sexual deviance:

> If you feel sympathy rather than fear towards a group which challenges the dominant social order its power may be diffused. Pity deflects the force of that group and redistributes its power in terms of a conventional relationship organized around notions of social conscience, compassion and philanthropy.[23]

Nead, drawing on a Barthesian model of mythological representation, posits the image of the fallen woman as helpless victim as part of the narrative of 'Temptation − fall − decline and death' which 'posed the 'problem' of deviant femininity which was then resolved through the process of narration . . . across a range of representations and practices operating through specific institutions'. Nead's survey concentrates on medical, social and religious structures; clearly, literature presents an additional institutional apparatus through which such mythology may be propagated. Elizabeth K. Helsinger, Robin Lauterbach Sheets and William Veeder note a corresponding ascendancy in the second half of the nineteenth century of the fallen woman figure in literature. They trace a shift in attitudes towards the fallen woman as the century progresses:

> Fallen women in early Victorian fiction . . . tend to conform to traditional type. They are denied the role of protagonist and are subjected to the death mandatory for women with extramarital relationships. What is potentially subversive about presenting such women appears in 1850 when a 'Magdalen' at last becomes a heroine . . . Despite the mandatory death Elizabeth Gaskell inflicts upon her fallen heroine, Ruth, she shows enough sympathy with unorthodox attitudes to spark immediate and extensive controversy.[24]

Pfeiffer's ruined heroine, who appears in 1876, is clearly of the second category. The poem ends with the speaker's suicide as she throws herself into the river, fallen literally and metaphorically. But, although punished for her transgression with ignominy and death, the speaker's moral status heightens as her material torture moves towards its climax. As Margaret Reynolds observes:

> The poem elevates the fallen woman to a saintly status, even going so far as to compare her to Christ . . . In giving her this sanctified role Pfeiffer follows the cleaning-up device used also by Procter in 'A Legend of Provence' and Elizabeth Barrett Browning in *Aurora Leigh*.[25]

As the speaker's martyrdom reaches its ritual culmination, so the pace and tone of her monologue achieve a peak of melodramatic declamation:

> Yet the world is all blurred as with tears: I am looking my last;
> I can still hear its moan, though the worst of its sorrow is dumb; –
> Farewell to the glimmer of lamps that grow pale in the blast,
> And the clock that will measure the time when my times shall be past!–
> See, he opens his arms – O my River-God, clasp me, I come![26]

The pathos, somewhat heavy for early twenty-first-century taste perhaps, seems rather laboured here, as the poet attempts to assert her heroine's integrity. And yet the piece demonstrates Pfeiffer's deftness of touch in her tonal manipulation of the dramatic monologue form. The speaker's descent into suicidal madness is rendered through a series of increasingly abrupt shifts backwards and forwards among a series of addressees; movements take place from reader, to self, to lost love, to her lover's new bride, the speaker's hysteria increasing with each shift. She finally feels herself caught between the river and life itself:

> What is done between us, river, must be seen by us alone.
> You are watching for me, waiting, let me be, my flesh recoils;
> What are you that you should sentence me – what evil have I done?
> You have ever been my fate; you have and hold me in your toils;
> Yet, O life, I cannot live you, with your fevers and turmoils;
> Come and take me, lest it find me at the rising of the sun.[27]

The poet metaphorizes the river, here, as her judge and lurking executioner, and as the bridegroom who is soon to 'have and hold' her, the speaker's madness thus expressing the elements of sexual transgression, marital promise and social condemnation which have combined to generate its own existence. In Pfeiffer's depiction, as in the case of Gaskell's Ruth and Barrett Browning's Marian Erle, the fallen woman is certainly constructed as the victim of an unscrupulous lover, and, by implication, of the prevalent double standard of sexual morality in Victorian society. In accordance with Nead's thesis, then, the poem can be read as a minor contributory strand in the narrative of 'Temptation – fall – decline and death' which served to neutralize the threatening power of the sexually transgressive woman. I would suggest, however, that 'From Out of the Night' is a text which at least complicates such an interpretation.

A characteristic theme of Victorian women's poetry, as I have already asserted, is that of the female speaker's or protagonist's search for self-identity. This quest may take many symbolic forms; Angela Leighton has identified one of the most common motifs as that of the meeting between heroine and other, 'usually figured as the fallen woman'.[28] Leighton cites Barrett Browning's *Aurora Leigh* and Christina Rossetti's *Goblin Market* as examples of this trend, 'both of which turn the idea of philanthropic rescue-work into something much more like a love story between women'.[29] In Pfeiffer's poem this meeting between pure and impure female figures occurs twice, in reality between the speaker and her lover's mother and in fantasy between the discarded mistress and the new bride:

> As he knelt before the altar with that woman at his side,
> Dressed in cobwebs spun in cellars where the spinners' eyes grow dim;
> How the devils in their triumph yelled aloud and drowned the hymn,
> When they lifted up the cobwebs and his mother kissed the bride.
>
> Hush, the river must not know that I had ever seen her face,
> Must not know she came and found me when my torturers had fled;
> Hah! for me she had no kiss, but sat aloof in pride of race,
> Though I yearned to her – his mother – till she offered me a place
> In the service of the living, never noting I was dead.[30]

The construction of 'From Out of the Night' through the first-person voice of the ruined heroine herself suggests an interesting variation on Leighton's observation that the fallen-woman motif represents a 'meeting between self and other'. In this case the first-person articulation forces an intense and immediate identification between speaker, poet and reader. The poet, and by implication the reader, is the fallen woman in this poem. This is a device which exceeds the self-exploratory potential of the more confrontational 'meetings' figured by either Barrett Browning or Rossetti, and, arguably renders the piece more radical in terms of class and gender analyses than *Aurora Leigh* or *Goblin Market*.

The speaker of 'From Out of the Night' observes her lover's wedding, and it is the distinction of class between herself and the bride which attracts her most bitter resentment. The bride's garment has been produced at the cost of the eyesight of many other women, who are ill-housed for their toil. The gossamer beauty of her gown has been born out of the drudgery of those who are afforded, for their skill and effort, no more value than the spiders which spin, unnoticed, beside them. The meeting depicted between the speaker and her lover's mother is also located in a tirade against class divisions, as the speaker recalls the older woman's visit, in which the inducement was offered of secure work in service in order to obtain her silence and submission. The mother is described as 'aloof in pride of race', unwilling to connect with the speaker physically or emotionally; her rigidity is situated by the speaker in a fundamental and deeply ingrained class-consciousness which conceives of the lower-born woman as belonging to an inferior breed.

The meeting between the speaker and her lover's new bride takes place in a strange region where memory and imagination merge, but it is informed by the earlier confrontation with the mother. The speaker recalls witnessing the marriage of her lover and fantasizes that she is speaking to the new bride:

> And she will be a growing power and potency, the years –
> The treacherous years will take her part and ravish him from me,
> And she will make a title out of daily smiles and tears,
> And will pass to a fuller blessedness through weakness which endears,
> And I shall be as one forbid before I cease to be.
>
> O thou blessed among women more than all of women born!
> Be my sister, be my comforter; nay wherefore cold and proud?
> We are bound as in one web of Fate, the garland that was worn
> Of thee to-day, but yestere'en from off my brows was torn,
> And that costly bridal robe of thine must serve me for a shroud.[31]

The device of oscillating address, here between self and her lover's bride, is once again used to evoke the speaker's emotional turmoil. In the first stanza quoted above the repetition of 'And' at the beginning of lines one, three, four and five serves to heighten the agitated tone and increasingly frantic pace of the diatribe. Repetition through hyphenated enjambement – 'the years – / The treacherous years' – adds to the impression of distracted agitation. The speaker's vision of her rival's future, secure and flourishing, is expressed in terms of an inherited sovereignty rather than earned respect. The bride will gain 'power and potency' by virtue of her mere presence over 'treacherous years'; she will 'make a title out of daily smiles and tears' and hence consolidate her position through the trivia of her privileged existence. The concepts of legitimacy and entitlement are problematized here in terms of moral and emotional justice. The emphasis on authority and entitlement offers a critique of the precarious species of power which is gained only vicariously through the fickle favour of a potentially unreliable husband. The bride has been given by one man to another; her presence in the marriage, ironically, provides financial security for her husband and his family; her emotional security depends on pleasing him through a 'weakness which endears'. The tone of the speaker's assessment of the new bride is scathing; the rival is constructed as feeble and undeserving, and the speaker's awareness of the vulnerability of the bride's position is overwhelmed by the bitterness and anger engendered by the desperation of her own circumstances. The poem thus challenges the concept of inherited privilege which supersedes systems founded in notions of moral merit.

The 'meeting' between fallen and pure female figures, which Leighton identifies as often representing in Victorian women's poetry 'a love story between women', occurs here rather differently. The speaker meets the new bride only in her imagination, and the confrontation which takes place is far from loving. The stanza begins by echoing the rhythm and diction of the 'Hail Mary', the supplicant's prayer to the mother of Christ.[32] The speaker entreats the bride to provide the motherhood promised by the iconography of St Mary, and the sisterhood depicted, for example, by Barrett Browning in *Aurora Leigh*, and more explicitly by Rossetti in *Goblin Market*. But in the speaker's fantasy the other woman rejects all connection with her impure counterpart, while the juxtaposition of the expectation of saintly and sisterly bonding with distinctly un-madonna-like and unsisterly qualities of coldness and pride indicates the poet's interest in the social and material distance between the two figures. When Pfeiffer deploys the favoured Victorian trope of a clash between the pure and impure bride, it is the fallen woman who holds the moral ascendancy and the reader's sympathy, whilst the pure bride's legal title to the role of wife is tainted with the stain of injustice and violence. In a direct reversal of the device used, for example, by Charlotte Brontë in *Jane Eyre*, Pfeiffer's 'true' but fallen bride sees her wedding veil brutally usurped by her chaste counterpart.[33] And tellingly, in an echo of the earlier scene, it is the economics of the situation which are located so as to draw maximum end-weighted emphasis in the stanza: 'And that costly bridal robe of thine must serve me for a shroud.' The vanity and comfort of the wealthy woman is purchased, then, at the cost of the life of her underprivileged counterpart. Though it is possible to read Pfeiffer's reversal of moral influence in 'From Out of the Night' as an inevitable result of her choosing to speak from the fallen woman's point of view, it is also clear that the moral integrity of the speaker is asserted throughout and remains intact, despite her eventual suicide.

Nead's argument that the image of the fallen woman as victim is a component of the repressive machinery of Victorian patriarchy is clearly problematized by a consideration of women's writing of the period. Critics such as Leighton and Reynolds have demonstrated that the fallen-woman figure in women's poetry may be read as symbolic of the expression of a range of forbidden desires. Helsinger, Lauterbach Sheets and Veeder have seen such contributions, more optimistically, as forcing middle-class men and women to 'face more honestly their responsibilities for the sexual ills of society and to view more humanely the passions which woman shares with man'.[34]

My reading of Pfeiffer's 'From Out of the Night' suggests that this is a woman writer who is interested in issues of class as well as of gender. Her depiction of the fallen woman indicates hostility between women, arising from inequities of class. The familiar theme of philanthropic rescue, noted by Leighton, is transmuted in this poem into a cold and patronizing exchange in which the fallen woman retains the moral high ground in the act of relinquishing all hope of worldly survival. Pfeiffer's heroine remains too angry and too justified to be easily assimilated into Nead's model of submissive decline; similarly the poet's concentration on class distance over gender commonality renders the poem difficult to read as an encoded exploration of female desire. Pfeiffer's deployment of the fallen-woman figure in this poem, I would argue, uses female sexual transgression as a vehicle through which to effect a critique of the unjust social system which subjugates women as much through material poverty as through gendered moral hypocrisy. In depicting the limited possibility for cross-class alliance among women, Pfeiffer asserts the ethical and social imperative of challenge to the edifice of Victorian patriarchal ideologies.

In a comparative reading of Pfeiffer's poems 'Martha Mary Melville' and 'The Love that Dares to Wait', and of her more contemporary depiction of cross-class relations in 'From Out of the Night', it is possible to detect a somewhat paradoxical attitude to the issue of class identity. I have discussed the poet's interrogation of gender roles in Victorian bourgeois patriarchy; in terms of class representation it is possible to argue that Pfeiffer does not fully identify with middle-class values as such, but neither is it possible to locate her position as unequivocally subversive. On the one hand, 'Martha Mary Melville' and 'The Love that Dares to

Wait' can be read as far more reactionary in terms of class politics than in those of gender. Martha Mary Melville and Helen Mortimer, whilst symbolic of problematic issues of culturally defined gender polarities, are nevertheless presented as honourable and attractive representatives of inherited social privilege. Both characters martyr themselves in order to preserve the moral high ground of the nobility's adherence to duty. By contrast, in 'From Out of the Night' it is the working-class woman who is depicted as the only martyr and victim of the hierarchical social system. The male lover, of indeterminate high-class position, ruins the heroine; his mother and bride are depicted as smugly privileged and self-serving, hypocritical in their endorsement of the sexual double standard and heartless in their condemnation of the fallen woman. Generally Pfeiffer's sympathies tend to lie, then, with either the old gentry class or the social underdog. It is possible that these contradictory impulses in Pfeiffer's approach to class issues may spring from her personal class status. Pfeiffer was descended from the venerable and landed Tilsley family, whose fortune was lost through an inability to deal effectively with the tide of Victorian capitalism. It is perhaps inevitable, then, that her affinity should lie with the old families, gentlefolk in terms of birth rather than wealth. Another possibility is that Pfeiffer's sense of her Welsh identity may have engendered in her a distance from the middle-class values of Victorian Britain. In his book *Mid-Victorian Wales: The Observers and the Observed*, Ieuan Gwynedd Jones notes the absence in Wales during the period of 'an integrated, self-conscious middle class'.[35] Certainly the rise of the middle class in Britain is associated with English as opposed to Celtic historical development. It may well be, then, that Pfeiffer's ambivalence towards the bourgeois ideologies of Victorian Britain is rooted in her Welshness as well as her womanhood. I turn now to a more detailed analysis of this aspect of the poet's work.

★ ★ ★

I have already examined ways in which Emily Pfeiffer's work may be read as interrogating the dominant middle-class and patriarchal ideology of Victorian Britain; as Catherine Hall notes, however, an integral component of that middle-class ethos was the celebration of a species of English/British national identity 'powerfully articulated by middle-class men . . . who claimed to speak for the nation and on behalf of others'.[36] Mary Poovey explores the ways in which the Victorian ideology of gendered difference was deployed in order to authorize not only the bourgeois dominance in terms of Britain's legal and social relations, but also to legitimize its imperial project.[37] Pfeiffer's position as Welsh by blood and birth, combined with her long residence in London and her success as a writer for the English literary market, suggest that an examination of her poetry on Welsh topics may offer an interesting site for an exploration of the place and function of the woman writer in the construction of national identity in both Welsh and British contexts. Pfeiffer certainly demonstrates an interest in life at the Celtic margins of British culture. Her collections of poetry contain a number of works which feature settings and characters in Scotland and Wales: for example on 'On Loch Katrine', 'Among the Hebrides' and 'Martha Mary Melville' all celebrate Scottish landscape and culture. 'The Love that Dares to Wait' does not explicitly refer to Wales, but focuses on the noble Mortimer family 'of a race that heralds glory'; the Mortimers are cited by Gwyn A. Williams in his volume *When Was Wales?* as having 'Welsh connections of long duration'.[38] Williams also traces the Mortimers' Welsh connections back to twelfth-century English colonial origins which embraced 'much of the best land and expropriat[ed] much of the potential for growth'.[39] In Pfeiffer's poem, the Mortimers appear to have been appropriated as a Welsh dynasty which, although used to problematize gender and class relations, as already discussed, is presented as heroic in terms of its ethnic identity.

In examining Pfeiffer's poems in relation to her position as a Welsh poet, it is important to consider the context of Victorian Wales against which she was writing. By the 1860s the process of immense political upheaval which had characterized Welsh society throughout the Victorian period had arrived at a point where 'political demonstrations were of an unprecedented kind; relatively peaceful, orderly and constitutional where before they had often been violent and disruptive'.[40] Ieuan Gwynedd Jones discusses the political impetuses which had brought about this profound change. He locates the Chartist rising in Newport in 1839 as a watershed in relations between Wales and the English government:

> Already by the summer of 1839 Chartism was a mass movement in industrial south Wales and the region was seething with unrest. Lord John Russell, Liberal Home Secretary . . . attributed the disorder to a fundamental lack of a proper system of education designed to deal with the challenge it posed.[41]

The Welsh language was identified as a particular problem in controlling the Welsh, especially in the aftermath of the Rebecca Riots, which had taken place throughout the early 1840s, when the rioters had managed to evade their pursuers more successfully by communicating in Welsh. Hence the emphasis on education as a means of propagating the English language and consequently 'civilizing' the unruly inhabitants of Wales. In 1846 the English government sent its inspectors to Wales in order to investigate the educational system which seemed to be the cause of so much trouble; in 1847 the report entitled *Reports of the Commissioners of Inquiry into the State of Education in Wales* was published. The report not only condemned the appallingly retarded system of education in Wales, but also denounced its inhabitants as generally uncivilized and uncouth. In particular, Welsh women were accused of sexual profligacy. The Reverend John Griffith, Anglican vicar of Aberdare and witness to the commissioners, was quoted thus: 'Nothing can be lower, I would say degrading, than the character in which the women stand relative to the men. Promiscuous intercourse is most common, is thought of as nothing, and the women do not lose caste by it.'[42] Welsh women's lax morality was taken as confirmation of the urgent need to civilize the Welsh. This in turn provided the English with justification for increased involvement in administering Welsh affairs, and particularly in ridding the country of its obstructive attachment to the Welsh language.

Ieuan Gwynedd Jones explores the way in which the publication of the report affected the political life of the country. The process he describes is a complex one, but, in general terms, the effects of the 1847 report upon Welsh self-confidence were devastating, resulting, in part, in the more disciplined political and social conduct witnessed from the 1860s and thereafter. It is against this background of turmoil and change that Emily Pfeiffer chose to publish her poems on Welsh topics.

In 1877, whilst still basking in the glow of critical and popular enthusiasm with which *Gerard's Monument* had been received a year earlier, Pfeiffer published an epic poem in blank verse entitled *Glan-Alârch: His Silence and Song*. The poem, as its author indicates in her 'Preface', depicts an ancient bardic culture, which is chosen, she claims, in order to reveal universal truths with resonance to her contemporary, and mainly English readership:

I have chosen a remote historic epoch for my subject; but in dealing with it, I have tried to penetrate beneath the veil of chivalry, which, however fair, I feel to be still a veil, to the homelier life which it in part conceals from us; and by the help of the few facts we possess, and the indications supplied by race, to revivify a typical moment of the past which lies at the heart of the present through which we are living, and the future to which we aspire.[43]

In view of this declaration of intent, the tone and content of the poem which follows is somewhat surprising; for *Glan-Alârch: His Silence and Song* is an overtly racist piece which vilifies the English as a breed, and may be read as an attempt to goad the Welsh into violent struggle against colonial oppression. More surprising still is the enthusiastic welcome which the piece received from the English press. The *British Quarterly* praises the poem for its 'vigorous picture' and 'profound lessons'. Being entirely convinced by Pfeiffer's preamble, the critic remarks: 'There is a powerful narrative bringing into relief a state of society and of manners very remote.'[44] None of the numerous positive reviews notices the anti-English sentiments expressed in the 'very ingenious plot'[45] or 'passages of great beauty'[46] of which *Glan-Alârch: His Silence and Song* is composed. A close reading of the poem in terms of its depictions of Welsh and English identities illustrates the scale of Pfeiffer's feat in achieving popular and critical success with its publication.

Glan-Alarch: His Silence and Song is set in an early medieval historical period; Pfeiffer is therefore describing a country which is in the process of being colonized. The Acts of Union, negotiated during the sixteenth century, established the rights of the Welsh to parity with the English under the law; before that, however, and during the period in which *Glan-Alarch: His Silence and Song* is placed, Wales was colonized by the Saxons (and later by the Normans) through processes of physical and legislative brutality. In locating her poem in a period of colonial aggression, Pfeiffer establishes a moral and ethical basis for her call to arms.

The poem opens in a flourish of fairly conventional Celtic colour, as the old bard Glan-Alârch marks the passing of time and his waning strength and talent:

> I am the bard Glan-Alârch, he who sings
> Beneath the morning cloud which wraps Crag Eryri
> Who basks upon his sun-kiss'd side at noon,
> And sleeps with him in silence when his crown -
> A beacon fire whose message hath been sped -
> Fades on the east where he prolonged the day.
> I am the bard Glan-Alârch, he whose day of life
> Is likewise hasting to its close . . .[47]

The bard acknowledges his declining life force, but, unlike many such nineteenth-century poetic renderings, his deterioration is not symbolic, here, of the degeneration of the culture he represents. Welsh culture is depicted as a still powerful force, and its reach, it is implied, extends to political as well as spiritual efficacy:

But not in sadness will I quench my song:
For joy still lives, if not for old Glan-Alârch
And pride of strength; what though its fountains rise
From other springs than his, – its droppings reach
Him in his drouth; and there is light in heaven
For him and every poorest thing that breathes;
And bardic fire for me, which, when it burns,
Mine ancient house still glows with deathless youth![48]

Immediately, then, the depiction of Welshness suggests an ancient and continuing tradition of poetry and power. If the poem is to be read as part of the Welsh 'invention of tradition',[49] its opening lines indicate a heroic version of history which is at once generative and self-sustaining. As an example of what Hall describes as 'disruptive relations of ethnicity', the extract presents evidence that such work may provide ample textual fabric through which to 'unpick the stories which gave meaning to the national and imperial project'.[50]

As the poem moves on, however, the reader is introduced to a motley cast of Welsh characters who serve to undercut the heroic resonances of the early passage; these include Eurien, the young lord; Mona, an Irish girl adopted by Eurien's family to whom he is betrothed; and the rather villainous members of his court – Weroc ('whom no man loved')[51] and his henchman Cynorac ('widows were his spoil').[52] Various allegiances and petty disputes between these figures are depicted in a long preamble to the main action, until, some thirty-seven pages into the poem, the true villains of the piece are revealed, at which point the vagaries of the assorted Welsh personalities pale into insignificance. A messenger delivers the news to the assembled lordly household that 'twelve hundred monks of Bangor' have been slain at their altar by 'the brutal Saxon Ethelfrith'.[53] The description of the massacre is melodramatic, the condemnation is passionate and, interestingly, located firmly in issues of race and territory:

The brutal Saxon Ethelfrith, the leader of
The vile scum which makes our wholesome borders
A foul morass, from out his swinish sleep
Awakened by the voices of these saints
Rising on morning breath with fragrant thyme
And all sweet savour of the dawning day
Cried out
'These monks, they fight us with their prayers,
Which we make bold to answer with our swords!'[54]

The identification of the perpetrator of this atrocity is founded on a bloodthirsty epithet which qualifies his race, with his name appearing as an afterthought; this device clearly mitigates the earlier boorish behaviour of several of the Welsh characters: the Welsh are only human, is the implication, but the English by contrast are more savage than beasts. The language in the passage juxtaposes the notion of domain with that of pollution; Welsh territory is distinct, legitimate and hygienic, until infiltration by the 'vile scum' renders the same marginal area an unclean, malodorous bog. Welsh identity, as defined by the parameters of its geographic jurisdiction, thus becomes blurred and equivocal the moment that territory is compromised by the Saxon invaders.

The bard's interjection which follows the revelation of the massacre is telling. The event is depicted as being the cause of the cultural vacuum which the poem itself in part attempts to fill:

> Our ancient Bangor levelled and despoiled,
> The records of our learning and our pride, –
> The story of the years that are no more, –
> Lapsed into sullen silence for all time![55]

The passage is clearly resonant of Glan-Alârch's first speech, in a direct reversal of the optimistic declarations there of continuity and strength. The sense of cultural and political potential described in the opening lines of the poem is entirely quenched here by the loss of historical archives, and it is this deprivation which outweighs in significance the deaths of over a thousand saintly monks:

> The God-worn flame of thought, inherited
> And fed by us to light the world to come,
> Blown out, with nought but ashes left to darken
> The storm, or trodden dust for us to heap –
> Heap on the mountain of our huge despair![56]

Prys Morgan notes the fact that 'Wales did not have a network of learned or academic institutions to check and balance myths and inventions with criticism. The reader and the writer could not hunt for the past symmetrically together.'[57] Pfeiffer alludes, in this passage, to the deficiency which both necessitates and allows her own intervention. In so doing so she appears to legitimize and contribute to the project of inventing a Welsh tradition; at the same time she produces a rupture in the nineteenth-century fabric of seamless Englishness. Another factor at work here is that of Christianity: Pfeiffer's poem is set during the post-Roman, pre-Norman period, when the Celts had been converted to Christianity but the Saxons had not.[58] The ancient learning which Pfeiffer depicts the Bangor priests failing to protect is therefore Christian as well as Welsh. In my chapter on Felicia Hemans I have discussed the importance of the Christian mission to nineteenth-century British understanding of the imperial drive. Pfeiffer's English audience may well have found it easy, then, to identify with the Welsh Britons in their struggle against Saxon pagans. In her construction of religious history Pfeiffer thus secures the complicity of her English readers in asserting the seniority and spiritual integrity of the Welsh Christian tradition.

The poem continues, however, with a depiction of misjudgement and indecision on the part of the Welsh lords, which compounds the cultural and political damage inflicted by Saxon villainy. The Irish maiden, Mona, stands as the voice of passionate nationalism, whose opinions are rejected, to the ultimate cost of her adoptive Welsh kin. As Eurien counsels caution, Mona's tirade is ironic and scathing:

'Forget your olden glory, ye men of Glyneth,
Cast the torch from the armed right hand ere it flickers or fails,
Stamp it out and end the story, O men of Glyneth,
Let Cambria fall like a stronghold that treasure assails,
And in tears of your shame shall your land be re-christened wild Wales!'

Wales, Wales, wild Wales! She ended with that cry,
A cry to haunt the memory, and to bring
Tears to the eyes in lieu of sleep at night.
Wales, Wales, wild Wales! Her hearers knew full well
The land she sung of was the bleeding heart
Of Britain, Britain mangled by the foe,
Torn limb from limb, the parts still quick with life,
Throbbing in all sad corners of the earth.[59]

The Irish character, here, is the prophetic voice which foretells the fall of Wales as a political, cultural and linguistic reality. She envisions suicidal capitulation which will result in the 'end of the story', already 'lapsed into silence' by English aggression; the narrative of Welsh history is seen as curtailed by the colonial experience. The annihilation of Wales is symbolized in its relinquishment of the capacity to name itself: Cambria becomes Wales, its identity subsumed by domination which is founded in naked English bellicosity, but exacerbated by Welsh torpidity. In figuring

Wales as 'the bleeding heart / Of Britain, Britain mangled by the foe', the poet draws on the notion of Britain as the land of the Ancient Britons, to whom the Anglo-Saxons are the enemy. She thus asserts kinship between Mona's valiant Irish people and the Welsh, and at the same time claims an ancient ethical precedent for the legitimacy of Welsh cultural identity. The representation of the Irish character, Mona, as encouraging the Welsh to revolt had additional political significance in 1877. Irish nationalist agitation was a thorn in the side of the English government throughout the mid-Victorian period. Any suggestion that the Welsh might be incited to emulate the rebellious Irish would have been perceived as threatening to the middle-class English establishment of the time. Pfeiffer's use of an Irish figure in this context is further evidence of her impulse to construct for herself an identity which articulates her sense of Welshness and the subversive potential of its marginality. It also renders all the more remarkable Pfeiffer's success in gaining wide applause for the poem in the context of mid-Victorian British culture.

A choric intervention by the bard follows Mona's lyric. Whereas Mona has provided the regretful voice of Celtic nationalism, Glan-Alârch himself assumes the position here of the 'British' overview. Once again, Pfeiffer is making a historical reference to the pre-Anglo-Saxon meaning of British here. Glan-Alârch speaks as an authentic Welsh Briton. The imagery used to express the bard's despair is physiological. Britain is metaphorized as a living body, symbol of organic interdependence, with Wales its 'bleeding heart'. The body of Britain is seen as having been ripped apart by 'the foe' which can be read in this context only as the Anglo-Saxon colonizing impulse.

From this perspective the colonization and Anglicization of Wales results in the violent destruction of an authentic British identity. Pfeiffer 'invents' a Welsh tradition in this poem, which draws attention to the practice it undertakes; it sets up a model of heroic bardic culture early on, only to undermine it in later passages, culminating in Mona's lacerating lyric quoted above. At the same time Pfeiffer posits the view that the Welsh can be seen as somewhat inadequate defenders of the Christian faith against the Saxon pagans. In so far as her nineteenth-century audience believed that Britishness was synonymous with Christianity, the poem would have been read as saying that Britain depended on Wales.

When, in her 'Preface', Pfeiffer declares her intention to 'revivify a typical moment of the past which lies at the heart of the present . . . and the future to which we aspire', it seems to me that she is indicating her interest in articulating the inadequacies of the available English/British identity in expressing her own complex sense of self. *Glan-Alârch: His*

Silence and Song suggests that Pfeiffer's work may be read as concerned less with constructing a satisfying Welsh tradition than with attempting to invent a British tradition which is based on Welshness. As such, I would argue that the piece offers convincing fuel for the argument, propounded by Catherine Hall, that the notion of English as a universal norm through which all parts of Britain may be represented is unsatisfactory. Pfeiffer's work is all the more valuable in these terms, I suggest, because it supplements Hall's restricted evidence with insights into the experiences of a white minority culture.

The other major work in Pfeiffer's oeuvre which deals with Welsh characters and themes is her verse 'Drama of Modern Life' *The Wynnes of Wynhavod*, published in 1882. This is an eccentric text, which draws on the Victorian theatrical vogue for melodrama. The play is sensational in plot and incident, complete with gun-wielding villain, dashing hero and proud but delicate heroine. It is also, like *Glan-Alârch: His Silence and Song*, extremely critical in its portrayal of the English as opposed to the Saxons. In this later text, however, the poet's condemnation of English colonial aggression is less sustained. In a work which surrenders rigorous political argument to the demands of a lurid storyline, Pfeiffer casts English figures as both heroes and villains of the piece. *The Wynnes of Wynhavod* tells the story of the beautiful Winifred Wynne and her brother, the noble Mostyn, who are the rightful heirs to the Wynhavod estate in Flintshire. Wynhavod has been acquired 'for a song' by the ruthless English businessman Sir Pierce Thorne, the Wynne family having fallen upon hard times. Mostyn and Winifred have vowed to devote their youth and strength to earning enough money to buy back Wynhavod and restore to the inheritance its proper Welsh stewardship. The convoluted plot includes a trumped-up charge of theft against Mostyn, Winifred's kidnap by the villainous English banker, Robert Murdoch, the much-tested true love between Winifred and Sir Pierce's disinherited son, Norman, and the intervention of a Welsh hound named Gelert. Needless to say, in the tradition of Victorian melodrama, virtue is rewarded in the play and all is resolved happily: Winifred and Norman marry, Robert thoughtfully commits suicide, and Wynhavod is restored to the Wynnes.

The moral high ground is located firmly with the Welsh characters in the text. At the beginning of the play, with the exception of Norman, all of the English characters are depicted as unattractive, at best. Sir Pierce's purchase of Wynhavod, though accomplished within the law, is depicted as an act of profiteering opportunism which privileges percentage return over considerations of history and humanity:

SIR PIERCE:

Did you say Wynne?

Welshmen have not many names,
And this is one of them. My place in Flintshire
Is called Wynhavod, and was once the seat
Of some of them. I bought it for a song.

ROBERT MURDOCH:

A song that was a threnody to them.

SIR PIERCE:

Aye, aye, I think it was. I got the homestead
And some few hundred acres, as I say,
For nearly nothing; paid the mortgage off,
And bought up all the land that used of old
To go with it . . .
That was a chance,

Seemly, safe and seasonable. There,
You have my motto . . .[60]

Sir Pierce's relationship with his sensitive and honourable son Norman is
ruined by Norman's insistence on immersing himself in European culture,
rather than business, when sent to Germany at his father's expense.
Tensions between father and son reach breaking point when Norman
announces on his return that he wishes to become a poet:

SIR PIERCE:

Mad! mad! – I thought it. Hah! poor fool! Poor father!

An only son, who might have had the world
Grovelling before him on bare knees. A POET!![61]

Robert Murdoch, the most depraved of Pfeiffer's English scoundrels in
the text, displays distinctly anti-Semitic tendencies. Carteret, one of
Robert Murdoch's companions, is in debt to Jewish bankers. Robert
refers to Carteret's creditors as 'cormorants [who] had picked him clean',

assuring Carteret that, providing he complies with Robert's dastardly plan to win the heart of Winifred, he 'will start you / As free a Gentile as if every Jew / Were gone to meet the eldest-born of Egypt'.[62] Relentless English commercialism, philistinism and anti-Semitism is thus established, early on, to be contrasted later in the text with Welsh devotion to music and poetry, embodied in the figure of Dafyth, the harper of Wynhavod. Dafyth is first encountered enduring the taunts of Sir Pierce's footmen. Interestingly, in addition to his credentials as musician and poet, Dafyth also boasts impressive Jewish connections:

FIRST FOOTMAN:

How, now, Taffy?

DAFYTH:

Dafyth's my name, which, being interpreted
Means David. We've been harpers, man and boy,
Since Wales became dry land, and Dwygifylchy
Rose from the flood.

SECOND FOOTMAN:

You chose a poor trade, Taffy.

DAFYTH:

Dafyth, I say! The name is well beknown;
One of my ancestors stood godfather
To Dafyth, King of Israel.[63]

In this scene the poet makes comic capital out of the supposed tendency of the Welsh towards obsession with their illustrious ancestors.[64] This humorous exchange sees the ill-mannered English servant deflating Dafyth's pretensions to grandeur by reducing his vocation to the level of failed commerce, referring to it as a 'poor trade'.

Within the parameters of the drama, however, Englishness is recovered to a certain degree of honour, though not without the improving influence of the Welsh, or the cleansing effects of Robert Murdoch's violent death. Winifred and Mostyn regain Wynhavod when Sir Pierce suffers a stroke and is shocked into reconciliation with his son. Realizing Norman's love for Winifred, Sir Pierce gifts Wynhavod to them; Norman

immediately hands over the management of the estate to Mostyn, much
to the grateful delight of both Winifred and Mostyn. Thus the land in
Wales passes into the stewardship of the Welsh, but remains the property
of powerful English patrons; and this state of affairs is welcomed by the
Welsh characters as the sought-after happy ending.

Interestingly, knowing Norman's distaste for capitalist acquisitiveness,
Sir Pierce convinces his son to accept the estate by explaining that
Wynhavod was a legacy to Norman from his dead mother:

SIR PIERCE:

Take this. See, here, her hand and deed, Wynhavod,
And all the land belonging thereunto,
Bought with her money, pure of any stain
From mine; her money and her father's, gathered
God knows from what foul quarries long ago,
But cleansed, maybe, by wholesome use.[65]

Pfeiffer makes a distinction here between commerce founded on the toil
of English hands on, presumably, English land, and the species of colonial
capital accumulation which wrests land and profit from its historical
Welsh owners. She also establishes a moral contrast based on gender-
difference. The maternal inheritance is free from the taint of colonial
aggression. Sir Pierce forgoes the tasty financial turnover he had been
anticipating and Wynhavod is safe in Mostyn's Welsh hands once more.
Moreover, Wynhavod is returned to the Wynnes in a better condition
than that in which it was lost. Through the 'pure' mechanics of this form
of non-aggressive gain, the estate is both restored and improved. This
conclusion carries a consolatory meaning in terms of Welsh relations with
England. Pfeiffer's message in the play is, ultimately, I would argue, to
reconcile the Welsh to 'marriage' with England.

Clearly, *The Wynnes of Wynhavod* is too bizarre a text on which to base
a systematic analysis of Pfeiffer's sense of her Welshness. Taken with the
evidence of *Glan-Alârch: His Silence and Song*, however, I would argue
that, just as in her representations of class relations, Pfeiffer's own position
is less than coherent. In her class depictions Pfeiffer shifts between
sympathy for the gentry in 'Martha Mary Melville', for example, and
condemnation of rigid and brutal class hierarchy in 'From Out of the
Night'. Similarly, in her depictions of Welshness she vacillates within
and among texts between provocation to rebellion, in the form of the
Irish character, Mona, and the bard's noble resignation to defeat in

Glan-Alârch: His Silence and Song; from depictions of English corruption and greed to happy reconciliation with English dominance in the marriage of Norman and Winifred in *The Wynnes of Wynhavod*. Whilst Pfeiffer tends to identify with the victimized in her poetry, it is not possible, it seems to me, to see her as a revolutionary in terms of class or national identity. There is a certain sense of defeatism about the poet's depictions of her favoured underdogs: just as it is impossible for the working-class woman in 'From Out of the Night' to live on after her ruin, so Glan-Alârch realizes that the Welsh will inevitably lose their battle with the Saxon invaders. The victims remain subdued. The poet demands the sympathetic understanding of the reader for the plight of the oppressed; she also requires the reader to recognize the brutal aspects of the system whose tyranny destroys them, but in this Pfeiffer's attitude is reformist rather than revolutionary.

★ ★ ★

I began this chapter by citing lines of Pfeiffer's which suggest her ambivalence to the mid-Victorian notion of progress. In this exploration of her work, the poet's equivocal attitude towards the dominant ethos of the era has emerged as a key component in her poetic sensibility. Like many Victorian women poets, Pfeiffer's work demonstrates a range of anxieties in relation to dominant patriarchal canons, both literary and social. Additionally I have discussed Pfeiffer's vacillating approaches to issues of class and national identity. In her representations of the 'flux and reflux' of developments in Victorian society, particularly through her rendering of Welsh perspectives, Pfeiffer, I would argue, may be read as less than entirely convinced of the moral integrity of the prevalent ideologies.

7

Anna Walter Thomas and the power of privilege

Anna Walter Thomas is chronologically the most recent and by far the most socially privileged of the seven poets considered in this study. Thomas was also the longest-lived of the seven writers; she died in 1925 at the age of eighty-one. Although she published only two poems, both prizewinning National Eisteddfod entries, Thomas was, nevertheless, a prominent scholar and public figure in the field of Welsh literary culture. She lived and worked through a period which spanned enormous and rapid developments in technology, philosophy and art, as well as in class and gender politics. In this chapter I am concerned to determine the ways in which Thomas's poetry can be seen to respond to the changes occurring in the world around her. I am also interested in the extent to which the advantages bestowed on the poet by the circumstances of her birth impinge upon her poetry in terms of class, gender, religious and national consciousness.

Thomas was born in Barningham, Suffolk 'on February 13th or 14th, 1839 or 1840'. This ambiguity over dates arose 'as the Baptismal Register was burnt [and] I was free to choose St Valentine's day in the forties'.[1] She was the youngest of twenty children fathered by Thomas Fison, a rural landowner with a 'devotion to his religion and Church work'.[2]

Thomas Fison married twice; he was a widower with seven young children when he married Charlotte Reynolds, the mother of Anna Walter Thomas. Charlotte Reynolds Fison died at the age of fifty-two, presumably exhausted after giving birth to thirteen children. The poet's maternal grandfather, according to her own reminiscences, was 'a great scholar and linguist', and her mother 'herself no mean scholar'.[3] The academic accomplishments of the Fison brood, in particular of the offspring of Charlotte Reynolds Fison, and specifically her daughters, are remarkable. All appear to have been endowed with natural ability as scholars, and to have received some formal schooling outside the home.[4] In addition, the Fison daughters were encouraged to read widely, including much material 'very unfit for a child'.[5] Anna Walter Thomas recalls, for instance, how, as a ten-year-old, 'In the winter evenings of 1850, I read a large Histoire de Russie, and Mill's Logic; as a reward for something or other, I was allowed to begin Italian and German.'[6] Anna Walter Thomas is known to have been sent at the age of twelve to a school in London and later to a 'finishing school' in Cheltenham which was run by a cousin. As women, however, the highly intellectual Fison daughters were denied the opportunity of formal university education for themselves, and appear to have developed a strategy of access through marriage to the rarefied academic atmosphere of the Oxbridge colleges. The poet's eldest sister, Charlotte, married George Waring, fellow of Hertford College, Oxford; Elizabeth, possessed of a 'masculine intellect' and 'well versed in general literature, particularly in French', married William Green, fellow of King's College and lecturer at Cambridge; Mary married Duncan Crooks Tovey, fellow of Trinity College, Cambridge; Jeannette married Robert Potts, also a fellow of Trinity College, Cambridge.

Anna Fison, as she then was, travelled with friends in Europe for a number of months after leaving school. Thereafter she spent her time making extended visits to the homes of two of her sisters, Charlotte at Oxford, and Jeannette at Cambridge. The poet's memoirist, W. Glynn Williams, remarks:

> To have passed, thus, every six months or so, from one University to the other, imbibing alternately the highest influences of each, is a privilege that few can have enjoyed; and that Anna Fison, with her singular natural abilities, and her self-disciplined and eagerly receptive mind, took full advantage of her unique opportunities is proved by the distinguished position she subsequently won in the literary world.[7]

The reputation of Thomas as a poet is perhaps exaggerated here; the respect with which she seems to have been universally regarded as a linguist and scholar, however, certainly demonstrates the extent of her determination to capitalize on the entrée presented by her sisters' connections. Thomas became a specialist in the ancient Classics, the Romance languages and German; she made a particular study of Anglo-Saxon, and, with her sister Charlotte Waring, assisted, unacknowledged, Professor Bosworth of the Bodleian Library in a major translation project which appeared under his name. Additionally, Thomas learned several other languages, including a 'thorough mastery of Welsh'.[8] Her interest in Welsh language and literature had begun some years earlier on a visit to Wales; she explains the growth of her unusual enthusiasm as having been inspired by the mentorship of a Welsh scholar at Oxford:

> On my return to Oxford from a visit to Wales I became an earnest student of the Welsh language. Dr Charles Williams, Principal of Jesus College, greatly assisted me . . . He unlocked for me the enchanted halls of the 'Mabinogion', and Wales became more and more to me a Fairyland.[9]

The guidance of Dr Williams was clearly influential in helping Thomas to develop a love of Welsh literature. Her initial interest, however, seems to have been sparked by an academic urge, understandable, perhaps, in so accomplished a linguist, to overcome the intricacies of what W. Glynn Williams refers to as 'one of the most difficult European tongues'.[10] I will return to an examination of Thomas's attitude to the Welsh language later in the chapter. At any rate, such was her academic excellence that she was engaged (presumably on an informal basis) to tutor undergraduates at Oxford for examinations.

In 1871 the poet married the Reverend David Walter Thomas MA, the vicar of St Ann's at Bethesda in Caernarfonshire; aside from accompanying her husband on a brief clerical placement in Italy, she subsequently remained in Wales until her death at the age of eighty-one. Thomas endeared herself to the local community at Bethesda through her willingness to perfect her spoken and colloquial Welsh. Already an authority on Welsh literature, she appears to have been immediately fascinated by the Eisteddfod, describing it as 'a new sensation, such as is felt at a Jewish Festival Service in a great London Synagogue, – a feeling that ages have rolled back, and that you are an anachronism in your modernity'.[11] By the mid-1870s, Anna Walter Thomas had become a regular speaker, contributor and adjudicator at the National Eisteddfod, as well as a vocal advocate for reform of the institution. In 1883 Thomas won the major poetry prize at the National Eisteddfod in Cardiff; she was the only woman to achieve this feat in the nineteenth century, and her accomplishment was not to be matched until 1953 when Dilys Cadwaladr took the Crown.[12] In 1880 the poet gave a paper to the Honourable Society of Cymmrodorion on 'The best method of improving the Eisteddfod'; W. Glynn Williams cites a contemporary newspaper report which describes how

The paper produced something very much like a sensation . . . and it was wonderful how many persons there were who discovered that they agreed with Mrs Thomas . . . and yet had hitherto maintained a strict silence. One result immediately followed . . . a Committee was appointed to consider the whole question of Eisteddfod reform.[13]

Williams asserts indeed that 'The ultimate result of the Paper was the establishment of the National Eisteddfod Association'.[14] In his monograph *The Eisteddfod*, in the Writers of Wales series, Hywel Teifi Edwards discusses the increasing agitation for reform of the National Eisteddfod during the second half of the nineteenth century, noting the situation ten years after the intervention by Thomas cited above:

In the aftermath of the Bangor National Eisteddfod in 1890, *Y Traethodydd* invited five prominent Welshmen to contribute to a symposium on the Eisteddfod, assessing its present condition and forecasting future developments . . . what most gave cause for concern was the pronounced Anglicization of 'the National'.[15]

Edwards does not credit Anna Walter Thomas with the achievement Williams claims on her behalf; indeed, there is no mention of her contribution in his account of the institution in the period. In reading the poems with which Thomas won the poetry prize at the National Eisteddfod on two separate occasions, however, it is possible to hypothesize that her involvement in the cause of improving the institution paradoxically contributed to the problem with which Welsh critics became most preoccupied. For not only are the two pieces, 'Llandaff' and 'Monody on Albert Victor Christian Edward, Duke of Clarence and Avondale', written in English, but both demonstrate a profoundly Anglocentric perspective. Hywel Teifi Edwards notes the emphasis placed by late nineteenth-century Eisteddfod reformers upon the choice of subject matter for the literature competitions. In order to arrest the much lamented Anglicization process, it was argued that there should be a return to 'the glories of the nation's old literature'.[16] A glance at the two poems by Thomas illustrates the extent of the problem. 'Llandaff', despite its title, which derives from the name of the ancient site of Christianity in Wales,[17] is, in fact, a virulent polemic on the demise of the English Church in Wales and, implicitly therefore, on contemporary Welsh Nonconformist culture in general. Not surprisingly, 'Monody on Albert Victor Christian Edward' is a sentimental eulogy on the late grandson of Queen Victoria, which celebrates in mawkish style the imperial 'family' of which the Welsh audience is assumed to be an obedient branch. Clearly, then, the enthusiasm Thomas displays for Wales, the Welsh language and people, and particularly for the Eisteddfod, is inflected by her position as a member of the English establishment.

In this chapter I intend to examine the two available poems, as well as the biographical details included by Williams in his *Memoir*, which represents the corpus of extant material on Thomas. I will analyse the poet's writing in terms of her approaches to questions of religion, class and gender, and in order to explore the complexities of her relationship with Wales. I begin with the question of religion.

★ ★ ★

Like Felicia Hemans, also an English-born and predominantly Wales-based poet, Anna Walter Thomas was a devout Anglican. Unlike Hemans, however, Thomas, fuelled by her position as a vicar's wife, appears to have seen her role within Anglicanism as an evangelizing one in relation to the people of Wales. In his book *Mid-Victorian Wales: The Observers and The Observed*, Ieuan Gwynedd Jones notes the attitude of the Anglican hierarchy to the provision of religious and moral ministry in the period amongst the insular and demographically shifting population of Wales: 'Shortly before [the Bishop of Llandaff, Charles Sumner] left for Winchester in 1827, he visited Dowlais . . . and on the way back . . . he bade . . . goodbye with the words, "I leave you as a missionary in blackest Africa".'[18] Jones also discusses the problems experienced by the Established Church in achieving a significant degree of influence in Wales during the nineteenth century, observing that it was 'beyond the power of the Anglicans to provide churches in sufficient numbers in the right places'.[19] It is clear from the memoir of Anna Walter Thomas by W. Glynn Williams that the poet's own approach to ministry in Wales entailed something of the same view of the Welsh as in need of missionary intervention, as well as a recognition of the Church's fast-disintegrating foothold in Welsh culture. Ieuan Gwynedd Jones makes the point that the failure of the Anglican Church in Wales was due in large part to its 'neglect of the language of the people'.[20] He notes that the evangelizing mission was unviable because of Anglican failure to preach and teach in the Welsh language. As I have already indicated, in addition to her zealous Anglicanism, Anna Walter Thomas was an accomplished Welsh-speaker. It is possible that the combination of her linguistic gifts and her privileged position may have affected the practice of her religious orientation in relation to the Welsh-speaking people of her husband's parish community.

Thomas spent the greater part of her life in Wales in devoted support of her husband's religious and pastoral duties. In addition, and tellingly, in view of the points made by Jones about language and sectarian development, she took up with enthusiasm the task of 'educating young people generally, and particularly [. . .] young men preparing for Holy Orders'.[21] W. Glynn Williams describes in some detail the extent and significance of this task:

> The vicar saw that exceptional zeal and perseverance were needed to put into order land that had lain fallow, or had been allowed to become a wilderness for so many years . . . but never did we see the least sign of slackening effort, or lack of patience, in either of our leaders.[22]

There is implicit in these remarks an assumption that the Anglican Church in Wales was, at the time, in urgent need of Thomas's attentions. The extent of the problem has been well-documented; the religious census of 1851 registered 1,180 places of Anglican worship compared with 2,769 Nonconformist chapels.[23] Eric Hobsbawm has detailed the way in which during the first half of the nineteenth century 'the established churches . . . neglected the new [industrial] communities';[24] Gwyn A. Williams notes that in terms of Church influence in the same period 'Wales seemed to be slipping away altogether'.[25] Also implicit in the memoirist's comments, however, is the premise that the exigency of Anglican intervention is sited in the moral and emotional poverty of Wales and the Welsh people. It was to this moral 'wilderness' that in 1847 HM Education Commissioners had been sent. The commissioners embarked on a mission to legitimize, through so-called statistical data, the use of educational mechanisms designed to reclaim the Welsh from the 'spiritual destitution' represented in part by the range of Nonconformist denominations to which the vast majority of them dedicated their religious allegiance. According to the Reverend John Griffith, Anglican vicar of Aberdare and respondent to the 1847 Inquiry: 'In religion they [the Welsh] are very excitable and lacking mental discipline . . . Properly speaking there is no religion whatever . . . The parish is retrograding educationally, and morally their condition is worsening.'[26] The spiritual poverty of the Welsh is a theme to which the poet herself warms in 'Llandaff', her winning entry in the 1883 National Eisteddfod poetry competition. Under the pseudonym 'Cyfeiliawg', Thomas entered a piece which was described variously by the adjudicators as 'a grand poem . . .

simple, pure, and elegant, and also strikingly clear . . . the similes are also well-chosen and chaste . . . the emanation of a pure mind'.[27] Clearly, the criteria by which poetry was judged at the National Eisteddfod in 1883 involved an element of moral discernment. Hywel Teifi Edwards notes the impulse of eisteddfod culture post-1847 towards promoting the image of the Welsh as, among other virtues, morally unimpeachable.[28] Although the adjudicators share with many of their contemporaries in Victorian literary criticism a tendency towards conflating literary and moral value, the imperative for these Welsh judges to assert the purity of mind of their chosen winner is perhaps more intensely pressing.

At any rate, the poem itself locates the problem of moral laxity in Wales as connected to the demise of the Anglican Church. In the account Thomas gives of the religious history of Wales, much like that of the informant to the commissioners cited above, Nonconformity does not exist, only godlessness.

'Llandaff' is the first-person meditation of a 'native of Llandaff living in London'.[29] The male speaker reflects retrospectively on his student days at King's College, Cambridge, on the philosophical discussions which took place there between himself and his friend, 'Lafone', and on the dream engendered by his reminiscences in which he envisions the religious history of his homeland. By establishing the speaker as an expatriate Welshman, the poet manipulates a Welsh readership, explicitly the original Eisteddfod audience, in an assumption of shared concerns. The piece is structured around the dream sequence, which is spoken in four hundred or so lines of heroic couplets, and is framed by opening and closing passages in blank verse.

In the section entitled 'The Dream' the speaker imagines himself inside a star, from which vantage point he is able to view the world in various stages of the past. The use of detailed descriptive subtitles throughout the poem allows no room for misinterpretation, directing the reader firmly towards a particular understanding of the work and of Welsh history: '*He looks towards Llandaff . . . And sees it at the time of the Roman invasion . . . The first Christian Church, circ.A.D. 180 . . .*' The headings become a potted history of Christianity in Wales, from the first century AD to the late nineteenth century when the poem was written. However, in her chronicle Thomas depicts a Christian heritage which is unequivocally Anglican in nature. The account describes an unbroken line from the first Christian church in Britain, erected at Llandaff by Lleurwg ap Coel ap Cyllin, to the arrival of Bishops Copplestone and Ollivant in the mid-nineteenth century, a line which is unequivocally Anglican throughout. This is an extraordinary version of Church history, given the well-documented circumstances of the development of Christianity in Britain. At the time of the Saxon conquest of Wales in the fifth century AD, the Celtic Church was already well established. When the Saxon, or English, invaders first entered south Wales, they were pagans, and it was the effects of their bloody incursion which posed the most serious threat to the survival of Christianity in Wales.

Despite the ravages of the Saxon occupation, Christianity survived in Wales. When power shifted to the hands of the Norman invaders in the eleventh century, the conquerors' priority was to assert control over the Welsh dioceses, and to force the so-called Celtic Church to conform with the rule of Rome.[30] In a curious distortion of historical fact, the Norman Conquest is seen by the speaker of 'Llandaff' as a profoundly negative influence on the life of the Anglican Church in Wales and the point at which its fortunes begin to wane:

> But soon an evil day dawns o'er the land.
> With pain good Urban sees the spoiler's hand
> Stretched o'er Llandavia's possessions fair,
> Heedless alike of threatening and of prayer.
> An evil day: for now the Norman bold
> Has crossed the sea, greedy of land and gold.
> Well were this all – but brethren false arose,
> And 'they of her own household were her foes'.
> Till stripped of her wealth and shorn of fair domain,
> Llandaff is left a prey to high disdain . . .[31]

Norman greed is depicted as infecting members of the Welsh establishment, whose collaboration ensures the demise of the Anglican Church in Wales. Tellingly, the significance of the Church is expressed in terms of its material resources. Without its property, Llandaff is seen as vulnerable to the contempt of the powerful, and consequently impotent to address the spiritual needs of the people. The link here between political and spiritual power is explicit:

> Darker and darker deepens down the night,
> Faith yields to rapine, freedom bows to might;
> Country and Church oppressed by alien lords,
> Who live by plunder, govern by their swords . . .[32]

What is of value, in the speaker's view, is the wealth and power of the Anglican Church in Wales; less positively encoded is the commercial development of secular interests. Later in the poem, when the speaker describes the effects of the Industrial Revolution, wealth is described in terms of parasitic despoilment:

> When . . . the two giant serfs
> Of commerce – Coal and Iron – were found to dwell
> Beneath Llandavia's soil, there flocked a throng
> Of men, hard-handed, to the rich-veined earth.
> Then roared the furnace where once waved the corn,
> And round the black pit's mouth sprang, fungus-like,
> Dwelling of miner and artizan . . .[33]

Clearly, although material wealth is desirable for the Anglican Church, the visible means by which material prosperity is acquired are abhorrent to the poet's moral sensibilities. The depiction of miner and artisan as fungus-like parasites on Welsh resources is an interesting image which implies that the people employed in these activities are all alien to Wales. This is statistically an untenable claim;[34] more importantly, the assertion indicates the complexity of the poet's attitude towards the relationship between Christian morality and the Welsh people. Later in the poem, when the speaker has woken from his dream and made his way to Llandaff cathedral, he muses on the role of the Welsh as world leaders in moral and spiritual affairs:

> No more shall *Cymru*'s sons, who cross the main,
> The wide Atlantic, for a distant shore,
> Where due reward will meet their toil, and where
> Their children will not vainly ask for bread;
> No more will they in deep heart sickness, pine
> In vain, ah! All in vain, to hear the grand
> Unrivalled speech of *Cymru* rise in prayer
> And psalm to God, within his chosen Church.
>
> . . .
>
> The day may dawn when *Cymru* will arise,
> Mother of nations yet unborn – beloved
> And honoured by them all . . .[35]

The rise of Wales as a world force depends, in the poet's vision, on the renewal of its allegiance to the Anglican Church. Welsh Anglicans in foreign worlds are seen as righteous pilgrims, justly welcomed and thriving. Without the benefit of Anglican absolution, they are depicted as parasitic aliens in their own country.

It is interesting, too, that in the poet's account of the evolution of the Church in Wales, it is the alien influence of the Norman invaders which is seen to corrupt the purity and potency of the native Church. In this skewed account, the native Church in Wales is figured as predominantly Anglican, although, as I have already discussed, before the Norman Conquest the Church in Wales cannot be said in any terms to have been 'English'. Indeed, in the narrative speaker of 'Llandaff', Thomas bizarrely cites St Dyfrig, the first saint of the Celtic Church, as the founder of Anglicanism. The Reformation, the moment at which in fact the Anglican Church came into existence, is depicted in the poem merely as a further example of ecclesiastical asset-stripping:

> Where once St Dyfrig ruled in glad content
> Now alien Bishops, by the monarch sent,
> Usurp the place, and view with proud disdain
> The sheep who look for guidance, but in vain.
> The revenues they seize, and bear them hence
> To minister to pride and vain expense;
> Spending on courtly dress and groaning board,
> What once sustained the servants of the Lord . . .[36]

The poet reduces a theological and spiritual watershed of epic proportions to an instance, among many throughout the Church's history, of worldly pillage. In placing the emphasis on the material destruction of the Reformation she also effectively elides the distinction between Christianity and the established Church; in the poet's model of Welsh history 'Christian' thus becomes synonymous with 'Anglican'. The emphasis once again is on 'alien' invasion. Paradoxically the bishops sent by the monarch in what marks the birth of Anglicanism are seen to be as foreign and corrupt as the Normans before them. Continuity of tradition is emphasized as vital to the spiritual health of Wales: from 'St Teilo's holy sway / The day shines bright as was the yester day'.[37] The divine authority of the Church's mission is also central: 'By angel hands in God's own city given / Calling man aye from thought of earth to heaven'.[38] The religious allegiances of the poet, then, unsurprisingly, given her attachments to Oxford, are decidedly Tractarian in their bias.[39] It is interesting that in her advocacy of a religious dogma which was regarded with hostility at the time for its closeness to the Church of Rome, and given her own apparent antipathy towards the Norman

(Roman Catholic) influence in Church history, Thomas deploys the discourse of alienation and foreignness. I would suggest that it is possible to read her use of the concept of 'alien' as an attempt to assert the patriotic Englishness of her religious observance. In advancing this argument Thomas is able to propose the spiritual and practical efficacy of administering her brand of Christian practice to the Welsh people. Given that the Nonconformist sects of Wales were at this period beginning to press for the disestablishment of the Anglican Church in Wales, her stance is overtly political and provocative.[40]

Gwyn A. Williams describes the importance of the Oxford movement in the efforts of the Church to regain prominence in Wales, noting that 'Keble gave a lecture to a church in Cardiganshire'.[41] This poem by Thomas may be interpreted as representing a contribution to the project, fuelled by Tractarian energy and already well under way in 1883, of 'revitalizing the Church in Wales'.[42] Gwyn A. Williams makes the point that:

> A striking and long-term consequence [of renewed Church involvement in Wales] was that it was Anglicans above all who moved into the surging eisteddfod movement and the national revival . . . and who were some of the most committed to a Welsh nationality. To [Nonconformists] and to many steeped in their history, the Church of England in Wales was to be *yr hen fradwres* (the old traitress).[43]

Anna Walter Thomas was clearly an Anglican who became enthusiastically involved in the hierarchy of the National Eisteddfod. How far it is possible to regard her as 'committed to a Welsh nationality' is an issue to which I will return. What is certain, however, is that her prizewinning poem 'Llandaff' demonstrates the poet's loyalties to a Christian form which involves the negation of contemporary indigenous worship as morally, spiritually or emotionally viable. In this she presents a striking contrast with a number of the other poets in this study. I have mentioned the less proselytizing approach of Felicia Hemans to Anglican practice; in the case of Sarah Williams, however, despite some defensive ambivalence which may arise out of her geographical proximity to the English centre, Nonconformist practice is depicted as a potentially viable model for personal spirituality and moral development. Thomas, though Welsh-speaking and based in Wales, and despite her understanding of herself as an enthusiast for Welsh language and literature, retains a resolutely antipathetic, not to mention colonial, attitude towards the religious culture of the majority of Welsh people. It seems to me that the stance

Thomas takes towards religion is heavily informed by her position as a member of the privileged and distinctly English elite issuing from the Oxbridge colleges during the second half of the nineteenth century. It is this perspective, I would argue, which primarily distinguishes her approach from those of the other poets considered in this book. In the section which follows I will attempt to analyse this phenomenon in detail, as I focus on the poet's approaches to the issue of class.

★ ★ ★

As a daughter of the landed gentry, Thomas was part of what Geoffrey Best describes as the 'unchallenged topmost strata of the British hierarchy in the mid-Victorian period':[44]

> Around the inner ring of the hereditary and titled blood group [were] gathered the 'county families' . . . the common characteristic of county families was land ownership. That mattered not just because farmland usually . . . brought in a good income . . . but more because ownership of land and nothing else made possible the playing of the roles that country gentry conventionally played: the landlordly role in respect of tenants, employees and economic dependants . . . the society role by diligent attention to the rite of visiting, house and garden parties, churchgoing, charitable work etc.[45]

This description seems to correspond with the social role indicated by Thomas in her memories of her father: 'a courteous squire with devotion to religion and Church work'.[46] Her 1892 Eisteddfod-winning 'Monody on Albert Victor Christian Edward, Duke of Clarence and Avondale' asserts unequivocally, if proof were needed, her loyalty to the established social order. The poem opens in hyperbolic elegy:

> O thrice beloved! O thrice lamented Son!
> Fair Soul, that from a royal race of Earth
> Art summoned to a nobler birth,
> What measure shall we give to our woe for these?
> What longing vain, what wild desire
> Once to reverse the immutable decree,
> And light once more the ever-quenched fire
> Within those wistful eyes, and part those lips
> Doomed to a lasting silence.[47]

The poet's representation of the prevalent hierarchy is clearly laudatory. The piece begins by articulating her impulse to question the Almighty's purpose in summoning the duke to the hereafter; it moves, inevitably, however, to an expression of trust in the divine plan:

> Yea, Pure in Heart, a fairer lot is thine,
> Who leav'st this earth, so full of joyless din,
> Crusted with selfishness, ingrained in sin,
> For the pure harmonies, the bliss divine,
> Of that immortal state
> Where, in the Beatific Vision ever blest,
> Thy happy soul doth ever wait
> To do His Will, Whose will to do is rest.[48]

The universe is thus presented as divinely ordered. Thomas suggests that anguish arising out of God's mandate must be borne by those assigned to the hierarchical summit; the implication is of a sanctified imperative for those who exist lower down the social scale to bear their lot with equally stoic acceptance.

W. Glynn Williams notes the pleasure taken by the Walter Thomases when, in the 'early nineties' the Reverend Walter Thomas was appointed to a 'Residentiary Canonry in Bangor Cathedral': 'both the Canon and his wife welcomed the change for three months in the year, from St Ann's to the more congenial life at the Canonry, where they had greater scope for their delightful hospitality'.[49] Clearly, according to Williams, whose credentials are established early on as a long-standing personal friend of Anna Walter Thomas and her family, life in the quarry parish of Bethesda presented certain social deprivations for the Walter Thomases. The poet's background as a daughter of the landed elite is emphasized by her biographer as an important element in the connection between herself and the community she sought to serve. It is from this position of privilege informed by duty that Thomas appears to have conducted her relations with social groupings subordinate to her own.

In his 'Preface' to the *Memoir*, Watkin Herbert Williams, DD, then bishop of Bangor, describes in extravagant terms the life of diligent 'visiting' and 'charitable work' which was embarked upon by Thomas on her marriage: 'When she came to her husband in his quarry parish, she brought up the loyalty and self-surrender, with which Ruth followed Naomi up the hills of Bethlehem. "Thy people shall be my people, and thy God my God".'[50] The bishop's citation from the book of Ruth here implies a level of dedication to the 'quarry' parishioners which is not documented in detail in the *Memoir* itself. Thomas is cited as having been encouraged on her arrival by the 'keenness of intellect and eagerness for knowledge' of the 'monoglot' local population; the favourable effect of her initial address in Welsh to the 'almost monoglot' parishioners is noted.[51] The area of her work in Wales which is most discussed in the *Memoir*, however, is that of her role in educating 'young men in the district who were desirous of taking Holy Orders'.[52] Williams cites a contemporary commentator:

> classes were established, one of which was conducted by Morfudd Eryri (Mrs Walter Thomas), in which were to be found the principles of true education, – the imparting of knowledge, a moral and religious atmosphere, and a sympathetic, uplifting influence . . . Mrs Walter Thomas . . . was a radiant source of moral and intellectual enlightenment.[53]

It is not clear whether the young men in question would have included members of the local monoglot Welsh-speaking community. Certainly, however, such aspirants to Holy Orders are likely to have been in need of the kind of training Anna Walter Thomas provided; they would have had to struggle not only with the English language, but also with the Latin which was required for Oxbridge entry at the time. In his book, *Mid-Victorian Wales*, Ieuan Gwynedd Jones notes the social significance of the Welsh/English linguistic distinction in the period:

> the language had become a way of expressing social difference: in particular it marked [the Welsh] off from the English aristocracy and the Anglicizing middle classes . . . This led on to the function of language as establishing class differences, or, put in another way, of stimulating the growth of class-consciousness.[54]

Ieuan Gwynedd Jones is concerned here with the functions of the two languages in the development of a social and political consciousness among the Welsh. The experience Thomas had of class relations in north Wales is clearly informed by the same sense of linguistic hierarchy. It is interesting to observe the rationalizing of the process from the perspective of a member of the 'English aristocracy' and/or 'Anglicizing middle class'. It is not clear from the account by Williams to what extent the poet's protégés were Welsh-speaking; what does emerge is that, for Thomas, a consequence of the linguistic hierarchy is that her understanding of the concept of parish ministry in large part involves the production of suitably qualified people who will propagate Anglican doctrines among the

Welsh. If her students initially belonged to the local lower classes, Thomas was prepared to help them, through her teaching, to become middle class and Anglicized. Ieuan Gwynedd Jones cites the Welsh-language periodical of the Church of England, *Yr Haul*, in illustrating the class implications of Anglican dogma: the periodical advocated 'resignation in the face of hardship: all must accept their diverse stations and be silent under the powerful hand of Providence'.[55] Clearly, the evangelizing project of Anglicanism in nineteenth-century Wales involved a strong element of sociopolitical control. In her poem 'Llandaff' Thomas articulates a view of religious history and practice which situates Anglicanism at the forefront of the quest to safeguard the moral welfare of the Welsh; a consideration of the mechanisms through which this work was to be accomplished suggests that the salvation she envisages also included the imperative to suppress the local population in terms of its potential for class dissent.

It is clear that the perspective taken by Thomas in the articulation of class relations differs from that of the other poets included in this book. Although, broadly speaking, a middle-class writer, Thomas's landed background and, more significantly perhaps, her educational privilege, imbue her poetry, I would argue, with the sense of an imperative not merely to endorse and/or celebrate the status quo. Rather, Thomas assumes the role of active crusader for a species of social improvement which will ensure the devoted compliance of its working-class subjects. In her vision, this involves the conversion of as many working-class people as possible to the cause of Anglican Christianity. This mission, of course, occurred in a Welsh-speaking and largely Nonconformist community, and I will return to discussion of her poems in relation to the issue of national identity later in this chapter.

★ ★ ★

The position taken by Thomas with regard to gender politics is also marked by her birthright of privilege. In her book *White, Male and Middle Class*, Catherine Hall discusses the marginalization of women from the public world of Victorian society. Hall considers the example of philanthropy, noting that

> As long as they [women] were concerned with private philanthropic work, visiting people in their homes in particular, there was no problem. The difficulties arose when they attempted to step outside of that domestic arena

and take on a more public role . . . The formalization of philanthropic and religious societies invariably marginalized women from the process of decision-making; their role was to support privately rather than engage publicly.[56]

Hall's work focuses on the development of the overwhelmingly middle-class ideology of Victorian Britain. Thomas's more aristocratic background inevitably made more complex her material and psychoemotional position in relation to the dominant bourgeois culture. Her role as vicar's wife presumably required paying substantial attention to the kind of 'visiting' work Hall identifies. Interestingly, however, this is not the employment celebrated by the poet's biographer in his account of her life as 'capable coadjutrix of her earnest and hard-working husband'.[57] W. Glynn Williams proclaims instead, as I have already noted, the efforts made by Thomas in teaching, writing and public speaking. The epithet Williams attaches to the Reverend Walter Thomas is telling in itself; the 'earnest and hard-working' husband represents a strong contrast to his wife, 'a singularly gifted woman of extraordinary erudition'.[58]

It is evident from the biographical material available that Thomas was able to negotiate the constraints imposed by dominant patriarchal ideology, and to establish for herself a role to which she was more suited. It was a role which allowed for the education of men, and, more significantly, men who were preparing for the most important of public roles, the priesthood. W. Glynn Williams cites the reminiscences of the poet's niece as evidence of her engaging sense of humour; from this evidence Thomas was less generous in her appreciation of Welsh efforts to speak English than she perceived the locals to be about her initial attempts at spoken Welsh:

> I was once present when she was coaching some young Welshman for a Theological College; she wanted to get the idea of the authority of the Church and the Bible into connection in his brain, I suspect. 'Now, Mr Jones, on whose authority do we believe that the books of the Bible are inspired?' Mr Jones (gazing helplessly at the title page of his Bible), 'Jemms the Firrst's!'[59]

Aside from illustrating her somewhat patronizing attitude towards first-language Welsh-speakers, the attempt by Thomas to convey the un-fortunate Mr Jones's difficulties with spoken English suggests that she did, indeed, tutor members of the local lower classes. What the extract also testifies to is the extent of her involvement in teaching theology. The celebration by W. Glynn Williams of the poet's public life clearly owes something to the twentieth-century perspective from which he writes, as does that of Watkin Herbert Williams. In her pursuit of a significant public role in the Anglican Church in Wales, however, Thomas did not confine herself to the strictly parochial sphere. In 1884 she applied, as W. Glynn Williams notes, 'with a courage rare among women in those days', to the new University College of North Wales in Bangor for the Chair of Modern Languages.[60] Thomas failed in her application, but was placed second out of the forty candidates, having presented, in support of her application, a number of glowing testimonials from 'some of the best judges in Oxford and Cambridge'.[61]

Such high respect from many of the most eminent churchmen and scholars of the era clearly owes a great deal to Thomas's personal qualities of intellect, energy and drive. W. Glynn Williams suggests that Thomas may be thus regarded as 'one of the noble army of pioneers in the advancement of her sex to the "status" it now holds'.[62] Undoubtedly, the high-profile achievements of a talented and capable woman may be seen as a positive contribution in themselves to the cause of women's equality in the period. The extent of her interest in the 'advancement of her sex', however, is more dubious. In his discussion of her work in education, Williams refers briefly to the tuition Thomas provided to the women of the area: 'Nor were the women neglected; women married and single, from both sides of the Ogwen river attended Mrs Thomas's Sunday School Class at Tanyssgrafell, for many years.'[63] It is not possible to determine the progressive potential of these sessions; Williams does not identify the class constituency of the groups, and it may well have been the case that through her education of local women Thomas provided for them empowering literacy not available elsewhere. Certainly the sense conveyed by Williams, however, is of a catechistic approach through which women received religious and moral instruction in much the same way as children. The poet's education of women, then, was not perceived to be a politically radical activity. It is tempting to see Anna Walter Thomas's pioneering spirit with regard to women's roles as extending only as far as her own advancement, remaining satisfied with more conventional mechanisms and methods where other women were concerned.

In terms of her poetry, engagement by Thomas with the 'woman question' is even less easy to detect. In neither of the two available poems is there explicit engagement with issues connected with the 'woman question', which was reaching a peak among the 'articulate classes' by 1883.[64] I have already discussed Angela Leighton's observations on the classic tropes of Victorian women's poetry. In her introduction to

Victorian Women Poets: An Anthology, Leighton discusses the preoccupa-
tion among women poets in the period with problems of poetic identity;
she identifies a number of images repeatedly employed in their work, for
example: the mask, the picture, the mirror, the meeting with the other –
usually the fallen woman – and the experience of mothering. In the two
poems by Thomas, 'Monody on Albert Victor Christian Edward, Duke
of Clarence and Avondale' and 'Llandaff', no use is made of any of these
devices. In the 'Monody' the poet refers to the mother who 'by a funeral
couch stands', but it is to eulogize the dead prince and his family, rather
than to explore issues of female subjectivity. Similarly in 'Llandaff' the
poet uses the biblical image of the woman cured of 'the spirit of infirmity'
in order to metaphorize the resurgence of the Church in Wales:

> But as of old, the woman, bowed to earth
> By him mankind's great foe, for eighteen years
> Had walked in pain and weakness and complaint;
> All those long years, her eyes still bent on earth,
> Unable quite to raise them up to heaven,
> Until one blessed day, when creeping on
> Beneath her weight of woe, she heard the words
> (How simple, yet how full of power divine!)
> 'Woman, from thine infirmity be loosed!'
> . . .
> So it was with the Church – Christ's chosen bride . . .[65]

The poet's deployment of the fallen-woman motif here does not
problematize the notion of woman as symbol of physical and moral disease.
The episode to which Thomas alludes occurs in St Matthew's Gospel:

> And behold, a woman, which was diseased with an issue of blood twelve
> years, came behind him, and touched the hem of his garment: For she said
> within herself, If I may but touch his garments, I shall be made whole. But
> Jesus turned him about and when he saw her, he said, Daughter, be of
> good comfort; thy faith hath made thee whole. And the woman was made
> whole from that hour.[66]

In 'Llandaff' the power of the woman's faith and love is elided in favour
of her 'weakness and complaint'. The physical haemorrhage referred to by
Matthew is figured in the poem as 'mankind's great foe'; with no apparent
sense of irony, Thomas transmutes gynaecological suffering into the
manifestation of Satan in the lives of 'men'. Her deployment of the fallen-

woman image does not, as Leighton suggests is common in Victorian women's verse, involve engagement between two aspects of the female self; it depicts, rather, a meeting between an extremely assured self and a distinctly othered female figure. In their comments on the anonymously submitted 'Llandaff', the adjudicators of the 1883 Eisteddfod certainly imply that they assumed the poet to be male.[67] This sense of alienated self-confidence pervades these poems by Thomas; it indicates, I would suggest, a strategy for expression borne out of her unusually privileged position in a patriarchal culture which, nevertheless, tends to problematize full articulation of female consciousness.

In her book *Victorian Women Poets: Writing Against the Heart* Angela Leighton expands on her thesis concerning women poets' struggle to articulate female identity. She argues that in their attempt to negotiate the spirit of the Victorian age, which involved 'a highly moralized celebration of women's sensibility', without becoming completely dissociated from the 'affairs of the world', women poets developed strategies for writing 'not from but against the heart'. Leighton continues:

> Without the heart to guarantee femininity, feeling and truth, the imagination enters a world of sceptically disordered moral and linguistic reference. While the aesthetic possibilities of such disorder are seductive, the moral cost, especially for women, is high. The tension between these two recurs, in various patterns, in the work of most of these poets, and becomes the hallmark of their common creativity.[68]

Anna Walter Thomas was a Victorian woman poet who clearly had no desire to dissociate herself from the 'affairs of the world'. Indeed, her proclivity to public oration, and her aspirations to high academic office, indicate an impulse on her part towards active involvement in the upper echelons of its hierarchy, a drive which far exceeds the arguably less materially ambitious aims of the poets Leighton examines. This impulse manifests itself in Thomas's poems, not in an imaginative 'world of sceptically disordered linguistic and moral reference', but in a highly structured environment whose organization mirrors the hierarchical arrangement of the material world of Victorian patriarchy.

In 'Llandaff', for example, the fashionable Victorian device of the dramatic monologue is deployed. Much feminist scholarship in recent years has been concerned with the 'ventriloquism' of Victorian women's verse; the dramatic monologue has been discussed as a form which allows experimentation with a range of speaking voices, and has been identified as an important device for women poets, for whom issues of authority and identity are of paramount concern. The first-person speaker, through whom Thomas mounts her discussion of the Anglican Church in Wales, derives authority, not merely through his male persona, but by virtue of the fact that he is a Cambridge scholar. The speaker's credentials are established early on:

> *He recalls the time when he and a College friend talked in the grounds of King's College, Cambridge.*
> When weary of our books, Lafone and I,
> Lafone, beloved alike of 'dons'★ and men,
> Lay idly on the velvet sward of Kings,
> And watched the drowsy Cam★★ slip slowly by . . .
>
> ★Tutors, etc., and undergraduates.
> ★★The Cam is a remarkably sluggish river.[69]

The title of the section sets up the context of the exchange very clearly; should there be any doubt of the legitimacy of the claims of speaker, and by implication, of the poet, to membership of this rarefied environment, the footnotes clarify his insider's understanding. Whilst emphasizing the knowledge possessed by both the speaker and the poet, the footnotes simultaneously delineate the reader's exclusion from it, assuming a lack of previous access on the part of the reader to these points of information, and thus locating poet and speaker as elevated in intellectual and social terms. It is interesting that, in constructing Cambridge as site of the privilege and authority she claims for herself, Thomas deploys the same image of the college grass which Virginia Woolf was to use to the opposite effect fifty years later.[70] For Woolf, writing in 1928, as a woman the lawns of 'Fernham College Oxbridge' are forbidden; for Thomas's male speaker in 1883, the lawns of King's College may be lain upon idly. I would argue that for Thomas, the desire to identify with her male speaker is so intense as to elide the abiding inequality noted by Woolf. It is difficult to think of the first-person speaker in 'Llandaff' as Welsh – much less female – so absolutely male, upper-class English does his confident placing of himself appear.

By scrupulously establishing the speaker's authority in this way the poet legitimizes her subsequent discussion of theology and church history. As a male academic, the speaker's stinging criticism of bishops and kings is sanctioned by reference to both his knowledge and his affinity with the privileged few who share it. This is an undertaking which few Victorian women poets would have been equipped to attempt. In terms of

Leighton's notion of 'writing against the heart', Thomas seems to me to represent a poet whose strategies for self-expression preclude the possibility of 'linguistic and moral disorder' precisely because the existing order suggests far greater opportunity for her personal development than the creative space promised by unruliness. The construction of 'Llandaff' suggests, I would argue, that Thomas took the opportunity afforded her by the anonymous adjudication system of the Eisteddfod to 'speak' from the position of a university academic, a role which, throughout 1884, she was actively pursuing for herself.

The platform offered by the National Eisteddfod allowed Thomas a public profile through a variety of media, as an active organizer and reformer, as an orator and as a poet. Hywel Teifi Edwards describes how the onslaught of Romanticism saw the end of 'rules-dominated criticism' at the National Eisteddfod.[71] The context of the Eisteddfod in the late nineteenth century, with its prescribed subject matter, might, nevertheless, suggest a sense of constraint in terms of artistic creativity. For Thomas, however, the competitive system of the 'National' seems to have provided a poetic 'voice' well suited to her privileged but inconveniently female subject position. Edwards comments on the advantage of educational privilege in the context of Eisteddfod poetry: 'That year [1888], Elfed . . . scooped the pot, taking four of the major prizes at Wrexham . . . It was the triumph of a naturally gifted man whose education gave him a headstart over his competitors.'[72] As a naturally gifted and highly educated woman taking part in a competition which, moreover, involved authorial anonymity, Thomas was clearly able to succeed over other contenders. More importantly, from the point of view of Victorian women's writing strategies, she was enabled, through the laureateship of the eisteddfodic model, to speak publicly with a level of authority otherwise unavailable to the woman poet of the period. This authority and, perhaps, the welcome with which it was received, may have been strengthened by her pre-eminent position as the only woman to have won one of the two major poetry prizes in the nineteenth-century National Eisteddfod.

This poet's variation on the tendency to 'write against the heart', then, involves a dogged adherence to the linguistic and moral systems of the established order. In her pursuit of what she deemed to be the highest prizes held out by Victorian patriarchy, that is, the prerogatives to speak and be heard publicly, and to have one's utterances deservedly respected, Thomas devised a strategy of writing entirely against prevalent understandings of the female heart, but entirely in tandem with the desires and ambitions of her own heart. Thomas seems to have devoted little of her formidable emotional or intellectual energy to the problems of gender for less privileged women. Ironically, it is in her attempt at distinguished conformity that she transgresses irredeemably against the order she seeks to lead. Thomas, for all her gifted erudition, found herself trapped in the double bind of Victorian patriarchal ideology: unable to rise to the top without conforming, unable, as a woman, to conform in her desire to rise to the top.

★ ★ ★

I have discussed the work of Anna Walter Thomas in relation to her approaches to the issues of religion, class and gender, and in doing so I referred extensively to her privileged position in terms of the power relations among the various interactive groups. In discussing the poet's connection with Wales it is necessary to consider the same issues of authority and dominion.

In his *Memoir*, W. Glynn Williams cites comments made by the poet's daughter on the attitude Thomas displayed towards the people and cultures she encountered during her husband's postings to parishes in Europe: 'She made the most of her time in getting to know the French and Italian peasants, and even learnt the language-signs of the Neapolitan beggars. She had an extraordinary flair for folklore, and peasant customs and dialects.'[73] In the same paragraph, Williams continues, 'On her return she devoted herself to a deeper study of Welsh and became a familiar figure on the platform of the National Eisteddfod.'[74] In an earlier chapter I have discussed ways in which the poetry of Ann Julia Hatton indicates an identification on the part of the poet with Welsh culture, which results in moments of genuine 'admiration and wonder' exceeding a colonial interest in exotic locations and lifestyles. I have also considered the contrasting response of Felicia Hemans to Welsh history and literature, which, I have argued, suggests a superficial appropriation of these resources for largely cosmetic purposes. However, the interest which Thomas is described – by one who knew her well – as exhibiting towards the marginal cultures of France and Italy is the academic curiosity of the trained linguist. Her preoccupation with folklore and peasant culture presumably owes something to the post-Romantic vogue for primitivism; it also, unlike Hatton's more dialogic affinity, clearly establishes the elevated status of Thomas in the interactive process of 'getting to know' the local people. The immediately subsequent reference by Williams to her study of Welsh suggests that the impression gained by the poet's memoirist and friend of her attitude towards Wales and the Welsh was that of another academic study of another group of peasants.

Anna Walter Thomas's own account of the process of learning colloquial Welsh is equally telling: 'the wild beauty and sweetness of the language fascinated me, and I set myself to master it; though the difficulties were great'.[75] The language interests the poet because of the challenges presented by its untamed qualities; the accomplished linguistic scholar is thus determined to command it. The verb to 'master' is interesting and, I would argue, significant in terms of Thomas's position in relation to Wales. I have suggested that her understanding of religious, class and, particularly, gender politics is inflected by her experience as part of the intellectual elite centred in the Oxbridge colleges. I have further proposed that her urge to dominate in these areas arises out of a supreme confidence in her capacity and entitlement, as a member of that elect, to do so. I want to explore the possibility that the resolve Thomas showed to 'master' the Welsh language may be read as evidence of the same assumption of cultural and political hegemony.

Post-colonial theorists have identified language as a 'fundamental site for post-colonial discourse'.[76] In the introduction to the section on language in their *Post-colonial Studies Reader*, Ashcroft et al., for example, make the point that

> The control over language by the imperial centre – whether achieved by displacing native languages, by installing itself as the 'standard' against other variants which are constituted as 'impurities', or by planting the language of empire in a new place – remains the most important instrument of cultural control.[77]

Ashcroft et al., in common with all of the writers included in their collection, consider the impact upon colonized peoples of the displacement of their native languages in favour of the language of the colonial power. This is the situation which pertained in Wales throughout the nineteenth century, of course; in discussing the case of Anna Walter Thomas, however, I suggest that the colonizer's 'mastery' of the indigenous language may act as an equally potent instrument of cultural control.

In his book *The Alchemy of English*, Braj B. Kachru makes the point that 'the English language is a tool of power, domination and elitist identity'.[78] Kachru is concerned to examine the emergence and functions of non-native English variants in a colonial context. I am interested in exploring the complexities of the notion of language as an instrument of imperial repression by focusing on the colonizer's 'mastery' of the native language.

I have already located Thomas's subject position as closely linked to the elite strata of the 'elitist identity' Kachru describes. Through her association with this intellectual grouping,[79] Thomas gained the means by which to command a number of languages; this capacity for linguistic dominance is a key component of her identity as a member of that elite. I would argue, therefore, that, in her urge to master the Welsh language, Thomas performs a crucial act of self-definition as a specifically English academic.

One immediate effect of her acquisition of the Welsh language was apparently to endear Thomas to the people of her parish community. W. Glynn Williams, an admittedly partial observer, comments that, on her arrival in Bethesda,

> Mrs Walter Thomas struck the right note amongst the almost monoglot Welsh parishioners by saying '*Yr oeddwn yn caru Cymru a Chymraeg eisioes, ond yn awr yr wyf yn caru Cymro hefyd!*' (I loved Wales and Welsh already, but now I love a Welshman too!).[80]

Regardless of the true extent of local affection for the poet, her ability to speak Welsh also gave her access to the Eisteddfod movement; this, combined with her high social and intellectual standing, allowed her to take a prominent role in the organizational hierarchy. Prys Morgan, in his paper 'From a Death to a View: The Hunt for the Welsh Past in the Romantic Period', considers the process of 'revival and myth-making' in Wales during the late eighteenth- and nineteenth-century period. Morgan focuses on the Welsh impetus to 'ransack the past and transform it with imagination, to create a new Welshness'.[81] Anna Walter Thomas clearly saw herself as a wholehearted friend of Wales and dedicated enthusiast of Welsh literature. Her work offers an opportunity to supplement an understanding of the process which Morgan identifies from the perspective of a Welsh-speaking Eisteddfod activist who is, nevertheless, an English writer with strong allegiances to the English imperial centre. I have already discussed the way in which the National Eisteddfod, with its initial brief of promoting interest in Welsh language and literature, had, by the mid-Victorian period, become a highly Anglicized institution which had developed into a vehicle for securing English approval of Wales and the Welsh. Although Thomas addressed the Eisteddfod on a number of occasions in Welsh, her two prizewinning poems were written in English.

As Hywel Teifi Edwards remarks, in the wake of the 1847 *Reports of the Commissioners of Inquiry into the State of Education in Wales*, the Eisteddfod became a vital instrument in the project of promoting an image of 'a God-fearing, Queen-loving, empire-supporting, self-improving, moral, earnest and wholesomely patriotic people whose National Eisteddfod annually displayed their worth'.[82] In 1847, the government commissioners who reported on the state of education in Wales had identified two central factors in what they considered to be the debased moral condition of the Welsh, namely, the effects of their widespread attachment to dissenting religious observance, and to their mysterious native tongue. I have already discussed the involvement of Thomas in the project of displacing Nonconformist practice in Welsh religious life; her enthusiasm for the Welsh language, and her activities in the National Eisteddfod movement, whilst apparently celebratory of Welsh culture, seem to me to represent the same, perhaps unconscious, drive to assert the superiority of English values. Her fluency in Welsh proclaims the pre-eminence of the English system out of which Thomas has emerged; simultaneously she is able to establish a space for herself, as part of the English elite, on an important public platform, a vantage point which also affords influence over the way in which the Welsh view themselves.

The two poems by Anna Walter Thomas which won prizes at the National Eisteddfod indicate the measure of her interest in promoting the cause of Welsh incorporation into the 'family' of the empire. The subject-setting and adjudication processes out of which these winning entries emerge is evidence of the extent to which the Eisteddfod itself was dominated by the same incorporative drive.

'Monody on Albert Victor Christian Edward' was written to commemorate the death in 1892 of the duke of Clarence and Avondale, son of the then prince of Wales and much-loved grandson of Queen Victoria. W. Glynn Williams includes extracts from the piece as an appendix to his *Memoir*, prefaced by the information that 'Queen Victoria ordered 100 copies of it for herself'.[83] Williams details this accolade with a degree of earnest pride which indicates the tenor of native Welsh responses to the push to incorporate Wales as part of the imperial family, an enterprise in which Thomas was an enthusiastic participant. The queen's approval is unsurprising; the poem consists of a hundred and fifty lines of hyperbolic panegyric on the virtues not only of the unfortunate duke himself, but also of the House of Saxe-Coburg, the institution of monarchy and the entire imperial project. It opens in a declaration of shared grief: 'O thrice beloved! O thrice lamented Son! . . . / What measure shall we give our woe for thee?'[84] The use of the personal pronoun 'we' immediately implicates the Welsh audience/readership in mourning the royal addressee. In detailing the tragedy of the duke's death the poet describes his fiancée as 'The fairest flower of our English spring'.[85] Here the possessive pronoun is explicitly Anglicized; the National Eisteddfod audience is thus designated as unproblematically English. The depiction which follows of the relationship between the duke and Princess Mary of Teck is heavily sentimental:

> thou didst gather to thy breast
> Upon thy heart to rest,
> And shelter safe for summer blossoming,
> Now – by the fury of the sudden blast
> Reft from her stay – beneath the pitiless rain
> She, earthward cast,
> Lies prostrate, as if ne'er to bloom again.[86]

The poet is clearly able to fulfil the role of laureate with some confidence. She is adept at deploying the conventions of hyperbole and rhetoric to ceremonial effect. The transience of the political moment which gives rise to ceremony, however, is illustrated by a historical footnote to the particular occasion marked here. The term 'as if ne'er to bloom again' turned out to be prophetically tentative; in later years, sentiment having been overtaken by political prudence, the same Princess Mary of Teck was expeditiously married to the duke's younger brother. W. Glynn Williams, writing in 1922, does not note the irony of this development.

The speaker goes on to declare the grief of the entire empire at the prince's demise, referring to the dead duke as 'Son of an Empire's sorrow!'[87] Again, in the public voice of laureate, Thomas blandishes the monarchy with details of the vastness of the British empire. All of the continents spanned by British imperial dominance are listed. The imperial project is celebrated and promoted to the Welsh audience as positive, powerful and all-encompassing. In an extremely interesting image, the empire's grief for the dead duke is metaphorized as 'Making of Babel tongues one harmony of woe'. This refers to the Old Testament book of Genesis in which the people of the earth built a tower in an attempt to reach heaven; but their plans were thwarted by God who confused the languages of the builders so that they could not understand one another. Although the people had hitherto spoken the same language, Genesis describes how 'the Lord did therefore confound the language of all the earth: and from thence did the Lord scatter them abroad upon the face of the earth'.[88] In the poet's deployment of the allusion, the British monarchical empire is able to reverse the effects of God's sanction. The implication is of an unlimited divinely appointed power with the potential to negotiate the most ancient heavenly ordinance. The notion of harmonizing the languages of the empire is extremely interesting in terms of the position Thomas holds in relation to the Welsh language. A harmony consists of a combination of different notes working together to produce a sweet sound. The poet advocates linguistic harmony, rather than a single voice, providing it works in order to uphold the imperial edifice. This is textual evidence, then, which supports my proposal that her command of the Welsh language could be brought to bear as a useful tool in the project, viewed unproblematically by Thomas and, perhaps, by a number of her fellows in the Anglicized elite of the National Eisteddfod, of homogenizing Wales as an eager participant in the kinship of empire.

I have already discussed the poet's depiction of Welsh religion in 'Llandaff' in terms of her negation of Nonconformist practice. I have argued that in this denial of Welsh religious culture Thomas attempts to assert the moral and historical primacy of Anglicanism as a spiritually viable force in Wales. The enterprise of reclaiming Wales as the rightful home of Anglican worship is reinforced in the poem by a number of tropes which draw on a view of Wales in relation to the imperial metropolis of London.

'Llandaff' opens with the Welsh speaker waxing lyrical in the grounds of Llandaff cathedral; but the speaker is immediately established as an inhabitant of London on a visit home to Wales:

> O fairest Day! the Summer in her prime
> Poured forth sweet scent of rose and bedded hay
> On faint warm airs that lightly touched the cheek,
> Like spirit hands of the beloved dead.
>
> . . .
>
> Across a stile I passed, and wandered through
> The fragrant meadows, ankle-deep in blooms.
> A toiler I, amid the rush and roar
> Of that great City, throned upon the Thames,
> Whose heart beat throbs through every land and clime.
> How sweet once more to breathe my native air!
> How blest the calm, the peace, as if of Heaven![89]

The use of the past tense in referring to Wales and present tense in referring to London indicates that the speaker's connection to London is firm and ongoing, whereas the time spent in Wales is a temporary retreat from every day life in the capital city of England. Llandaff is figured as a pastoral idyll, its peace is encoded as stasis, filled with 'faint warm airs . . . / Like spirit hands of the beloved dead'. The depiction is sedentary rather than death-dealing; but this is in strong contrast to the dynamic vitality of London in the piece. It is also in strong contrast to the documented condition of Cardiff during the period when the poem was written. John Davies describes the extent of the city's growth by the end of the nineteenth century:

> Cardiff in 1890 was the largest port in the world and the centre of a commercial empire which stretched to the farthest reaches of the globe . . . the position of Cardiff as the headquarters of the coal industry and as the pinnacle of the urban hierarchy of south Wales was wholly secure.[90]

The poet's inaccurate depiction of Cardiff as pastoral retreat in relation to the English metropolis is telling. In advancing this view of Wales as isolated and sedate, Thomas implies that the country is in material and spiritual need of the energy and drive represented by London's commercial intensity. The metaphor of London's throbbing heart connotes strength and circulation, as well as sincerity and compassion; the commercial and political imperialism represented by the city is thus depicted as a crucial and highly desirable counterpart to Welsh tranquillity. It is also a source of pride to the Welsh speaker, and, by implication, to his Welsh audience. Later in the poem, the speaker considers the development of other areas into centres of commerce and industry, and this is seen as a far less positive phenomenon:

> At home, the people more and more increased.
> Commerce and Art and Science made their thrones
> In countless places of our island fair.
> Where once the rural hamlet, 'mid green trees
> And waving cornfields, stood from age to age,
> In ten short years would rise a busy mart,
> With straight unlovely streets thick thronged with men.
>
> . . .
>
> . . . From the hour
> When suddenly there started forth to sight
> The treasures *Mynwy* and *Morganwg* hid
> Within their breasts; when the two giant serfs
> Of commerce – Coal and Iron – were found to dwell
> Beneath Llandavia's soil, there flocked a throng
> Of men, hard-handed to the rich-veined earth.[91]

The poet acknowledges the connection between commerce, which she has celebrated in her depiction of London, and the industry required to sustain it. But paradoxically she sees the industrialization of Wales as a matter to be deplored. Such inconsistency is symptomatic, I would argue, of the urge Thomas displays to celebrate Wales as a site of spiritual and emotional nurture, but simultaneously to recruit this resource to the project of English supremacy. The two crucial elements of her Welsh vision are that Wales sees itself, and is seen to be, delightfully different from, but is entirely unthreatening to the established order.

'Llandaff' also deals explicitly with the issue of religious and cultural imperialism. In a section entitled *Neglect of Missions*, the speaker considers the condition of peoples before the advent of Anglicanism and, by implication, Anglicization:

> In far lands
> Where devil-gods to fiercest crimes spurred on
> Their wretched worshippers, in that dark night
> Of monstrous heathendoms – pierced by no beam
> Of that most blessed Sun Divine, whose rays
> Disperse all ill and quicken all good things;
> Where foulest wrong was king, and Hate and Fear
> And Strife reigned lords over each hapless race.[92]

The poet locates Wales early on as the birthplace of Anglican Christianity; the Welsh are thus implicated in the particularly noxious species of evangelizing invective promoted here.[93] As already discussed, however, the poem also identifies the current godless condition of Wales; the graphic description of 'far lands' by implication depicts the dire moral consequences for Wales of resisting a revival in Anglican practice. In discussing the state of the Church 'at home', the poet makes explicit her attitude to Nonconformist Christian practice. According to the poet this is a decline which can be arrested only by a rejection of indigenous Welsh religious culture in favour of the Anglican and distinctly Anglicized variety offered by Thomas and the imperial cohort she represents.

* * *

Anna Walter Thomas is a remarkable figure whose biography seems to represent a triumph for the political interests of women in the period. However, the extraordinary intellectual endowments and achievements which elevate her to the status of pioneer contain the seeds of a force which is reactionary rather than revolutionary. She is a writer who also presents an interesting study of the English imperial project at work in mid-Victorian Wales. In her apparent enthusiasm for Welsh cultural life, and in her acquisition of the Welsh language, she appears to be a part of what Prys Morgan refers to as 'the invention of tradition' in Welsh culture of the mid to late nineteenth-century period.[94] However, in her mastery of Welshness rests her capacity for damaging the development of Welsh identity. It is precisely because of her great gifts and enthusiasms that Anna Walter Thomas remains a dangerous woman to those causes she appears to endorse.

Conclusion

My purpose in this book has been twofold: firstly, I have been concerned to make a survey of the field of English-language poetry by nineteenth-century Welsh women. In introducing the book I remarked on its limitations in terms of scope, and in concentrating on only seven poets I am aware that the study is by no means comprehensive. However, what it does represent is a cross-section of the range of texts available, and one which includes all the better-known poets, in so far as any nineteenth-century Welsh woman may be said to be well known as an English-language poet. Each of the women I have studied wrote at a different point in the nineteenth century, a period of rapid and intense social change; each maintained her own particular and deeply held connection with Wales. In their diversity of perspective, these poets present a spectrum of points of view which has been a challenging, but ultimately fruitful, site for exploration.

The second part of my project here has been to establish the extent to which a consideration of the poets' various species of Welshness may add to current understandings of women's experience in relation to nineteenth-century patriarchal ideologies, and it is in this respect that the explorations made in this book have been most rewarding.

Like all women writing for public consumption during the nineteenth century, the poets examined here are concerned with ideas about authority and poetic identity. In discussing Felicia Hemans, for example, I have been able to include a poet whose work has already been widely debated in terms of gender issues. Hemans is considered to be both architect and archetype of Victorian domestic ideology, and her poetry has been analysed extensively by critics concerned to explore the complexities inherent in her apparent promotion of these values. My examination of the Welsh poems by Hemans has endorsed current feminist readings which problematize the poet's reputation as the acquiescent embodiment of Victorian patriarchy. The Welsh works indicate that her sense of herself as a 'naturalized Welsh woman' provided the poet with additional resources through which to articulate her prevailing preoccupation with ideas about women, writing and home.

At the later end of the chronological spectrum, Anna Walter Thomas represents a complete contrast with the somewhat fraught gender-consciousness expressed by Felicia Hemans. Thomas's poems do not suggest a problematic sense of contemporary gender relations. The highly privileged position from which Thomas wrote manifests itself in the poetry through a supremely self-confident and implicitly or explicitly 'male' voice. Her status as a prominent member of the cultural elite in late nineteenth-century Wales allowed Thomas access to the National Eisteddfod movement. This in its turn provided her with a forum in which not merely to explore but authoritatively to pronounce her poetic and political vision. This poet's Welshness, then, in direct contrast with that of Hemans, allowed her space to express not troubled marginality but assured dominance.

With one exception, the seven poets studied belong to the middle social ranks of nineteenth-century society, but their own viewpoints on social hierarchies differ, in a manner which is significantly related to their attitude towards their Welsh inheritance or connection. I have argued that the poems of Jane Cave, for example, the first and earliest of them, writing at a time when the emergent middle class had yet to establish itself as the dominant force it would later become, suggest a class identity which is defensive rather than confident. The poet's Calvinistic Methodist faith – an inheritance from her Welsh upbringing – instilled in her an egalitarian approach to class hierarchy which emerges through the poetry, but which is at odds with her persistent stylistic conservatism. Similarly Sarah Williams, another Welsh Nonconformist by upbringing, for all that she was writing much later, during the mid-Victorian era of middle-class dominance, uses her Welsh poems to explore a range of anxieties about bourgeois life in Victorian London. I have also examined the work of Maria James, the working-class emigrant to America, and suggested that, although her Methodism cannot be seen as a marker of class in the American context, the poet's Welsh identity nevertheless informs and facilitates exploration of ideas about freedom and confinement, potential and frustration, which are pertinent to an understanding of class structures in the period.

The cultural context out of which these women poets emerged was not only patriarchal and predominantly middle class, but also, increasingly as the century progressed, imperial. An important aspect of this study has been to explore the ways in which the poetry engages with ideas about empire. In this context I have referred to a number of post-colonial theorists and suggested that readings of English-language works by Welsh women add to this currently developing body of thought. The issue of language is central to post-colonial criticism, but the nineteenth-century Welsh context clearly problematizes the prevalent exclusion of European minority-language literatures from contemporary theoretical post-colonial debate. Maria James, for example, was uprooted from her home in Wales and compelled to learn English in order to survive in America. I have argued that the fabric of her poetry reveals the complex nature of James's position as a linguistically colonized subject who is also implicated in the project to colonize the New World.

Just as the English imperial drive was adversely affecting linguistic communities across the globe, its increased cultural colonization was also proving particularly destructive to the native Celtic languages of the British Isles. The English government's 'Blue Books' report of 1847 represented a watershed of epic proportions in Welsh cultural life, linking supposed moral laxity in Wales, particularly in its women, with the prevalence of the Welsh language. My readings of poetry written after 1847, such as that by Anna Walter Thomas, for example, indicate the extent of the impact of this crisis in Wales. Anna Walter Thomas was born in England but determined to 'master' the Welsh language, a feat which she managed spectacularly well. Though Thomas wrote in English, her accomplishments in Welsh, along with her elevated class status, enabled her to achieve an important position in the National Eisteddfod movement. In her two poems, importantly both rewarded with prizes at the National Eisteddfod, Welshness is celebrated, but only in so far as it is seen to contribute to Anglocentric dominance. I have suggested that the adjudicators' selection of those poems indicates the force of the imperative felt in Wales in the aftermath of the 1847 report to assert the unimpeachably submissive loyalty of the Welsh in the project of British imperialism.

It is interesting that all of the women included in this study were exiles of one sort or another: even Sarah Williams, who never left her birthplace, may be considered in exile in so far as she belonged to the London-Welsh. In most cases they were exiles for pragmatic reasons; their parents' employment or their marriages took them from Wales to England, or, in the case of Maria James, to America. Welsh-born poet Emily Pfeiffer lived for most of her adult life in London, and an ambivalence towards Welshness is evident in her poems. In *Glan Alârch: His Silence and Song* Pfeiffer celebrates Welsh culture and urges political action to revive its potency. In *The Wynnes of Wynhavod* she invests Welsh identity with a moral authority; at the same time, however, the Welsh culture depicted in *Glan Alârch: His Silence and Song* is in decline, and at the end of *The Wynnes of Wynhavod* she urges Welsh acceptance of a subordinate position in marriage with the English colonizers. For Ann Julia Hatton, exile in Wales was an enforced condition of her material survival. I have argued that in her identification with Wales and Welsh culture, Hatton finds a resource through which to articulate ideas about marginality and subjection which challenge prevalent patriarchal ideologies in terms of gender and imperialism. But the claims made by Felicia Hemans to a 'naturalized' Welsh identity do not appear to have mitigated the pernicious jingoism of her English imperialistic loyalties.

★ ★ ★

I began this survey by referring to Gillian Clarke's assertion that the literature of Wales represents evidence that 'the nation has always existed'. My readings of poetry written by these nineteenth-century women suggests, perhaps unsurprisingly, given their geographic distance from Wales and their dependence on the English literary marketplace, that Welsh identity for them was an often contradictory and fragmented consciousness. Nevertheless, I would argue that these women's expression in verse of their respective varieties of Welshness offers substantial material with which to complement current understandings of women's history during the nineteenth-century apogee of British imperialism. My analyses further suggest that Welshness functions in the poems both to inform and to resource explorations of other aspects integral to the project of Victorian patriarchy.

Implicit in Gillian Clarke's call for the invention of a new Welsh consciousness is the imperative for an elite group of 'brilliant' Welsh artists to take the lead. Also implicit in it, I would argue, is an assumption that the evidence of such nationhood as exists today is contained in canonical works now included on examination syllabuses 'throughout Britain'. But it seems to me that from a more comprehensive view of Welsh literature, one which encompasses work by writers who may never achieve the recognition enjoyed by R. S. Thomas and Dylan Thomas, may proceed an understanding of Welsh identity which will galvanize contemporary artists into creating a genuinely new nation.

Notes

Notes to Introduction

1   Gillian Clarke, 'Ffiw: Referendum Reactions', *The New Welsh Review*, 38 (Autumn 1997), p.11.
2   Ibid.
3   Bill Ashcroft, Gareth Griffiths and Helen Tiffin, *The Empire Writes Back: Theory and Practice in Post-colonial Literatures* (London: Routledge, 1989).
4   Sandra M. Gilbert and Susan Gubar (eds), *Shakespeare's Sisters: Feminist Essays on Women Poets* (Bloomington: Indiana University Press, 1979), p.xv.
5   Virginia Woolf, *A Room of One's Own* (1928) in *A Room of One's Own and Three Guineas*, ed. Michele Barrett (Harmondsworth: Penguin, 1993), p.44.
6   Gilbert and Gubar, *Shakespeare's Sisters*, p.xvi.
7   Ibid., p.xx.
8   Angela Leighton, *Victorian Women Poets: Writing Against the Heart* (London: Harvester Wheatsheaf, 1992), p.2.
9   Virginia Woolf, *Three Guineas* (1938) in *A Room of One's Own and Three Guineas*, p.34.
10 Ibid.
11 See, for example, Toril Moi, *Sexual Textual Politics: Feminist Literary Theory* (London: Routledge, 1985), pp.1–18.
12 Woolf, *Three Guineas*, p.232.
13 Elaine Showalter, *A Literature of Their Own: From Charlotte Brontë to Doris Lessing* (London: Virago, 1978), p.8.
14 Eric Hobsbawm, *Nations and Nationalism Since 1780: Programme, Myth, Reality* (Cambridge: Cambridge University Press, 1990), p.5.
15 John Davies, *A History of Wales* (Harmondsworth: Penguin, 1993), p.339.
16 Ieuan Gwynedd Jones, *Mid-Victorian Wales: The Observers and the Observed* (Cardiff: University of Wales Press, 1992), p.19.
17 Ibid., p.20.
18 Ibid., p.55.
19 Frederic Jameson, *Marxism and Form* (Princeton: Princeton University Press, 1971), p.413.

20 Mary Poovey, *The Proper Lady and the Woman Writer: Ideology and Style in the Works of Mary Wollstonecraft, Jane Austen and Mary Shelley* (Chicago: University of Chicago Press, 1984), pp.156–7.

21 Cora Kaplan, 'Pandora's Box: Subjectivity, Class and Sexuality in Socialist Feminist Criticism', in Gayle Green and Coppelia Kahn (eds), *Making a Difference: Feminist Literary Criticism* (London: Routledge, 1985), p.152.

22 Ibid.

23 Ibid., p.166.

24 Gayatri Chakravorty Spivak, 'Three Women's Texts and a Critique of Imperialism', in Catherine Belsey and Jane Moore (eds), *The Feminist Reader: Essays in Gender and the Politics of Literary Criticism* (London: Macmillan, 1989), p.175.

25 Spivak is profoundly concerned in this essay to interrogate Western feminist criticism for its tendency to 'reproduce the axioms of imperialism'. See ibid., p.175.

26 Benedict Anderson, *Imagined Communities: Reflections on the Origin and Spread of Nationalism* (London: Verso, 1983), *passim*.

27 Hobsbawm, *Nations and Nationalism,* p.12.

28 Ibid., p.9.

29 Ibid., p.46.

30 Ibid., p.10.

31 Gwyn A. Williams, *When Was Wales? The History, People and Culture of an Ancient Country* (Harmondsworth: Penguin, 1985), p.304.

32 Bill Ashcroft, Gareth Griffiths and Helen Tiffin (eds), *The Post-Colonial Studies Reader* (London: Routledge, 1995), p.2.

33 Davies, *A History of Wales*, p.161.

34 Williams, *When Was Wales?*, pp.88–9

35 Davies, *A History of Wales*, p.161.

36 Ashcroft, Griffiths and Tiffin, *The Empire Writes Back*, p.2.

37 A minor industry has been generated in the past decade or so by theorists who are interested in Felicia Hemans in terms of her importance for Victorian literary culture. Feminist and non-feminist critics have been drawn to Hemans as a major figure in the construction of Victorian domestic ideology. See, for example, Leighton, *Victorian Women Poets*; Jerome J. McGann, 'Literary History, Romanticism and Felicia Hemans', and Susan Wolfson, '"Domestic Affections" and "The Spear of Minerva": Felicia Hemans and the Dilemma of Gender', both in Carol Shiner Wilson and Joel Haefner (eds), *Revisioning Romanticism: British Women Writers 1776–1837* (Philadelphia: University of Pennsylvania Press, 1994).

38 A recent exception to this neglect is included in Jane Aaron's Welsh-language study of nineteenth-century Welsh women writers, *Pur Fel y Dur: Y Gymraes yn Llên Menywod y Bedwaredd Ganrif ar Bymtheg* (Cardiff: University of Wales Press, 1998), pp.89–95.

39 For a discussion of the impact of the 1832 Act on the formation of middle-class consciousness in Britain see, for example, Leonore Davidoff and Catherine Hall, *Family Fortunes: Men and Women of the English Middle Class 1780–1850* (London:

Hutchinson, 1987), pp.18–19; David Thomson, *England in the Nineteenth Century* (Harmondsworth: Penguin, 1950), pp.21–3.

[40] Thomson, *England in the Nineteenth Century*, p.117.

[41] Geoffrey Best, *Mid-Victorian Britain 1851–75* (London: Fontana, 1971), pp.252–4.

[42] For a discussion of the effects of enclosure on patterns of emigration from Wales see, for example, Davies, *A History of Wales*, p.335.

[43] Williams, *When Was Wales?*, p.161.

[44] Ibid., p.170.

[45] See, for example, Joel Haefner, 'The Romantic Scene(s) of Writing', in Shiner Wilson and Haefner (eds), *Revisioning Romanticism*, pp.256–73.

[46] Davidoff and Hall, *Family Fortunes*, p.13.

[47] Elizabeth K. Helsinger, Robin Lauterbach Sheets and William Veeder, *The Woman Question: Society and Literature in Britain and America 1837–83*, vol. 1 (Chicago: University of Chicago Press, 1983), pp.4–5.

[48] Ibid., vol. 2, p.40.

[49] Davidoff and Hall, *Family Fortunes*, passim.

[50] For a range of feminist perspectives on women and Victorian institutional discourses see, for example, Lynda Nead, *Myths of Sexuality* (Oxford: Blackwell, 1988); Helena Michie, *The Flesh Made Word: Female Figures and Women's Bodies* (Oxford: Oxford University Press, 1987); Jane M. Ussher, *Women's Madness: Misogyny or Mental Illness?* (London: Harvester Wheatsheaf, 1991).

[51] Angela Leighton, Introduction II, in Angela Leighton and Margaret Reynolds (eds), *Victorian Women Poets: An Anthology* (Oxford: Blackwell, 1995), p.xxxv.

[52] See, for example, McGann, 'Literary History'; Wolfson, '"Domestic Affections"'.

[53] Linda Colley, *Britons: Forging the Nation, 1701–1837* (London: Pimlico, 1994), p.370.

[54] Jane Aaron, 'A National Seduction: Wales in Nineteenth-Century Women's Writing', *The New Welsh Review* 27 (Autumn/Winter, 1994–5), p.32.

[55] See, for example, Williams, *When Was Wales?*, passim; Davies, *A History of Wales*, passim.

[56] See, for example, Jane Aaron, 'Finding a Voice in Two Tongues: Gender and Colonization', in Jane Aaron, Teresa Rees, Sandra Betts and Moira Vincentelli (eds), *Our Sisters' Land: The Changing Identities of Women in Wales* (Cardiff: University of Wales Press, 1994).

[57] Thomson, *England in the Nineteenth Century*, p.107.

[58] Ibid., p.108.

[59] Jones, *Mid-Victorian Wales*, p.15.

[60] Ibid., p.108.

[61] Williams, *When Was Wales?*, p.155.

[62] Jones, *Mid-Victorian Wales*, pp.6–7.

[63] Ibid., p.5.

[64] Ibid., p.7.

[65] Davies, *A History of Wales*, p.391.

[66] Williams, *When Was Wales?*, p.208.

[67] Jones, *Mid-Victorian Wales*, p.7.

Notes to Chapter 1

1   Roland Mathias, 'Poets of Breconshire', *Brycheiniog: The Journal of the Brecknock Society*, XIX (1980–81), 36–8.

2   Claire Tomalin, in the *Independent*, cited in Roger Lonsdale (ed.), *Eighteenth-Century Women Poets: An Oxford Anthology* (Oxford: Oxford University Press, 1989), dust jacket.

3   Alice Browne, *The Eighteenth-Century Feminist Mind* (Brighton: Harvester Wheatsheaf, 1987), p.27.

4   Jane Cave, *Poems on Various Subjects, Entertaining, Elegiac and Religious* (4th edn, Bristol: N. Biggs, 1794), p.1.

5   See Showalter, *A Literature of Their Own, passim*.

6   Cave, *Poems* (4th edn), p.1.

7   Ibid., p.2.

8   See, for example, Browne, *The Eighteenth-Century Feminist Mind*, p.1.

9   Cave, *Poems* (4th edn), p.2.

10   Ibid., p.119.

11   Ibid.

12   Ibid.

13   Ibid., p.126.

14   Ibid.

15   Ibid.

16   Ibid.

17   Ibid., p.202.

18   Adrienne Rich, 'Compulsory Heterosexuality and Lesbian Experience', in E. Abel and E. K. Abel (eds), *The Signs Reader: Women, Gender and Scholarship* (Chicago: University of Chicago Press, 1983), pp.156–7.

19   For Freud's early work on the unconscious see Sigmund Freud and Josef Breuer, *Studies on Hysteria*, trans. by James and Alix Strachey, Penguin Freud Library 3 (Harmondsworth: Penguin, 1974), *passim*.

20   Hélène Cixous, 'Sorties: Out and Out: Attacks/Ways Out/Forays', in Hélène Cixous and Catherine Clement, *The Newly Born Woman*, trans. by Betsy Wing (Manchester: Manchester University Press, 1986), p.63.

21   Graham Smith, *Something to Declare: 1,000 Years of Customs and Excise* (London: Harrap, 1980), p.33.

22   Ibid.

23   Davidoff and Hall, *Family Fortunes*, p.20.

24   Ibid., p.172.

25   Cave, *Poems* (4th edn), p.46.

26   Ibid., p.27.

27   Ibid., p.46.

28   Colley, *Britons*, p.192.

29   Ibid., p.238.

30   Lonsdale, *Eighteenth-Century Women Poets*, p.xxiv.

31   Colley, *Britons*, p.5.

32   See Geraint H. Jenkins, 'The New Enthusiasts', in Trevor Herbert and Gareth

Elwyn Jones (eds), *The Remaking of Wales in the Eighteenth Century* (Cardiff: University of Wales Press, 1988), p.45.

33 Mathias, 'Poets of Breconshire', p.35.

34 Quoted in ibid., p.35.

35 Cave, *Poems* (4th edn), p.190.

36 Jenkins, 'The New Enthusiasts', p.43.

37 T. Evans, *The History of Modern Enthusiasm* (London, 1752), cited in ibid., p.61.

38 Colley, *Britons*, p.61.

39 Ashcroft et al., *The Empire Writes Back*, p.4.

40 For an account of the primacy of 'heart over head' in eighteenth- and nineteenth-century Welsh Methodist culture, see, for example, Jane Aaron, 'Daughters of Dissent', *Planet* 94 (1992), pp.33–43.

41 Jane Cave, *Poems on Various Subjects, Entertaining, Elegiac and Religious* (3rd edn, Shrewsbury: Printed for the Author, 1789), p.174.

42 William Wordsworth, *The Prelude* (1805), Book XIII, ll.1–119.

43 See, for example, Jane Austen, *Catherine and Other Writings*, ed. Margaret Doody and Douglas Murray (Oxford: Oxford University Press, 1993).

44 Cave, *Poems* (3rd edn), p.174.

45 See Alexander Pope, *Poetical Works*, ed. Herbert Davis (Oxford: Oxford University Press, 1966), p.37–50.

46 Cave, *Poems* (3rd edn), p.174.

47 Ibid., p.175.

48 Ibid.

49 Ibid., p.103.

50 Ibid.

51 Ibid.

52 Frantz Fanon, *Black Skin, White Mask* (1952), trans. by C. L. Markmann (London: Pluto 1986), pp.18, 38.

53 Ibid., p.38.

Notes to Chapter 2

1 Ann Julia Hatton, *Scrap Book* MS, 1833–4 (City and County of Swansea: Swansea Museum Collection), cited in Ivor J. Bromham, 'Ann of Swansea', *Glamorgan Historian*, 7 (1971), pp.173–86.

2 For biographical material on the Kemble family see Yvonne Ffrench, *Mrs Sarah Siddons: Tragic Actress* (London: Derek Verschoyle, 1954); Kathleen Mackenzie, *The Great Sarah: The Life of Mrs Siddons* (London: Evans Brothers, 1968); Roger Manvell, *Sarah Siddons: Portrait of an Actress* (London: Heinemann, 1970).

3 Bromham, 'Ann of Swansea', p.174.

4 Manvell, *Sarah Siddons*, p.117.

5 Ffrench, *Mrs Sarah Siddons*, p.80.

6 Mackenzie, *The Great Sarah*, p.97.

7 Ibid., *passim*.

8   See Aaron, 'A National Seduction', pp.31–8.
9   Janet Todd, *Sensibility: An Introduction* (London: Methuen, 1986), p.2.
10 Ibid., p.23.
11 Ibid., p.19.
12 Ibid., p.21.
13 Ibid., p.15.
14 Ibid.
15 Manvell, *Sarah Siddons*, p.4.
16 Ivor Bromham relates how, between 1806 and 1809, Hatton embarked on a short-lived enterprise of running a 'school for dancing and deportment' at Kidwelly. See Bromham, 'Ann of Swansea', pp.176–7.
17 Todd, *Sensibility*, p.28.
18 Ann of Swansea (Ann Julia Hatton), *Poetic Trifles* (Waterford: Printed for the Authoress, 1811), p.54.
19 Ibid.
20 Ibid., p.262.
21 Todd, *Sensibility*, p.3.
22 Hatton, *Poetic Trifles*, p.148. The emphasis is by Hatton.
23 Hatton, *Poetic Trifles*, p.148. The emphases are by Hatton.
24 Bromham, 'Ann of Swansea', p.175.
25 Hatton, *Poetic Trifles*, p.137.
26 Ibid., p.138. The emphasis is by Hatton.
27 Ibid., p.8.
28 Ibid.
29 Bridget Orr, 'The Only Free People in the Empire: Gender Difference in Colonial Discourse', in Chris Tiffin and Alan Lawson (eds), *Describing Empire: Post-coloniality and Textuality* (London: Routledge, 1994), p.156.
30 Ibid.
31 Thomas Chatterton's *Felix Farley's Bristol Journey* (1768), and James MacPherson's *Fragments of Ancient Poetry Collected in the Highlands of Scotland and Translated from the Gaelic or Erse Language*.
32 Williams, *When Was Wales?*, p.69.
33 Ibid., p.262.
34 Ibid.
35 Ibid., p.263.
36 Ibid., p.68.
37 Ibid.
38 Orr, 'The Only Free People in the Empire', p.154.
39 Anthony D. Smith, *National Identity* (Harmondsworth: Penguin, 1991), pp.16–17.
40 Hatton, *Poetic Trifles*, p.68.
41 Ibid., p.70.
42 See Norman Lewis Thomas, *The Story of Swansea's Districts and Villages*, vol. II, iv–viii, with an abridged vol. I (Swansea: Qualprint (Wales), 1969), p.iv.
43 Moira Dearnley, 'Condem'd to wither on a foreign strand', *The New Welsh Review* 41, XI/i (1998), 56–9.
44 Ibid., p.58.

[45] Hatton, *Poetic Trifles*, p.75.

[46] Ibid.

[47] Ibid.

[48] *The Cambrian*, 29 December 1838, quoted in Bromham, 'Ann of Swansea', p.178.

[49] Colley, *Britons*, p.5.

Notes to Chapter 3

[1] Leighton, *Victorian Women Poets*, p.20.

[2] Wolfson, '"Domestic Affections"', p.128.

[3] Jane Williams (Ysgafell), *The Literary Women of England* (London: Saunders, Otley and Co., 1861), p.420.

[4] In her essay 'Hemans and Home: Victorianism, Feminine "Internal Enemies", and the Domestication of National Identity', Tricia Lootens alludes briefly to the issue of national identity in relation to Hemans's Welsh poems. But the essay focuses primarily on the tensions between gender identity and English patriotism. See Angela Leighton (ed.), *Victorian Women Poets: A Critical Reader* (Oxford: Blackwell, 1996), pp.1–23.

[5] Peter W. Trinder, *Mrs Hemans*, Writers of Wales series (Cardiff: University of Wales Press, 1984), p.3.

[6] See, for example, Leighton and Reynolds (eds), *Victorian Women Poets*, *passim*.

[7] Catherine Hall, *White, Male and Middle Class: Explorations in Feminism and History* (Cambridge: Polity Press, 1992).

[8] Leighton, *Victorian Women Poets*, p.19.

[9] George Gilfillan, 'Female Authors No. 1, Mrs Hemans', *Taits Edinburgh Magazine* (1847), quoted in Helsinger, Lauterbach Sheets and Veeder, *The Woman Question*, vol. 3, p.3.

[10] Leighton, *Victorian Women Poets*, p.19.

[11] William Michael Rossetti (ed.), *The Poetical Works of Mrs Felicia Hemans* (London: Ward Lock and Co., 1873), p.xi.

[12] Leighton, *Victorian Women Poets*, p.19.

[13] Trinder, *Mrs Hemans*, pp.18, 20.

[14] See, for example, Leighton, *Victorian Women Poets*, p.23.

[15] Colley, *Britons*, p.265.

[16] Felicia Hemans, *The Poetical Works of Mrs Hemans*, Albion Edition (London: Frederick Warne and Co., n.d.), p.404.

[17] Ibid.

[18] Ibid.

[19] Ibid. The emphasis is by Hemans.

[20] For an analysis of the effects of foreign policy and domestic upheaval in the period, see, for example, Eric Hobsbawn, *The Age of Revolution 1789–1848* (London: Abacus, 1962), *passim*.

[21] Thomson, *England in the Nineteenth Century*, p.40.

[22] Hemans, *The Poetical Works*, Albion edn, p.629.

[23] Ibid.

[24] Hall, *White, Male and Middle Class*, p.82.

25 See William Wordsworth, Preface to the *Lyrical Ballads with Pastoral and Other Poems* (1802), in Stephen Gill (ed.), *William Wordsworth* (Oxford: Oxford University Press, 1984), pp.595–615.

26 Wolfson, '"Domestic Affections"', p.128.

27 Elizabeth Barrett Browning, 'Felicia Hemans' (1837), in Leighton and Reynolds, *Victorian Women Poets*, p.67.

28 See Meredith B. Raymond and Mary Rose Sullivan (eds), *The Letters of Elizabeth Barrett Browning to Mary Russell Mitford: 1836–1854* (Winifield: Wedgestone Press, 1983), p.425.

29 William Wordsworth to Dorothy Wordsworth, August 1830, in Alan G. Hill (ed.), *Letters: The Later Years, 1821–1853* (Oxford: Clarendon Press, 1978–88), p.311.

30 Francis Jeffrey, Review of *Records of Woman* (2nd edn) and *The Forest Sanctuary* (2nd edn), *The Edinburgh Review*, 50 (1829), 24.

31 Maria Jane Jewsbury, 'Original Papers Literary Sketches No.1, Felicia Hemans', *The Athenaeum*, 171 (February 1831), 187.

32 Henry F. Chorley, *Memorials of Mrs Hemans with Illustrations of Her Literary Character From Her Private Correspondence*, vol. 1 (London: Saunders, Otley and Co., 1836), p.137.

33 Rossetti (ed.), *Poetical Works*, p.xxxvii.

34 Hemans, *The Poetical Works*, Albion edn, p.30. The emphasis is by Hemans.

35 Ibid., p.30. Emphasis by Hemans.

36 Ibid., p.31.

37 Ibid., p.30.

38 Ibid., p.35.

39 Ibid., p.30.

40 Ibid., p.33.

41 Helsinger et al., *The Woman Question*, p.128.

42 See Norma Clarke, *Ambitious Heights: Writing, Friendship, Love – The Jewsbury Sisters, Felicia Hemans and Jane Welsh Carlyle* (London: Routledge, 1990); Cora Caplan, *Salt and Bitter and Good: Three Centuries of English and American Women Poets* (New York: Paddington, 1973).

43 Helsinger et al., *The Woman Question*, p.128.

44 Wolfson, '"Domestic Affections"', p.140.

45 Leighton, *Victorian Women Poets*, p.8.

46 Wolfson, '"Domestic Affections"', p.140.

47 Lootens, 'Hemans and Home', pp.1–23.

48 Jerome J. McGann, 'Literary History', p.220.

49 See Gwyn Jones (ed.), *The Oxford Book of Welsh Verse in English* (Oxford: Oxford University Press, 1977), p.282.

50 Hemans, *The Poetical Works*, Albion edn, p.122.

51 Ibid., p.441.

52 Hemans, *The Poetical Works*, Albion edn, p.122.

53 Ibid.

54 Ibid., p.451.

55 McGann, 'Literary History', p.223.

56 Wolfson, '"Domestic Affections"', p.141.
57 For a discussion of the use of so-called primitive ancient Celtic settings and culture as a resource for sentimental poetry, see Todd, *Sensibility*, pp.57–60.
58 Gwyn A. Williams, *When Was Wales?*.
59 Hemans, *The Poetical Works*, Albion edn, p.124.
60 Ibid.
61 Ashcroft et al., *The Empire Writes Back*, p.125.
62 Harriet Mary Hughes (Browne), *Memoir of the Life and Writings of Felicia Hemans: By Her Sister; With an Essay on Her Genius: By Mrs Sigourney* (Philadelphia: Lea and Blanchard, 1839), pp.83–4.
63 Ibid., p.300.
64 Hemans, *The Poetical Works*, Albion edn, p.459.
65 Hall, *White, Male and Middle Class*, p.208.
66 Ibid., p.219.
67 Hemans, *The Poetical Works*, Albion edn, p.413.
68 Ibid., pp.605–6.
69 Ibid., p.304.

Notes to Chapter 4

1 In Methodist terminology 'professor' refers to one who has found Christ and professes Him – as all good converts are expected to do.
2 Mary Garretson, letter to Mrs A. Potter, 26 May 1836, quoted in A. Potter, 'Introduction', Maria James, *Wales and Other Poems* (New York: John S. Taylor, 1839), p.41.
3 Ibid.
4 See, for example, Leighton and Reynolds (eds), *Victorian Women Poets*.
5 Carol Shiner Wilson, 'Lost Needles, Tangled Threads: Stitchery, Domesticity and the Artistic Enterprise in Barbauld, Edgeworth, Taylor and Lamb', in Shiner Wilson and Haefner (eds), *Revisioning Romanticism*, p.183.
6 Joel Haefner, 'The Romantic Scene(s) of Writing', in ibid., pp.265–67
7 Ashcroft et al., *The Empire Writes Back*, p.133.
8 Ibid., p.135.
9 Ibid., p.136, refers to Renata Wasserman, 'Reinventing the New World: Cooper and Alencar', *Comparative Literature* 2 (Spring 1984).
10 Ashcroft et al. (eds), *The Post-colonial Studies Reader*, p.249.
11 See Erna Olafson Hellerstein, Leslie Parker Hume and Karen M. Offen (eds), *Victorian Women: A Documentary Account of Women's Lives in Nineteenth-Century England, France and the United States of America* (Stanford: Stanford University Press, 1981), p.281.
12 James, *Wales and Other Poems*, pp.14–15.
13 Ibid., p.17.
14 Ibid., p.18.
15 Ibid., p.35.

16 Ibid., p.45.
17 Ibid., p.41.
18 Ibid., p.79.
19 Ibid.
20 Ibid.
21 Ibid.
22 Ibid., p.162.
23 Ibid., p.162–3.
24 Ibid., p.163–4.
25 Terry Coleman, *Passage to America: A History of Emigrants from Great Britain and Ireland in the Mid-Nineteenth Century* (Harmondsworth: Penguin, 1972), p.23.
26 Ibid., p.50.
27 Maldwyn Allen Jones, *American Immigration* (Chicago: University of Chicago Press, 1960), p.95.
28 Ibid., p.96.
29 James, *Wales and Other Poems*, p.34.
30 See Karen L. Kilcup (ed.), *Nineteenth-Century American Women Writers: An Anthology* (Oxford: Blackwell, 1977), *passim*.
31 Leighton, Introduction II, Leighton and Reynolds (eds), *Victorian Women Poets*, p.xxxv.
32 Jones, *Mid-Victorian Wales*, p.20.
33 See Jane Aaron, 'The Way Above the World: Religion and Gender in Welsh and Anglo-Welsh Women's Writing, 1780–1830', in Shiner Wilson and Haefner (eds), *Revisioning Romanticism*, pp.111–27.
34 James, *Wales and Other Poems*, p.36.
35 See ibid., pp.34–8.
36 Ibid., p.35.
37 Ibid., p.83.
38 Ibid.
39 Ibid., p.74.
40 Ibid.
41 Ibid., p.75.
42 Ibid., p.109.
43 Ibid., p.110.
44 Ibid.
45 See Coventry Patmore, *The Angel in the House* (1854–6) (London: George Bell and Son, 1885).
46 Kilcup (ed.), *Nineteenth-Century American Women Writers*, p.xiv.
47 For an account of the extent of Welsh emigration to Pennsylvania, New England, etc., see Coleman, *Passage to America*, *passim*.; Jones, *American Immigration*, *passim*.
48 James, *Wales and Other Poems*, p.47.
49 Ibid.
50 Ibid.
51 Ibid., p.48.
52 See William Wordsworth, *The Prelude* (1805), Book XIII.
53 James, *Wales and Other Poems*, pp.48–9.
54 Ann Julia Hatton and Felicia Hemans are two examples of this trend.

55 James, *Wales and Other Poems*, p.49.
56 Ibid., p.41.
57 Ashcroft et al. (eds), *The Post-colonial Studies Reader*, p.283.
58 Chinua Achebe, 'The African Writer and the English Language', quoted in Ngugi Wa Thiong'o, *Decolonizing the Mind: The Politics of Language in African Literature* (London: James Currey, 1986), p.8.
59 Ngugi, ibid., p.9. Ngugi has, in fact, written on post-coloniality in the Welsh context. In a 1993 essay he notes that 'the Third World is not the only place where English tried to grow on the graveyard of other people's languages . . . The decline of the Welsh language has roots in the inequality prevailing between the nationalities that inhabited the two linguistic regions.' Ngugi Wa Thiong'o, 'Imperialism of Language: English, a Language for the World?', in *Moving the Centre: The Struggle for Cultural Freedoms*, Studies in African Literature series (London: James Currey, 1993). I am grateful to Victor Golightly for bringing this connection to my attention.
60 See James, *Wales and Other Poems*, p.38.
61 Ibid., p.49.
62 Ibid.
63 Ibid., p.69.
64 Ngugi, *Decolonizing the Mind*, p.13.
65 James, *Wales and Other Poems*, p.50.
66 Ibid., p.51.
67 Ibid., p.52.
68 Ibid., p.94.

Notes to Chapter 5

1   E. H. Plumptre, Memoir, in Sarah Williams (Sadie), *Twilight Hours: A Legacy of Verse* (London: Strahan and Co., 1868; 2nd edn 1872), p.xv.
2   Quoted in ibid., p.xxx. The emphases are by Williams.
3   Elaine Showalter (ed.), *Daughters of Decadence: Women Writers of the Fin-de-Siècle* (London: Virago, 1978), p.x.
4   Ibid.
5   Williams, *Twilight Hours*, p.viii.
6   ' "Sadie": In Memory of an Esteemed Contributor', *Good Words* (June 1868), 379.
7   Quoted in Williams, *Twilight Hours*, p.viii.
8   Ibid., p.xv.
9   Ibid., p.xiv.
10 For a discussion of the state of the medical profession in the nineteenth century, see, for example, Davidoff and Hall, *Family Fortunes*, pp.262–4.
11 Eliza Cook, 'The Surgeon's Knife' (1874), in Leighton and Reynolds (eds), *Victorian Women Poets*, p.183.
12 Ibid.

13 Williams, *Twilight Hours*, p.135.

14 Ibid.

15 In ibid., p.xii.

16 Ibid., p.108.

17 Ibid., p.85.

18 Ibid., pp.86–7.

19 In ibid., p.xx.

20 Ibid., p.xxiii.

21 Robert Buchanan, 'The Fleshly School of Poetry', *The Contemporary Review* (1871), in Joseph Bristow (ed.), *The Victorian Poet: Poetics and Persona* (London: Macmillan, 1987), p.142.

22 In Williams, *Twilight Hours*, p.xx.

23 Ibid., p.xxiv.

24 See F. L. Cross (ed.), *Oxford Dictionary of the Christian Church* (London: Oxford University Press, 1974), pp.765–6.

25 Algernon Charles Swinburne, 'Hymn to Proserpine', *Poems and Ballads* (London, 1866).

26 Williams, *Twilight Hours*, p.140.

27 Ibid.

28 Ibid., p.149.

29 For an account of the passionate expression involved in Welsh Nonconformist practice in the period, see, for example, Jenkins, 'The New Enthusiasts', p.45.

30 Jane Aaron, 'The Way Above the World', p.116.

31 Ibid., p.117.

32 Gareth Stedman Jones, *Outcast London: A Study in the Relationship Between the Classes in Victorian Society* (Oxford: Clarendon Press, 1971), p.239.

33 Ibid.

34 Williams, *Twilight Hours*, p.x.

35 See, for example, the piece 'He Never Smiled Again', in which Hemans describes the tragedy of King Henry I, who, 'after the death of his son William, who perished in a shipwreck off the coast of Normandy . . . was never seen to smile'. Felicia Hemans, footnote in *The Poetical Works* (Albion edn, n.d.), p.313.

36 Williams, *Twilight Hours*, p.x.

37 Ibid.

38 Ibid., p.xx.

39 See, for example, Hall, *White, Male and Middle Class*, passim.

40 See Davidoff and Hall, *Family Fortunes*, passim.

41 See Raymond Williams, *The Country and the City* (London: Hogarth, 1985), passim.

42 Quoted in Jones, *Outcast London*, p.241.

43 Ibid.

44 Ibid., p.245.

45 Williams, *Twilight Hours*, p.viii–ix.

46 Ibid., p.viii.

47 Karl Marx and Friedrich Engels, *Manifesto of the Communist Party* (1848), trans. by Samuel Moore (Woodbridge: Merlin Press, 1998), p.2.

48   Leighton, Introduction II, in Leighton and Reynolds (eds), *Victorian Women Poets*, p.xxxviii.

49   Williams, *Twilight Hours*, p.viii.

50   Ibid., p.32.

51   Dickens's novel opens: 'London. Michaelmas term lately over . . . Fog everywhere. Fog up the river . . . fog down the river, where it rolls defiled among the tiers of shipping, and the waterside pollutions of a great (and dirty) city . . .'. Charles Dickens, *Bleak House* (1852–3) (London: Hazell, Watson & Viney Ltd., n.d.), p.9.

52   See William Blake, *Complete Writings*, Geoffrey Keynes (ed.), (Oxford: Oxford University Press, 1966), p.170.

53   Williams, *Twilight Hours*, p.32.

54   *Good Words*, p.380.

55   Ibid.

56   In Williams, *Twilight Hours*, p.xv.

57   Ibid., p.xxvii.

58   Ibid., p.xxi.

59   Ibid., p.xx.

60   Ibid., p.xxix.

61   Elizabeth Barrett Browning, *Aurora Leigh: A Poem in Nine Books* (London: Smith Elder and Co., 1887), Book I, p.1.

62   See, for example, Poovey, *The Proper Lady and the Woman Writer*; Elaine Showalter, *A Literature of Their Own*.

63   In Williams, *Twilight Hours*, p.xviii.

64   In ibid.

65   See, for example, Sandra M. Gilbert and Susan Gubar, *The Madwoman in the Attic: The Woman Writer and the Nineteenth-Century Literary Imagination* (New Haven: Yale University Press, 1979); Gilbert and Gubar (eds), *Shakespeare's Sisters*; Leighton, *Victorian Women Poets*.

66   Williams, *Twilight Hours*, p.130.

67   George Henry Lewes, 'The Lady Novelists', *The Westminster Review*, 58 (1852), pp.133–4.

68   For a comprehensive analysis of the ways in which Victorian medical discourse linked intellectual activity in women with hysterical symptoms, see Elaine Showalter, *The Female Malady: Women, Madness and English Culture, 1830–1980* (London: Virago, 1987), *passim*.

69   See Pierre Brunel (ed.), *Companion to Literary Myths, Heroes and Archetypes* (London: Routledge, 1992).

70   See Leighton, *Victorian Women Poets*, pp.31–2.

71   Hemans, *The Poetical Works*, Albion edn, p.523.

72   For a discussion of Victorian women writers and poetic identity, see, for example, Gilbert and Gubar, *The Mad Woman in the Attic*; eadem (eds), *Shakespeare's Sisters*; Leighton, *Victorian Women Poets*.

73   Plumptre, Preface, in Williams, *Twilight Hours*, p.ii.

74   Leighton and Reynolds (eds), *Victorian Women Poets*, p.xxxvi.

75   Williams, *Twilight Hours* (1868 edn), p.25.

[76] Leighton, *Victorian Women Poets*, p.xxxvii.
[77] *Good Words*, p.382.
[78] Williams, *Twilight Hours* (1868 edn), p.31.
[79] Ibid.
[80] Ibid.
[81] See Williams, *The Country and the City, passim*.
[82] Williams, *Twilight Hours* (1868 edn), p.33.
[83] Ibid., p.37.
[84] Ibid., pp.37–8.
[85] Ibid., p.45.
[86] Ibid., p.42.
[87] Ibid., p.47.
[88] Ibid., p.55.
[89] Ibid, p.56–7.
[90] Williams, *The Country and the City*, p.154.
[91] Williams, *Twilight Hours* (1868 edn), pp.58–9.

Notes to Chapter 6

[1]   For discussion of Victorian complacency see, for example, Thomson, *England in the Nineteenth Century*; Best, *Mid-Victorian Britain 1851–75*; Denis Judd, *Empire: The British Imperial Experience from 1765 to the Present* (London: Fontana, 1996).
[2]   Emily Davis (Pfeiffer), *The Holly Branch: An Album for 1843* (London), p.ii.
[3]   See W. Gareth Evans, *Education and Female Emancipation: The Welsh Experience, 1847–1914* (Cardiff: University of Wales Press, 1990), pp.1–35.
[4]   Review of *Gerard's Monument and Other Poems, The Times* (1873).
[5]   Review of *Gerard's Monument and Other Poems, Liverpool Albion* (1873).
[6]   Leighton and Reynolds (eds), *Victorian Women Poets*, pp.338–43.
[7]   Hall, *White, Male and Middle Class*, p.60.
[8]   Ibid., p.207.
[9]   Leighton and Reynolds (eds), *Victorian Women Poets*, p.339.
[10] Leighton, Introduction II, in ibid., p.xxxvii.
[11] Pfeiffer, *Gerard's Monument and other Poems*, p.173.
[12] Ibid.
[13] Ibid.
[14] For discussion of Victorian constructions of motherhood see, for example, Helsinger et al., *The Woman Question*, vol. 3, pp.13–14; Hall, *White, Male and Middle Class*, p.59.
[15] Pfeiffer, *Gerard's Monument and Other Poems*, p.173.
[16] Mary Poovey, *Uneven Developments: The Ideological Work of Gender in Mid-Victorian Britain* (Chicago: University of Chicago Press, 1989), p.9.
[17] Hall, *White, Male and Middle Class, passim*.
[18] Poovey, *Uneven Developments*, p.10.
[19] Pfeiffer, *Gerard's Monument and Other Poems*, p.123.

20 Poovey, *Uneven Developments*, p.10.
21 Sarah Lewis, *Woman's Mission* (1839), in Helsinger et al., *The Woman Question*, vol. 3, p.7.
22 Nead, *Myths of Sexuality*, p.18.
23 Ibid., pp.140–1.
24 Helsinger et al., *The Woman Question*, vol. 3, p.113.
25 Margaret Reynolds, introductory notes on Emily Pfeiffer, Leighton and Reynolds (eds), *Victorian Women Poets*, p.339.
26 Emily Pfeiffer, *Poems* (London: Strahan and Co., 1876), in ibid., pp.341–2.
27 Ibid., p. 341.
28 Leighton, Introduction II, in ibid., p.xxxvii.
29 Ibid.
30 Pfeiffer, *Poems*, p.xxxvii.
31 Ibid., pp.340–1.
32 The prayer begins 'Hail Mary, full of grace / Blessed art thou amongst women / And blessed is the fruit of thy womb, Jesus'. See, for example, *The Sunday Missal* (London: Collins Liturgical Publications, 1975), p.798.
33 See Charlotte Brontë, *Jane Eyre* (1847) (Harmondsworth: Penguin, 1966), p.311.
34 Helsinger et al., *The Woman Question*, vol. 3, p.111.
35 Jones, *Mid-Victorian Wales*, p.10.
36 Hall, *White, Male and Middle Class*, p.207.
37 Poovey, *Uneven Developments*, pp. 164–98.
38 Williams, *When Was Wales?*, p.104.
39 Ibid., p.67.
40 Jones, *Mid-Victorian Wales*, p.103.
41 Ibid., p.114.
42 See 'The Rev. John Griffith and the Survival of the Established Church in Nineteenth-Century Glamorgan', *Morgannwg*, XIII (1969), quoted in Jones, *Mid-Victorian Wales*, p.146.
43 Emily Pfeiffer, Preface to *Glan-Alârch: His Silence and Song* (London: Henry S. King and Co., 1877), p.i.
44 *The British Quarterly* (1877) quoted in Emily Pfeiffer, *Under the Aspens: Lyrical and Dramatic* (London: Kegan, Paul, Trench and Co., 1882), p.4.
45 *Carmarthen Journal* (1877), quoted in ibid., p.5.
46 *English Independent* (1877) quoted in ibid., p.5.
47 Pfeiffer, *Glan-Alârch*, p.1.
48 Ibid.
49 For discussion of the invention of tradition in Welsh cultural life during the nineteenth century, see Prys Morgan, 'From a Death to a View: The Hunt for the Welsh Past in the Romantic Period', in Eric Hobsbawm and Terence Ranger (eds), *The Invention of Tradition* (Cambridge University Press, 1983), pp.43–100.
50 Hall, *White, Male and Middle Class*, p.206.
51 Pfeiffer, *Glan-Alârch*, p.32.
52 Ibid., p.37.
53 Ibid.
54 Ibid., p.38.

55 Ibid.
56 Ibid.
57 Morgan, 'From a Death to a View', p.99.
58 For an account of the development of the early Celtic Church in Wales see, for example, Davies, *A History of Wales*, *passim*.
59 Pfeiffer, *Glan-Alârch*, pp.47–8.
60 Emily Pfeiffer, 'The Wynnes of Wynhavod', in Pfeiffer, *The Wynnes of Wynhavod: A Drama of Modern Life* (London: Kegan Paul and Co., 1882), pp.139–40.
61 Ibid. p.165.
62 Ibid., p.291. For a discussion of Victorian attitudes to Jewishness, see Vivian D. Lipman, *The Social History of the Jews in England, 1850–1950* (London: Watts and Co., 1954), pp.134–64.
63 Pfeiffer, 'The Wynnes of Wynhavod', p.291.
64 See, for example, the character of Mrs Woodcourt in Dickens, *Bleak House*, p.327.
65 Pfeiffer, 'The Wynnes of Wynhavod', pp.306–7.

Note to Chapter 7

1   Quoted in W. Glynn Williams, *Memoir of Mrs Anna Walter Thomas (Morfudd Eryri)* (Holywell: W. Williams and Son, n.d. [1922]), p.5.
2   Ibid., p.8.
3   Ibid., p.6.
4   See ibid., pp.8–9.
5   Ibid., p.9.
6   Ibid.
7   Ibid., p.14.
8   Ibid., p.15.
9   Ibid., p.21.
10 Ibid., p.15.
11 Ibid., p.22.
12 See Hywel Teifi Edwards, *The Eisteddfod*, Writers of Wales series (Cardiff: University of Wales Press, 1990).
13 In Williams, *Memoir*, p.23.
14 Ibid.
15 Edwards, *The Eisteddfod*, p.40.
16 Ibid.
17 See, for example, Davies, *A History of Wales*, *passim*.
18 Jones, *Mid-Victorian Wales*, p.5.
19 Ibid.
20 Ibid., p.63.
21 Williams, *Memoir*, p.19.
22 Ibid., p.20.
23 See Williams, *When Was Wales?*, p.205.

24   Hobsbawm, *The Age of Revolution*, p.241.
25   Williams, *When Was Wales?*, p.204.
26   Quoted in Jones, *Mid-Victorian Wales*, pp.147–8.
27   In David Tudor Evans (ed.), *Transactions of the Royal National Eisteddfod of Wales Held at Cardiff . . . in 1883* (Cardiff: Printed for the Association, 1884), pp.66–7.
28   Edwards, *The Eisteddfod*, p.26.
29   Anna Walter Thomas, 'Llandaff', in Evans, *Transactions 1883*, p.71.
30   For a discussion of the emergence of the Celtic Church in Wales, see, for example, Davies, *A History of Wales*, passim.
31   Thomas, in Evans, *Transactions 1883*, p.79.
32   Ibid.
33   Ibid., pp.84–5.
34   See, for example, Davies, *A History of Wales, 1883*, pp.443–4.
35   Thomas, in Evans, *Transactions 1883*, p.86.
36   Ibid., p.79.
37   Ibid., p.78.
38   Ibid.
39   The Oxford, or Tractarian, movement was a school of thought within the Church of England, centred at Oxford from around the middle of the nineteenth century. The movement aimed to defend the Church as a divine institution with an independent spiritual status, and to revive High Church traditions of the seventeenth century.
40   The Anglican Church in Ireland was disestablished in 1869. For an analysis of the links between this and the Welsh context, see, for example, Davies, *A History of Wales*, pp.433–4.
41   Williams, *When Was Wales?*, p.204.
42   Ibid.
43   Ibid.
44   Best, *Mid-Victorian Britain*, p.261.
45   Ibid., p.267.
46   In Williams, *Memoir*, p.9.
47   Anna Walter Thomas, 'Monody on Albert Victor Christian Edward, Duke of Clarence and Avondale', in *Transactions of the Royal National Eisteddfod 1892 (Rhyl)* (Oswestry: Printed for the Association, 1895), p.148.
48   Ibid., p.149.
49   Williams, *Memoir*, p.26.
50   Watkin Herbert Williams, Preface in ibid., p.3.
51   Williams, *Memoir*, p.19.
52   Ibid.
53   Ibid., p.20.
54   Jones, *Mid-Victorian Wales*, p.77.
55   Quoted in ibid., p.76, trans. by Ieuan Gwynedd Jones.
56   Hall, *White, Male and Middle Class*, pp.164–5.
57   Williams, *Memoir*, p.19.
58   Ibid., p.35.
59   Ibid., p.24.

60   Ibid., p.70.
61   Ibid., p.61.
62   Ibid., p.24.
63   Ibid., p.20.
64   See, for example, Helsinger et al., *The Woman Question, passim.*
65   Thomas, in Evans, *Transactions 1883*, p.83.
66   Matthew: 9:20–2, *The Holy Bible*, King James Version (1611).
67   See Evans, *Transactions 1883*, pp.66–70.
68   Leighton, *Victorian Women Poets*, p.3.
69   Thomas, in Evans, *Transactions 1883*, p.72.
70   See Woolf, *A Room of One's Own*, p.5.
71   Edwards, *The Eisteddfod*, p.37.
72   Ibid., p.39.
73   In Williams, *Memoir*, p.22.
74   Ibid.
75   In ibid., p.21.
76   Ashcroft et al. (eds), *The Post-colonial Studies Reader*, p.283.
77   Ibid.
78   Braj B. Kachru, *The Alchemy of English: The Spread, Functions and Models of Non-native Englishes* (Oxford: Pergamon Institute, 1996), quoted in ibid., p.291.
79   I use the term 'association' advisedly here. Despite her many gifts and accomplishments, as a woman Thomas was excluded from full membership of this formally educated cohort. Her ambitions to senior academic office, which she was not alone in believing her talents deserved, were ultimately disappointed. This suggests that in the case of Anna Walter Thomas, despite her apparent lack of interest in gender politics, the issue of her sex may inflect the experience and expression of class and national subject positions.
80   In Williams, *Memoir*, p.19.
81   Morgan, 'From a Death to a View', p.99.
82   Edwards, *The Eisteddfod*, p.50.
83   Williams, *Memoir*, p.22.
84   Thomas, in *Transactions 1892*, p.148.
85   Ibid.
86   Ibid.
87   Ibid., p.149.
88   Genesis 11: 9, *The Holy Bible*, King James Version (1611).
89   Thomas, in Evans, *Transactions 1883*, p.72.
90   Davies, *A History of Wales*, p.469.
91   Thomas, in Evans, *Transactions 1883*, p.84.
92   Ibid.
93   Thomas clearly sees Wales as implicated in a specifically Anglican form of religious colonialism, but the issue is a complex one. Welsh Nonconformity also did its share of foreign missionary work in the period. For a discussion of Welsh women's experience of Nonconformist missions to the New World during the nineteenth century see Jane Aaron, 'Slaughter and salvation', *The New Welsh Review*, 38 (Autumn 1997), 38–46.
94   Morgan, 'From a Death to a View', *passim.*

Selected Bibliography

Primary works

Cave, Jane, *Poems on Various Subjects, Entertaining Elegiac and Religious* (Winchester: Printed for the Author, 1783; 2nd edn, Bristol: Printed for the Author, 1786; 3rd edn, Shrewsbury: Printed for the Author, 1789; 4th edn, Bristol: N. Biggs, 1794).

Hatton, Ann Julia (Ann of Swansea), *Cambrian Pictures, or Every-One Has Errors*, 3 vols. (London: E. Kirby, 1810).

——, *Poetic Trifles* (Waterford: Printed for the Authoress, 1811).

——, *Scrap Book* MS (1833–4) (City and County of Swansea: Swansea Museum Collection).

Hemans, Felicia Dorothea, *Poems* (Liverpool: T. Cadell and W. Davies, 1808).

——, *The Domestic Affections and Other Poems* (London: T. Cadell and W. Davies, 1812).

——, *Tales and Historic Scenes in Verse* (London: John Murray, 1819).

——, *The Sceptic: A Poem* (London: John Murray, 1820).

——, *A Selection of Welsh Melodies, with symphonies and accompaniments by John Parry and characteristic words by Mrs Hemans*, 3 vols. (London: J. Power, 1822–9).

——, *The Siege of Valencia: A Dramatik Poem* (London: John Murray, 1823).

——, *The Forest Sanctuary and Other Poems* (London: John Murray, 1825).

——, *Records of Women with Other Poems* (Edinburgh and London: Blackwood and T. Cadell, 1828).

——, *Songs of the Affections, with Other Poems* (Edinburgh and London: Blackwood and T. Cadell, 1830).

——, *National Lyrics, and Songs for Music* (Dublin: William Curry, Jr. and Co., 1834).

——, *Scenes and Hymns of Life, with Other Religious Poems* (Edinburgh and London: Blackwood and T. Cadell, 1834).

——, *The Poetical Works of Mrs Felicia Hemans*, ed. by William Michael Rossetti (London: Ward Lock and Co., 1873).

——, *The Poetical Works of Mrs Hemans*, Albion edn (London: Frederick Warne and Co., n.d.).

——, *The Works of Mrs Hemans; with a memoir of her life, by her sister*, 7 vols. (Edinburgh and London: Blackwood and T. Cadell, 1813).

James, Maria, *Wales and Other Poems* (New York: John S. Taylor, 1839).

Pfeiffer, Emily Jane (Emily Davis), *The Holly Branch: An Album for 1843* (London, 1843).

——, *Valisnera: Or a Midsummer Day's Dream. A Tale* (1857).

——, *Gerard's Monument and Other Poems* (London: 1873; 2nd edn London: Kegan Paul and Co., 1878).

——, *Poems* (London: Strahan and Co., 1876).

——, *Glan-Alârch: His Silence and Song* (London: Henry S. King and Co., 1877).

——, *The Wynnes of Wynhavod: A Drama of Modern Life* (London: Kegan Paul and Co., 1882).

——, *Sonnets*, ed. J. E. Pfeiffer (London: Field and Tuer, 1886).

——, *Under the Aspens: Lyrical and Dramatic* (London: Kegan Paul and Co., 1887).

——, *Women and Work: An Essay Treating on the Relation to Health and Physical Development of the Higher Education of Girls* (London: Trubner and Co., 1888).

Thomas, Anna Walter (Morfudd Eryri) [and David Thomas], 'The Eisteddfod of the future', *Y Cymmrodor*, 2 (1878), 40–6.

——, 'Llandaff', in *Transactions of the Royal National Eisteddfod of Wales Held at Cardiff . . . in 1883*, ed. by David Tudor Evans (Cardiff: Printed for the Association, 1884), pp.65–88.

——, 'Monody on Albert Victor Christian Edward, Duke of Clarence and Avondale', in *Transactions of the Royal National Eisteddfod 1892 (Rhyl)* (Oswestry: Printed for the Association, 1895), pp.147–51.

Williams, Sarah (Sadie), *Twilight Hours: A Legacy of Verse* (London: Strahan and Co., 1868; 2nd edn 1872).

Secondary works

Aaron, Jane, *Pur Fel y Dur: Y Gymraes yn Llên Menywod y Bedwaredd Ganrif ar Bymtheg* (Cardiff: University of Wales Press, 1998).

——, 'Daughters of Dissent', *Planet*, 24 (1992), 33–42.

——, 'Finding a Voice in Two Tongues: Gender and Colonization', in Jane Aaron, Teresa Rees, Sandra Betts and Moira Vincentelli (eds), *Our Sisters' Land: The Changing Identities of Women in Wales* (Cardiff: University of Wales Press, 1994), pp.183–98.

——, 'The Way Above the World: Religion and Gender in Welsh and Anglo-Welsh Women's Writing, 1780–1830', in Carol Shiner Wilson and Joel Haefner (eds), *Revisioning Romanticism: British Women Writers, 1716–1837* (Philadelphia: University of Pennsylvania Press, 1994), pp.111–27.

——, 'A National Seduction: Wales in Nineteenth-Century Women's Writing', *The New Welsh Review*, 27 (1994–5), 31–8.

——, 'Seduction and Betrayal: Wales in Women's Fiction, 1785–1810', *Women's Writing*, 1, 1 (1994), 65–76, (1994–5), 31.

——, 'Slaughter and Salvation', *The New Welsh Review*, 38 (1997), 38–46.

Anderson, Benedict, *Imagined Communities: Reflections on the Origin and Spread of Nationalism* (London: Verso, 1983).

Ashcroft, Bill, Gareth Griffiths and Helen Tiffin, *The Empire Writes Back: Theory and Practice in Post-colonial Literatures* (London: Routledge, 1989).

—— (eds), *The Post-colonial Studies Reader* (London: Routledge, 1995).

Austen, Jane, *Catherine and Other Writings*, ed. by Margaret Doody and Douglas Murray (Oxford: Oxford University Press, 1993).

Barrett Browning, Elizabeth, *Aurora Leigh: A Poem in Nine Books* (1857) (London: Smith Elder and Co., 1887).

——, *The Letters of Elizabeth Barrett Browning to Mary Russell Mitford, 1836–1854*, ed. by Meredith B. Raymond and Mary Rose Sullivan (Winifield: Wedgestone Press, 1983).

Beddoe, Deirdre, 'Images of Welsh Women', in Tony Curtis (ed.), *Wales: The Imagined Nation* (Bridgend: Poetry Wales Press, 1986), pp.225–38.

——, 'Munitionettes, Maids and Mams: Women in Wales, 1914–1939', in Angela V. John (ed.), *Our Mothers' Land: Chapters in Welsh Women's History, 1830–1939* (Cardiff: University of Wales Press, 1991), pp.189–209.

Best, Geoffrey, *Mid-Victorian Britain, 1851–75* (London: Fontana, 1971).

Blake, William, *Complete Writings*, ed. by Geoffrey Keynes (Oxford: Oxford University Press, 1966).

Bromham, Ivor J., ' "Anne of Swansea" (Ann Julia Hatton): 1764–1838', *Glamorgan Historian*, 7 (1971), 173–86.

Brontë, Charlotte, *Jane Eyre* (1847) (Harmondsworth: Penguin, 1966).

Browne, Alice, *The Eighteenth-Century Feminist Mind* (Brighton: Harvester Wheatsheaf, 1987).

Buchanan, Robert, 'The Fleshly School of Poetry', *The Contemporary Review* (1871), in Joseph Bristow (ed.), *The Victorian Poet: Poetics and Persona* (London: Macmillan, 1987), p.142.

Chorley, Henry F., *Memorials of Mrs Hemans with Illustrations of Her Literary Character From Her Private Correspondence*, vol. 1 (London: Saunders, Otley and Co., 1836).

Cixous, Hélène and Catherine Clement, *The Newly Born Woman*, trans. by Betsy Wing (Manchester: Manchester University Press, 1986).

Clarke, Gillian, 'Ffiw: Referendum Reactions', *The New Welsh Review*, 38 (Autumn 1997), 11.

Clarke, Norma, *Ambitious Heights: Writing Friendship, Love – The Jewsbury Sisters, Felicia Hemans and Jane Welsh Carlyle* (London: Routledge, 1990).

Coleman, Terry, *Passage to America: A History of Emigrants from Great Britain and Ireland in the Mid-Nineteenth Century* (Harmondsworth: Penguin, 1972).

Coleridge, Samuel Taylor, *Poetical Works*, ed. by Ernest Hartley Coleridge (Oxford: Oxford University Press, 1912).

Colley, Linda, *Britons: Forging the Nation, 1707–1837* (London: Pimlico Press, 1992).

Davidoff, Leonore and Catherine Hall. *Family Fortunes: Men and Women of the English Middle Class, 1780–1850* (London: Hutchinson, 1987).

Davies, John, *A History of Wales* (Harmondsworth: Penguin, 1993).

Davies, Russell, *Secret Sins: Sex, Violence and Society in Carmarthenshire, 1870–1920* (Cardiff: University of Wales Press, 1996).

Dearnley, Moira, 'Condem'd to wither on a foreign strand', *The New Welsh Review*, 41, XI/i (1998), 56–9.

——, *Distant Fields: Eighteenth-century Fictions of Wales* (Cardiff: University of Wales Press, 2001).

Dickens, Charles, *Bleak House* (1852–3) (London: Hazell Watson and Viney Ltd., n.d.).

Edwards, Hywel Teifi, *The Eisteddfod*, Writers of Wales series (Cardiff: University of Wales Press, 1990).

Evans, W. Gareth, *Education and Female Emancipation: The Welsh Experience, 1847–1914* (Cardiff: University of Wales Press, 1990).

Fanon, Frantz, *Black Skin, White Masks* (1952), trans. by C. L. Markmann (London: Pluto, 1986).

Foucault, Michel, *The History of Sexuality Volume 1: An Introduction*, trans. by Robert Hurley (Harmondsworth: Penguin, 1978).

Ffrench, Yvonne, *Mrs Siddons: Tragic Actress* (London: Derek Verschoyle, 1954).

Freud, Sigmund, *Introductory Lectures on Psychoanalysis* (1916–17), trans. by James Strachey, Penguin Freud Library 1 (Harmondsworth: Penguin, 1963).

—— and Josef Breuer, *Studies on Hysteria*, trans. by James and Alix Strachey, Penguin Freud Library 3 (Harmondsworth: Penguin, 1974).

Gilbert, Sandra M. and Susan Gubar, *The Madwoman in the Attic: The Woman Writer and the Nineteenth-Century Literary Imagination* (New Haven: Yale University Press, 1979).

—— (eds), *Shakespeare's Sisters: Feminist Essays on Women Poets* (Bloomington: Indiana University Press, 1979).

Good Words, '"Sadie": In Memory of an Esteemed Contributor' (June 1868).

Gray, Thomas and William Collins, *The Poems of Gray and Collins*, ed. by Austin Lane Poole (Oxford: Oxford University Press, 1919).

Greer, Germaine, *Slip-shod Sybils: Recognition, Rejection and the Woman Poet* (Harmondsworth: Penguin, 1995).

Haefner, Joel, 'The Romantic Scene(s) of Writing', in Carol Shiner Wilson and Joel Haefner (eds), *Revisioning Romanticism: British Women Writers, 1776–1837* (Philadelphia: University of Pennsylvania Press, 1994), pp.256–73.

Hall, Catherine, *White, Male and Middle Class: Explorations in Feminism and History* (Cambridge: Polity Press, 1992).

Hellerstein, Erna Olafson, Leslie Parker Hume and Karen M. Offen (eds), *Victorian Women: A Documentary Account of Women's Lives in Nineteenth-Century England, France and the United States of America* (Stanford: Stanford University Press, 1981).

Helsinger, Elizabeth K., Robin Lauterbach Sheets and William Veeder, *The Woman Question: Society and Literature in Britain and America, 1837–83*, 3 vols. (Chicago: University of Chicago Press, 1983).

Hobsbawm, Eric, *The Age of Revolution, 1789–1848* (London: Abacus, 1962).

——, *Nations and Nationalism Since 1780: Programme, Myth, Reality* (Cambridge University Press, 1990).

Holledge, Julie, *Innocent Flowers: Women in the Edwardian Theatre* (London: Virago, 1981).

The Holy Bible, King James Authorized Version (1611) (Oxford: Oxford University Press, 1886).

Homans, Margaret, *Bearing the Word: Language and Female Experience in Nineteenth-Century Women's Writing* (Chicago: University of Chicago Press, 1986).

Hughes, Harriet Mary (Browne), *Memoir of the Life and Writings of Felicia Hemans: By*

Her Sister; With an Essay on Her Genius: By Mrs Sigourney (Philadelphia: Lea and Blanchard, 1839).

Jameson, Frederic, *Marxism and Form* (Princeton: Princeton University Press, 1971).

Jeffrey, Francis, Review of *Records of Woman* (2nd edn) and *The Forest Sanctuary* (2nd edn), *The Edinburgh Review*, 50 (1829), 24.

Jenkins, Geraint H., 'The New Enthusiasts', in Trevor Herbert and Gareth Elwyn Jones (eds), *The Remaking of Wales in the Eighteenth Century* (Cardiff: University of Wales Press, 1988), pp.42–5.

Jewsbury, Maria Jane, 'Original Papers. Literary Sketches No. 1 Felicia Hemans', *The Athenaeum*, 171 (February 1831), 187.

Jones, Gareth Stedman, *Outcast London: A Study in the Relationship Between the Classes in Victorian Society* (Oxford: Clarendon Press, 1971).

Jones, Gwyn (ed.), *The Oxford Book of Welsh Verse in English* (Oxford: Oxford University Press, 1977).

Jones, Ieuan Gwynedd, *Mid-Victorian Wales: The Observers and the Observed* (Cardiff: University of Wales Press, 1992).

——, 'People and Protest: Wales 1815–1880', in Trevor Herbert and Gareth Elwyn Jones (eds), *People and Protest: Wales 1815–1880* (Cardiff: University of Wales Press, 1988).

Jones, J. Graham, *The History of Wales* (Cardiff: University of Wales Press, 1990).

Jones, Maldwyn Allen, *American Immigration* (Chicago: University of Chicago Press, 1960).

Judd, Denis, *Empire: The British Imperial Experience from 1765 to the Present* (London: Fontana, 1997).

Kachru, Braj B., *The Alchemy of English: The Spread, Functions and Models of Non-Native Englishes* (Oxford: Pergamon Institute, 1996).

Kaplan, Cora. *Salt and Bitter and Good: Three Centuries of English and American Women Poets* (New York: Paddington, 1973).

——, 'Pandora's Box: Subjectivity, Class and Sexuality in Socialist Feminist Criticism', in Gayle Greene and Coppelia Kahn (eds), *Making a Difference: Feminist Literary Criticism* (London: Routledge, 1985), pp.146–76.

Kenyon, Olga, *800 Years of Women's Letters* (Stroud: Alan Sutton, 1992).

Kilcup, Karen L. (ed.), *Nineteenth-Century American Women Writers: An Anthology* (Oxford: Blackwell, 1997).

Leighton, Angela, *Victorian Women Poets: Writing Against the Heart* (London: Harvester Wheatsheaf, 1992).

Leighton, Angela and Margaret Reynolds (eds), *Victorian Women Poets: An Anthology* (Oxford: Blackwell, 1995).

Lewes, George Henry, 'The Lady Novelists', *The Westminster Review*, 58 (1852), 133–4.

Lipman, Vivian D., *The Social History of the Jews in England, 1850–1950* (London: Watts and Co., 1954).

Lonsdale, Roger (ed.), *The New Oxford Book of Eighteenth-Century Verse* (Oxford: Oxford University Press, 1987).

—— (ed.), *Eighteenth-Century Women Poets: An Oxford Anthology* (Oxford: Oxford University Press, 1989).

Lootens, Tricia, 'Hemans and Home: Victorianism, Feminine "Internal Enemies",
    and the Domestication of National Identity', in Angela Leighton (ed.), *Victorian
    Women Poets: A Critical Reader* (Oxford: Blackwell, 1996), pp.1–23.

McGann, Jerome J., 'Literary History, Romanticism and Felicia Hemans', in Carol
    Shiner Wilson and Joel Haefner (eds), *Revisioning Romanticism: British Women
    Writers, 1776–1837* (Philadelphia: University of Pennsylvania Press, 1994),
    pp.210–27.

Mackenzie, Kathleen, *The Great Sarah: The Life of Mrs Siddons* (London: Evans
    Brothers, 1968).

Maitland, Sara, *A Map of the New Country: Women and Christianity* (London:
    Routledge, 1975).

Manvell, Roger, *Sarah Siddons: Portrait of an Actress* (London: Heinemann, 1970).

Marx, Karl and Friedrich Engels, *Manifesto of the Communist Party* (1848), trans. by
    Samuel Moore (Woodbridge: Merlin Press, 1998).

Mathias, Roland, 'Poets of Breconshire', *Brycheiniog: The Journal of the Brecknock
    Society*, XIX (1980–1), 26–49.

Michie, Helena, *The Flesh Made Word: Female Figures and Women's Bodies* (Oxford:
    Oxford University Press, 1987).

Moi, Toril, *Sexual Textual Politics: Feminist Literary Theory* (London: Routledge, 1985).

Morgan, Prys, 'From a Death to a View: The Hunt for the Welsh Past in the
    Romantic Period', in Eric Hobsbawm and Terence Ranger (eds), *The Invention of
    Tradition* (Cambridge: Cambridge University Press, 1983).

Nead, Lynda, *Myths of Sexuality* (Oxford: Blackwell, 1988).

Ngugi, Wa Thiong'o, *Decolonizing the Mind: The Politics of Language in African Literature*
    (London: James Currey, 1986).

——, 'Imperialism of Language: English, a Language for the World?', in *Moving the
    Centre: The Struggle for Cultural Freedoms*, Studies in African Literature series
    (London: James Currey, 1993).

Orr, Bridget, 'The Only Free People in the Empire: Gender Difference in Colonial
    Discourse', in Chris Tiffin and Alan Lawson (eds), *Describing Empire: Post-
    Coloniality and Textuality* (London: Routledge, 1994).

Parry, Benita, 'Problems in Theories of Colonial Discourse', *The Oxford Literary
    Review*, 9, 1–2 (1987), 27–57.

Patmore, Coventry, *The Angel in the House* (1854–6) (London: George Bell and Son,
    1885).

Paxton, Nancy L., 'Complicity and Resistance in the Writings of Flora Annie Steel
    and Annie Besant', in Nupur Chaudhuri and Margaret Strodel (eds), *Western
    Women and Imperialism: Complicity and Resistance* (Bloomington: Indiana
    University Press, 1990), pp.158–70.

Poovey, Mary, *The Proper Lady and the Woman Writer: Ideology and Style in the Works of
    Mary Wollstonecraft, Jane Austen and Mary Shelley* (Chicago: University of Chicago
    Press, 1984).

——, *Uneven Developments: The Ideological Work of Gender in Mid-Victorian England*
    (Chicago: University of Chicago Press, 1989).

Pope, Alexander, *Poetical Works*, ed. by Herbert Davis (Oxford: Oxford University
    Press, 1966).

——, 'Popular Objections Considered', in *The Magdalen's Friend and Female Homes'*
    Intelligence, 2 (1861).
Rich, Adrienne, 'Compulsory Heterosexuality and Lesbian Existence', in E. Abel and
    E. K. Abel (eds), *The Signs Reader: Women, Gender and Scholarship* (Chicago:
    University of Chicago Press, 1983), pp.139–68.
Ruether, Rosemary Radford, *Womenguides: Towards a Feminist Spirituality* (Boston:
    Beacon Press, 1985).
Sackville-West, Vita, 'The Women Poets of the 'Seventies', in Harley Granville-
    Barker (ed.), *The Eighteen-Seventies: Essays by Fellows of the Royal Society of
    Literature* (Cambridge: Cambridge University Press, 1929).
Shelley, Mary, *Frankenstein: Or the Modern Prometheus* (1818), in Peter Fairclough (ed.),
    Three Gothic Novels (Harmondsworth: Penguin, 1968).
Shiner Wilson, Carol, 'Lost Needles, Tangled Threads: Stitchery, Domesticity and the
    Artistic Enterprise in Barbauld, Edgeworth, Taylor and Lamb', in Carol Shiner
    Wilson and Joel Haefner (eds), *Revisioning Romanticism: British Women Writers,
    1776–1837* (Philadelphia: University of Pennsylvania Press, 1994).
Showalter, Elaine, *A Literature of Their Own: From Charlotte Brontë to Doris Lessing*
    (London: Virago, 1978).
——, *The Female Malady: Women, Madness and English Culture, 1830–1980* (London:
    Virago, 1987).
—— (ed.), *Daughters of Decadence: Women Writers of the Fin-de-Siècle* (London: Virago,
    1993).
Shuttleworth, Sally, 'Demonic Mothers: Ideologies of Bourgeois Motherhood in the
    Mid-Victorian Era', in Linda M. Shires (ed.), *Rewriting the Victorians: Theory,
    History and the Politics of Gender* (London: Routledge, 1992).
Smith, Anthony D., *National Identity* (Harmondsworth: Penguin, 1991).
Smith, Graham, *Something to Declare: 1000 Years of Customs and Excise* (London:
    Harrap, 1980).
Spivak, Gayatri Chakravorty, 'Three Women's Texts and a Critique of Imperialism',
    in Catherine Belsey and Jane Moore (eds), *The Feminist Reader: Essays in Gender
    and the Politics of Literary Criticism* (London: Macmillan, 1989).
Stephens, Meic (ed.), *The Oxford Companion to the Literature of Wales* (Oxford: Oxford
    University Press).
The Sunday Missal (London: Collins Liturgical Publications, 1975).
Swinburne, Algernon Charles, 'Hymn to Proserpine', *Poems and Ballads* (London,
    1866), in Edmund Gosse and Thomas James Wise (eds), *Selections from A. C.
    Swinburne* (London: Heinemann, 1919), pp.25–30.
Thomas, Norman Lewis, *The Story of Swansea's Districts and Villages,* 2 vols. (Swansea:
    Qualprint (Wales), 1969).
Thompson E. P., *The Making of the English Working Class* (Harmondsworth: Penguin,
    1963).
Thomson, David, *England in the Nineteenth Century* (Harmondsworth: Penguin, 1950).
Todd, Janet, *Sensibility: An Introduction* (London: Methuen, 1986).
Trinder, Peter, *Mrs Hemans,* Writers of Wales series (Cardiff: University of Wales
    Press, 1984).
Ussher, Jane M., *Women's Madness: Misogyny or Mental Illness?* (London: Harvester
    Wheatsheaf, 1991).

Williams, Gwyn A., *When Was Wales? The History, People and Culture of an Ancient Country* (Harmondsworth: Penguin, 1985).

Williams, Jane (Ysgafell), *The Literary Women of England* (London: Saunders, Otley and Co., 1861).

Williams, Raymond, *The Country and the City* (London, Hogarth, 1985).

——, *Culture and Society: Coleridge to Orwell* (London: Hogarth, 1987).

Williams, W. Glynn, *Memoir of Mrs Anna Walter Thomas (Morfudd Eryri)* (Holywell: W. Williams and Son, n.d. [1922]).

Wolfson, Susan, '"Domestic Affections" and "The Spear of Minerva": Felicia Hemans and the Dilemma of Gender', in Carol Shiner Wilson and Joel Haefner (eds), *Revisioning Romanticism: British Women Writers, 1776–1837* (Philadelphia: University of Pennsylvania Press, 1994), pp.128–66.

Woolf, Virginia, 'Professions for Women' (1931) in Michele Barrett (ed.), *Virginia Woolf: Women and Writing* (London: Women's Press, 1979).

——, *A Room of One's Own* (1928) in *A Room of One's Own and Three Guineas*, ed. Michele Barrett (Harmondsworth: Penguin, 1993).

——, *Three Guineas* (1938) in *A Room of One's Own and Three Guineas*, ed. Michele Barrett (Harmondsworth: Penguin, 1993).

Wordsworth, William, *William Wordsworth*, ed. by Stephen Gill (Oxford: Oxford University Press, 1984).

—— and Dorothy Wordsworth, *Letters: The Later Years, 1821–1853*, ed. by Alan G. Hill (Oxford: Clarendon Press, 1978–88).

Wu, Duncan (ed.), *Romanticism: A Critical Reader* (Oxford: Blackwell, 1995).

Index